D1264361

Banking, Politics and Global Finance

Für meine Eltern

Hans-Peter und Renate

Banking, Politics and Global Finance

American Commercial Banks and Regulatory
Change, 1980-1990

Wolfgang H Reinicke
The Brookings Institution
Washington, D.C.

Edward Elgar

Published by

Edward Elgar Publishing Limited
Gower House
Croft Road
Aldershot
Hants GU11 3HR
England

Edward Elgar Publishing Company
Old Post Road
Brookfield
Vermont 05036
USA

British Library Cataloguing in Publication Data

Reinicke, Wolfgang H.
  Banking, Politics and Global Finance:
  American Commercial Banks and Regulatory
  Change, 1980-90. - (Studies in
  International Political Economy)
  I. Title II. Series
  332.120973

Library of Congress Cataloguing in Publication Data

Reinicke, Wolfgang H.
    Banking, politics and global finance: American commercial banks
  and regulatory change, 1980-1990 / Wolfgang H. Reinicke.
      p.   cm. - (Studies in international political economy)
    Includes bibliographical references and index.
    1. Banks and banking—Deregulation—United States. 2. Investment
  banking—Deregulation—United States. 3. Banking law—United States.
  4. International finance. 5. International economic integration.
  I. Title. II. Series: Studies in international political economy
  (Aldershot, England)
  HG2491.R428   1995
  332.1′0973—dc20   94-34103
                                                                CIP

ISBN 1 85898 176 X

Printed and Bound in Great Britain by
Hartnolls Limited, Bodmin, Cornwall.

Contents

Figures and Tables

Figures

Tables

Abbreviations

ABA	American Banking Association
ABHC	Association of Bank Holding Companies
BHC	Bank holding company
BIS	Bank for International Settlements
CRS	Congressional Research Service
EC	European Community
ECU	European Currency Unit
FDIC	Federal Deposit Insurance Corporation
Fed	Federal Reserve Board
FFIEC	Federal Financial Institution Examination Council
FRS	Federal Reserve System
IBAA	Independent Bankers Association of America
ICI	Investment Company Institute
ILSA	International Lending Supervisory Act
IMF	International Monetary Fund
MBHC	Multibank holding company
MMDA	Money Market Deposit Account
MMMF	Money Market Mutual Fund
MNB	Multinational bank
OBHC	One bank holding company
OCC	Office of the Comptroller of the Currency
OECD	Organization for Economic Cooperation and Development
OPEC	Organization of Petroleum Exporting Countries
OTA	Office of Technology Assessment
OTS	Office of Thrift Supervision
S&Ls	Savings and loan institutions
SEC	Securities and Exchange Commission
SIA	Securities Industry Association
CQ	Congressional Quarterly
NYT	New York Times
WSJ	Wall Street Journal
WP	Washington Post

Foreword

This book examines the U.S. banking system's response to the progressing globalization of financial markets. Studies in comparative political economy and new institutionalism have tended to emphasize macro-structural aspects of politics by concentrating on elements of stability and consistency in the policy responses by advanced industrial countries to external economic pressures. Based on a micro-political analysis of policymaking, the study reveals a multitude of changes in the interests, coalitions, and power constellations among private and public sector actors and institutions in the U.S. financial system, in the absence of any macro-structural adjustment. These changes open alternative channels for policymaking and eventually do lead to substantial adjustments in the regulatory framework governing U.S. financial markets by circumventing traditional mechanisms for policymaking.

The book also explains why the *same* policy network can respond very *differently* to an external economic challenge — a phenomenon usually neglected in the literature on comparative political economy. The conflict that erupted over the attempt to repeal the law that separates commercial from investment banking in the U.S. — the Glass-Steagall Act — led to the familiar legislative gridlock associated with the decentralized public policymaking structure in the U.S. In sharp contrast to this dynamic, U.S. regulators and the legislature not only succeeded in raising the capital standards of U.S. commerical banks, but took the lead in brokering an international agreement that harmonized the capital standards of financial institutions in the major financial markets of the world.

In its original form, this study was submitted to the faculty of the Graduate School of Yale University for the attainment of a Ph.D. I am grateful to David Cameron, David Lumsdaine and Sylvia Maxfield for their advice. In addition, I would like to thank the public and private sector officials in the U.S. and abroad who took the time to discuss details of the domestic and international politics of banking. Many conversations were granted on the condition that I preserve their anonymity.

The study has since undergone several revisions and has been updated. Phil Cerny, Ann Henderson and Christopher Allen provided helpful comments on an earlier version of the manuscript. The environment provided by the Foreign Policy Studies Program at the Brookings Institution and the research assistance by Patricia Lecerf, Christian Reeber and Jim Schoff were instrumental in completing the work. The entire book benefited from the encouragement and help of Jennifer Mitchell, who edited and typeset the manuscript. Finally, I am grateful for the financial support provided by the Brookings Institution for the completion of this book.

Wolfgang H. Reinicke

1. Introduction

SCOPE OF STUDY

In the 1980s, the major industrialized countries witnessed a sharp acceleration in the integration of their financial markets. This trend towards international financial integration manifested itself in a variety of ways, among them: increasingly mobile international capital flows, the convergence of Euro and domestic interest rates, cross-national mergers and strategic alliances among financial institutions, growing foreign participation in national financial markets, and the internationalization of institutional investors' asset portfolios.

This study examines how the United States' public and private sector institutions responded to the challenges posed by global financial integration. By analysing two case studies of domestic response to external financial pressures, the book examines a critically important component of the domestic and international political economy: the financial system. Contemporary aspects of the politics of banking in the United States, and among advanced industrial countries generally, have not been sufficiently studied by political scientists.[1] By examining the responses of U.S. commercial banks and their regulatory authorities to the challenges presented to them by the increasing integration of financial markets, the book identifies the public and private sector institutions involved in financial markets. It analyses their interests and the coalitions that form around the distributional conflicts over political and economic power among financial institutions in U.S. financial markets, as well as with their regulatory, jurisdictional and legislative counterparts in the government.

The study also examines the existing literature on domestic political response to external economic pressures developed by scholars working in the tradition of comparative political economy and new institutionalism. It concludes that the existing literature overemphasizes elements of both stability and consistency in national policy responses to external economic pressures, and in its stead develops a three phase dynamic model to arrive at a more nuanced understanding of the politics of domestic response to international economic integration. The purpose of the model is to account for divergence in policy responses and results among individual countries, in light of increasing international economic integration, *and* to understand

1

why and how these responses change over time. The origin and nature of change in the responses is analysed by examining the evolution of the policymaking process in two case studies of U.S. financial regulatory reform in response to the increasing international integration of financial markets. Divergences in policymaking processes and outcomes are examined by comparing the two cases.

Finally, the study's theoretical discussion specifically focuses on the field of comparative political economy and the role of external pressures on the domestic political economy. However, the theoretical critique provided here can be applied to a larger set of literature that tends to focus on the broader macro-structural aspects of the political process, often neglecting the micro-foundations of politics and the policymaking process.[2]

International financial integration created two distinct sets of challenges to the political economies of advanced industrial countries: one to the economic interests of private sector financial institutions, the other to the political capacity of state actors and institutions. Financial integration and the increasing interpenetration of financial systems greatly intensified the competitive pressures faced by financial institutions in both domestic and international markets. Financial integration posed particularly acute competitive challenges to the economic interests of those financial institutions operating in relatively more restrictive national financial regulatory environments, as regulatory differences across nations were transformed into competitive asymmetries in a single integrated market. More specifically, to financial institutions, the breakdown of the regulatory and geographic barriers between national financial markets meant that lenders and borrowers could seek out — at little or no extra cost — financial markets which provided the widest array of products at the most attractive terms.[3] As a consequence, financial firms operating in a more restrictive regulatory environment were placed at a competitive disadvantage.[4] They could not provide the same wide range of products and services at the same low costs as their competitors, and therefore were likely to lose market shares and customers to financial institutions operating in less regulated environments.[5] In response to the competitive pressures emanating from the growing integration of financial markets, financial institutions operating in a more restrictive regulatory environment pressed domestic regulatory authorities to deregulate the national financial system.[6]

In addition to challenging the economic interests of private sector financial institutions, international financial integration also threatened the political authority of state actors.[7] More specifically, international financial integration posed a threat to national regulatory authorities because it undermined the efficacy of existing national regulations and eventually challenged the regulatory capacity of domestic political authorities. As the barriers which insulated national financial systems from one another crumbled, so did the effectiveness of their respective national regulations.[8]

Against this background of diminished autonomy faced by domestic policymakers, concern grew that financial systems had become intrinsically more vulnerable to developments in other economies, such as the sharp fluctuations in interest rates, violent swings in stock markets, and downturns in economic activity prevalent in the 1970s and 1980s.[9] Most importantly, national regulatory provisions designed to ensure the safety and viability of the domestic financial system could no longer achieve their objectives, because domestic financial stability became affected by factors which lay outside the control of national regulatory authorities.[10] For example, a crisis arising from lax regulatory supervision in one national financial market could quickly spread to other financial systems.[11] In short, because financial activities became globalized, developments in one market could be transmitted very quickly to other major financial centres. Any discrepancy in the degree of prudence among different financial markets could lead to the globalization of imprudent practices. Given the heightened competition among financial institutions in the increasingly integrated global market, the spillover of increased risk from one national market into others rose.[12] National regulatory authorities could no longer ensure the safety and viability of the domestic financial system, because the financial system became vulnerable to externally-induced destabilization.[13] In sum, state institutions were no longer able to prevent a crisis in other financial markets from spreading to their own financial systems.

This problem was further complicated because a unilateral move to tighten domestic regulations would put financial institutions at a competitive disadvantage. It generated the kinds of challenges to the private sector described above and/or induced financial institutions to move their assets and activities abroad, beyond the direct control of domestic authorities, reducing the amount of capital readily available for productive investment in the domestic economy.[14] Since national regulatory authorities *alone* could no longer ensure the safety of the domestic financial system, the challenge to the regulatory capacity of state actors could only be resolved through international-level cooperation to reassert regulatory control over financial markets.[15] Reflecting the degree to which states had in fact lost control over their own financial systems, and responding to the charges that global regulatory cooperation results in an unacceptable loss of sovereignty, one report stated, '[N]ations do not lose sovereignty by reaching an agreement with other sovereign nations to reassert some measure of political control over the evolution of economic events.'[16] In the words of an official from the Federal Reserve:

The decade ahead thus promises to be a most challenging period for the Federal Reserve and for central banks throughout the world.... It is, therefore, imperative that central banks throughout the world share information, consult with each other about the possible consequences of monetary policies among countries, and devise innovative approaches to the supervision and regulation of financial institutions. The 'last war', both in the United States and in most other industrial countries, was deregulation and innovation in domestic financial markets. The challenges of the next war are more difficult, however, because they entail deregulation and innovation in international financial markets.[17]

In the United States, the challenges to the regulatory authority of state actors, and to the market position of private sector institutions, manifested themselves most clearly in two separate cases. One case revolved primarily around a threat to the competitive strength of U.S. commercial banks in domestic and foreign markets; the other around a threat to the regulatory powers of U.S. policymakers.

The principal threat to the competitive position of U.S. commercial banks arose from the domestic regulations embodied in the Glass-Steagall Act. This legislation was originally passed in 1933 as a major element of the New Deal financial legislation, and restricted the product range commercial banks were allowed to offer to their customers. The basic aim of Glass-Steagall was to eliminate universal banking in the U.S., as it was considered a major factor in the stock market collapse of 1929 and the subsequent Great Depression. By prohibiting U.S. commercial banks from offering investment banking services (among other things), Glass-Steagall separated commercial from investment banking and vice versa.

For three decades after World War II, commercial banks showed little concern for the Glass-Steagall Act. By the 1980s, however, some commercial banks began to exert strong pressure for its repeal. These banks argued that in the context of an increasingly integrated global financial market, this prohibition proved increasingly restrictive upon the ability of U.S. commercial banks to adapt to changing market circumstances, and thus placed U.S. commercial banks at a considerable competitive disadvantage vis-à-vis foreign universal banks and investment banks, which are permitted to offer a full range of financial services.[18]

As will be discussed in greater detail in Chapter 4, two of the major trends contributing to the process of global financial integration were the growth of securitization and the attendant internationalization of financial activities, and the growing interpenetration of national financial markets by foreign investors and institutions. Both of these trends threatened the position of U.S. commercial banks in domestic and international financial markets.[19] In the domestic market, the trend towards securitization undermined the commercial banks' market share. It shifted the focus of financial activity away from commercial bank lending and towards direct-debt instruments which, due to the Glass-Steagall Act, only investment banks were allowed to provide. The trend towards internationalization of financial transactions, as well as the process of integration, further eroded U.S. banks' market shares, both at home and abroad.

The growing international competition associated with global financial integration posed a threat not only to the market shares of U.S. commercial banks, but also to the regulatory authority of U.S. policymakers. International competition put pressure on banks in all countries to cut their expenses and offer more competitive prices in order to attract customers. Beginning in the late 1970s, U.S. commercial banks responded to this intensification of international financial competition by attempting to cut their operating costs. Many banks cut their costs by reducing their capital reserves, which were set aside to guard against unexpected losses. This erosion in banks' capital reserves, which are considered a major regulatory instrument, generated growing concern among U.S. regulators, who feared that declining capital reserves posed a threat to the safety and stability of the financial system. Yet U.S. regulators could not resolve this threat through traditional domestic financial regulation. They soon realized that national banking systems had become so integrated that higher capital standards in the U.S. alone could not insulate the American financial system from a crisis in another financial market, and that domestic regulatory measures alone would not achieve their goal. In addition, U.S. policymakers concurred that a unilateral move to raise capital standards would place U.S. banks at a disadvantage in international capital markets by forcing them to conform to stricter regulations than their competitors. The recognition by U.S. authorities that domestic regulation alone was no longer sufficient to guarantee the safety of their financial system in the context of a globally integrated financial market led to the initiation of a process of global regulatory coordination and cooperation to strengthen and harmonize capital standards across the major financial markets.

ORGANIZATION OF STUDY

Clearly, global financial integration in the 1980s created two different challenges to the interests and powers of U.S. private and public sector institutions. It is the purpose of this study to analyse the nature of these two challenges and the ways in which U.S. institutions responded to them. In order to carry out such an analysis, Chapter 2 develops a theoretical framework for examining the process of policy response to external economic pressures. In doing so, it draws extensively from existing theories that have examined the politics of domestic adjustment to international economic pressures. However, it will also incorporate new elements in order to construct an analytical framework which explains in a more comprehensive way national political responses to the challenges of global financial integration.

Chapter 3 provides the necessary historical background and a brief analysis of the contemporary regulatory structure of the U.S. financial system. In essence, the institutional structure of the United States has undergone several major transformations throughout the last century. Today the U.S. financial policy network is a highly fragmented and decentralized system, characterized by multiple regulators both at the state and federal level as well as numerous private sector interests, each pursuing their own particular concerns. Chapter 4 examines the degree to which national financial markets had become integrated by the late 1980s. While banks have been active internationally for a long time, several factors during the 1970s and 1980s contributed not only to a sharp increase in the internationalization of financial markets, but also to the actual integration of national financial markets.

The following four chapters contain an in-depth analysis of the United States' response to the globalization of financial markets. Chapters 5 and 6 examine the commercial banks' effort to repeal the Glass-Steagall Act, which obstructed their ability to compete effectively in the emerging global financial markets. Chapter 5 discusses the multiple conflicts and the resultant policy gridlock that erupted during the first half of the 1980s. Chapter 6 analyses the way in which increasing external pressure induced necessary changes in the policy network that led to a partial resolution of the challenge. Chapters 7 and 8 examine the attempts to internationalize capital standards, the second challenge to the U.S. financial policy network. Just as in the case of Glass-Steagall, increasing external pressure during the second half of the 1980s eventually generated a policy resolution. But although it was caused by the same external pressure, this case examines a challenge not to the private sector, as in the case of Glass-Steagall, but to the public sector. As a result, the pattern and degree of conflict that emerged differed substantially. In addition, the nature of the policy resolution generated by the network was different.

In conclusion, Chapter 9 provides a comparative analysis of the two cases and explains both the differences in the policymaking process in response to the external pressures and the divergent policy resolutions that were sought in each particular case.

NOTES

1. Kelly (1977); Hawley (1987); Pauly (1988); Rosenbluth (1989); Frieden (1991).
2. Evans, Rueschemeyer, Skocpol (1985); Krasner (1978); Zysman (1983).
3. Freeman (1987); Giddy (1985).
4. Denning (1986); Pardee (1987); Lamfalussy (1989).
5. Congress of the United States, Office of Technology Assessment (1987), see especially Chapter 3, 'International Competition in Banking and Financial Services'.
6. Pardee (1987).
7. As a former (1982-86) Vice Chairman of the Board of Governors of the Federal Reserve stated, '...[T]oday's central banker must navigate in uncharted waters. The global financial system is changing so rapidly that the old rules of the game no longer apply.' Martion and Higgins (1986).
8. Ogata, Cooper, Schulmann (1989).
9. Bank for International Settlements (1986).
10. Pecchioli (1983, 1987); Dale (1986).
11. Bellanger (1987); Giddy (1985).
12. Lamfalussy (1989).
13. Cooke (1983).
14. The fact that financial institutions do respond to unilateral regulations by moving part of their assets abroad has been clearly demonstrated in the case of Regulation Q and the Interest Equalization Tax.
15. Corrigan (1987); Freeman (1987); Kane (1987); Lamfalussy (1989); de Larosière (1989).
16. Ogata et al. (1989).
17. Martion and Higgins (1986).
18. Angermüller (1988); Crane and Hayes (1983-84).
19. Congress of the United States, Office of Technology Assessment (1987).

2. The Politics of Domestic Response to External Economic Pressure

CURRENT THEORETICAL FRAMEWORKS

Comparative Political Economy

One of the most influential approaches to the study of domestic political responses to external economic shocks has been developed by scholars working within the field of comparative political economy. These scholars generally explain domestic policy responses to external economic pressures in terms of the characteristics of national policy networks, which, according to Peter Katzenstein, are generally defined as a set of relationships linking public and private sector institutions in the formulation of policy. The policy network reflects the structure of the state and the society, particularly the degree of centralization of state institutions and private sector organizations, and the degree of differentiation between state and society.[1] Generally speaking, this literature holds that the level of centralization and state/society differentiation embedded in the policy network determines the way in which the network responds to external economic challenges.

This study builds upon the comparative political economy analysis by examining the critical role played by domestic policy networks in shaping policy responses to external economic pressures. However, this study differs from the literature in its central analytical focus. The main purpose of comparative political economy literature is to explain cross-country differences in policy responses to a common external shock. Accordingly, it attributes such divergences in national responses to differences in the structure of national policy networks; it assigns each nation a particular type of policy network, which determines national reactions to external economic pressures and creates for each country a distinctive national pattern of response. In order to posit that each nation's policy network generates a certain distinctive response pattern, comparative political economy literature must assume that the structures and processes of the policy network remain relatively fixed and stable. In other words, in order to posit the national policy network as the factor which explains variations in policy outcomes *across* countries, it is necessary to hold the policy network constant *within*

8

each individual country.[2]

This assumption of stable policy networks has two implications for the way in which this literature analyses domestic responses to external economic pressures. First, change in the policy network is defined in terms of broad macro-structural transformations which occur so infrequently that they do not enter as causal factors in the short- to medium-term analysis of policy networks. Change occurs in policy networks only when underlying social structures undergo transformations, such as a major shift in the degree of centralization of state or economy, or a major realignment in the nature of the relationship between state and society.[3] In the absence of such structural transformations, comparative literature assumes a broad continuity in policy responses and outcomes.

Secondly, and related to the first implication, comparative political economy literature's postulation of stability in policy networks necessitates a further assumption that an external shock will lead each country's policy network to generate an internally consistent set of policy outcomes. It presumes that each nation's policy network is only capable of producing a single type of policy response and ignores the possibility that a single policy network might react to an external economic shock in several different ways.[4]

This approach to change is appropriate for the particular set of issues which the comparative literature addresses. While the comparative approach is valuable for short-term, broad cross-national analyses, it is less useful for in-depth studies of the process of policy response within a particular country over a longer period of time. As this study will demonstrate, the assumptions of stability in the policy network — and therefore consistency and continuity in the responses it generates — do not bear close scrutiny in longer-term case studies of individual countries.

For example, over time shifts do occur in the responses of a particular policy network to external economic shocks. These shifts occur in the absence of the profound macro-structural transformations which the comparative approach sees as the only sources of change in policy networks and policy outcomes. Instead, these shifts reflect changes in the policymaking process arising from evolving patterns of conflict and coalition-building which take place within the existing societal and institutional structure of the policy network.

Also, the processes of policy response to an external shock can proceed along divergent paths. As the case of global financial integration will demonstrate, *one* external shock often poses *several* challenges to the domestic policy network. Each of the challenges is resolved through a different policymaking process culminating in a different policy outcome, a situation not anticipated by comparative political economy literature.

In sum, the comparative political economy analysis does not provide a satisfactory explanation for several of the most important issues raised by the study of responses to external economic pressures within a single policy network. More specifically, its explanation of the process of response to a particular external shock is inadequate because it cannot account for *change* in the way the policy network responds over time.[5] Furthermore, its capacity to contrast and compare responses to different challenges which arise from a common external shock is impaired by its assumption of consistency in response to external pressures over time. Thus it cannot explain *divergence* in either the policymaking process or the policy outcomes it generates.

New Institutionalism

By focusing on policy responses of an individual country to external economic pressures, this study also places itself within the literature known as 'new institutionalism'. This body of work reflects the renewal of interest in the role of institutions in 'political life' and the way these institutions structure and direct the political conflicts that ultimately affect policy outcomes.[6] New institutionalism emphasizes the partially independent nature of systemic characteristics (i.e. institutions) as opposed to the more atomistic perspective contained in pluralist analyses of the political process. At the same time, it avoids the broad superficiality and determinism often present in functionalist and systems theory perspectives by emphasizing the differences in domestic political systems that are caused by variations in each country's unique historical development.

Like earlier works that have emphasized the importance of institutions in shaping foreign economic policy, this study demonstrates the importance and analytical value of a more refined and disaggregated approach than that taken by most comparative political economy analyses.[7] However, unlike the institutional literature, this study does not merely explain variations in political conflict and the policymaking process by distinguishing between issue areas (e.g. trade and finance) and the differences in the institutional settings and the respective private and public sector interests that emanate from these settings.[8] Rather, it examines variations in the policy process that exist within the *same* issue area and develops an analytical framework for explaining these differences in the policy conflicts and their ultimate outcomes.

More importantly, this study differs from new institutionalism in its approach to the analysis of change in policy networks. Like most comparative political economy analyses, the institutional literature offers explanations of stability and continuity in policy responses and consequently defines change in broad macro-structural terms. Institutions and the relationships among them are characterized by long periods of stability. This steady state is only interrupted during times of crisis which result in the breakdown of the institutions, the relationships among them and the policy responses they generate.[9] For example, Ikenberry states that 'the institutional approach...gives special attention to specific historical junctures when economic or political crises reshape social relations and the institutions of policymaking...[D]epression and war are critical catalysts of change from this perspective.'[10] Similarly, Peter Hall, in accordance with the comparative political economy literature, writes:

> [We] can construct an institutionalist analysis of politics that is capable of explaining historical continuities and cross-national variations in policy....While they exist, institutional structures exercise a profound impact on the action of those who operate within them, and such structures are not particularly open to dramatic change except in the critical conjunctures of a nation's history, often associated with war or prolonged recession, that call into question the existing societal arrangements.[11]

The institutional approach thus shares with the comparative political economy literature the assumption that significant changes in a policy network occur only at infrequent historical junctures involving major structural transformations of the institutions that characterize the organization of state and society. In the absence of such structural transformations, both the institutional and comparative literature assume a broad continuity and consistency in policy responses.[12] In fact, some scholars subscribing to the institutionalist perspective of politics have acknowledged that the approach does not lend itself to the explanation of change. As Ikenberry states, '...theories of institutional change do not provide clear guidance on the thresholds necessary to induce change...'[13]

To summarize, while new institutionalism provides a constructive alternative to both society-centred and state- and/or system-centred explanations of politics, it has not provided an adequate *theory* of change. While the approach recognizes that institutions can break down in times of crisis, it does not explain the 'politics' of breakdown. However, disaggregating the state into a distinct set of political institutions, which is the major asset of new institutionalism, must serve the analytical purpose of examining how those institutions relate to each other and how their relationship changes over time as it evolves towards crisis and eventual breakdown. In other words, how does an external pressure that is considered the cause of the eventual breakdown feed through the institutional structure of policymaking? What changes that are in the interests of the institutional actors, and the coalitions among them, might take place? How is political power within and among the institutions redistributed so that a state of long-term stability suddenly deteriorates into crisis and institutional breakdown?

In addition, and related to the above, politics does not end with the breakdown of institutions. Rather, policymaking continues in a new institutional setting. How does this new institutional framework for policymaking — the policy network — emerge? What are the characteristics of institutional transition? If new institutions are created, how does this occur? If old ones adapt to the pressures that would otherwise lead to their breakdown, what are the mechanisms of adjustment and how are these institutions transformed? These questions need to be addressed in order to arrive at a comprehensive understanding of the process of change in both the overall policy network and the institutions which comprise the policy network.

Finally, by restricting its focus to instances of crisis defined as institutional breakdown, new institutionalism is biased in the cases it selects. If institutions can change short of breakdown, or if policy responses that have a major impact on society change without the actual transformation of institutions themselves, then institutionalists have neglected a large number of cases where institutions are central to the analysis of change. In such circumstances, institutions themselves are the mediators of change. In other words, rather than being the object of change induced by an external shock, institutions have now become (at least partially) the agents of change.[14]

As this book demonstrates, significant changes in policy responses on the part of the policy network do occur over time. First, these changes can occur in the absence of institutional breakdown but require some institutional adjustment. Secondly, if there is institutional breakdown, it is ultimately those changes in the institutional patterns of conflict and coalition-building within the policy network that lead to the eventual breakdown of the institutions and thus ultimately the structure of the policy network itself. *In other words, the incremental process of policy change, which the comparative political economy and institutional analyses neglect, is the very source of the broad macro-structural transformations which those analyses define as central to their conception of change.*

In the second case study, for example, there was a fundamental transformation in the mechanisms of regulatory supervision. But this change did not lead to a breakdown of the institutions themselves. Moreover, although the principal stimulus to change was the external pressure of global financial integration, the principal agents of change were the institutions in the U.S. financial policy network themselves. Similarly, in the case of Glass-Steagall, institutions, rather than external pressure, determined the direction of change. Today, this change has undermined the separation of commercial and investment banking to the degree that Glass-Steagall is *de facto* — though not *de jure* — repealed, even though the institutional structure that supports the act remains in place.

ANALYSING CHANGE AND DIVERGENCE IN DOMESTIC RESPONSE TO EXTERNAL PRESSURE

This study develops a framework to explain the way in which policy responses, as well as the institutional setting in which they are formed, change over time.[15] Also, it explains divergent policy responses and outcomes by a single domestic policy network to an external economic shock. In order to explain change in the process of response to each individual challenge, and ultimately change in the institutional setting that generates the policy response, the study constructs a time-dependent model for analysing domestic adjustment to external pressures. The origins and causes of divergence in policy responses are determined through a comparative analysis of two specific challenges posed to the U.S. financial system that grew out of the process of global financial integration.

The adjustment model will be built around an analysis of the following three questions:

1. How do external challenges *mobilize* the policy network?
2. What are the dynamic processes of *conflict* through which the policy network responds to such challenges?
3. How do these processes of conflict culminate in the eventual *resolution* of challenges?

These three questions are arranged in a sequence which is designed to build a causal chain of explanation. The model of the adjustment process will flow from the sequence of questions posed above, addressing each question in turn and building upon each answer to construct a progression linking the mobilization of the policy network to the process of conflict, and finally to the eventual resolution of the challenge generated by an external economic shock.

Each of the questions posed above corresponds to a particular phase in the process of adjustment. The first phase is that of **mobilization**, in which the external challenge penetrates the domestic policy network and activates a specific set of institutions in that network to respond. The second phase is that of **conflict**, in which the institutions mobilized by the challenge form coalitions, promote policy initiatives, and engage in political bargaining aimed at formulating responses to the challenge. Over time, this process involves shifts in the interests, coalitions, and powers of the institutions in the policy network, which in turn give rise to changing policy responses. The final phase is that of **resolution**, in which the process of institutional coalition-building and bargaining culminates in a policy outcome which is seen as resolving the particular challenge.

The three phase model of the adjustment process is utilized to explain not only change over time, but also divergence across challenges. By applying the model to two separate case studies involving two discrete challenges, this study identifies the sources of divergence in policy responses, compares the phases through which such divergent responses evolve and contrasts the institutional changes necessary to resolve the external challenge.

Mobilization

In order to explain the initial phase of the adjustment process, it is crucial to begin by disaggregating an external economic shock into the separate challenges which it poses. Each challenge threatens the political and/or economic power of a certain set of institutions. The identity of the institutions most threatened by a particular challenge determines the way in which the policy network initially mobilizes to confront the challenge; institutions whose interests are directly harmed by the challenge are the first to respond to it. Their response takes the form of pressure for policy changes which will redress the loss in political and/or economic power which the challenge has generated. By taking the initiative in responding to the challenge, those institutions determine the initial political and policy agenda for the adjustment process.

The pressure for policy changes generated by the initially-mobilized institutions in turn activates additional public and/or private sector institutions in the policy network whose own interests would be affected by the proposed policy changes. These newly-mobilized institutions attempt to defend their own interests by forming coalitions which either support or oppose the proposed policy changes. Thus each challenge sets off two waves of mobilization. Each leads the institutions that are most threatened by the challenge to seek compensatory policy changes; their efforts to bring about policy changes then mobilize other segments of the policy network into the debate on policy response.

Thus, the nature of the challenge shapes the initial mobilization phase of response by determining:

a. whose interests are threatened
b. what kind of compensatory policy changes those threatened will seek
c. which other institutions will next be mobilized into the debate on policy response.

The significance of the mobilization phase lies in the fact that it sets the stage for the subsequent process of adjustment to external challenges and provides the basis for understanding the origins of divergence within the policy network. With respect to divergence, the mobilization phase determines how different challenges activate different segments of the policy network and thus initiate divergent paths towards policy response and eventual resolution.

Thus, the sources of divergence in policy responses can be explained through a comparison of (a.), (b.), and (c.) across cases:

a. Broadly speaking, each challenge poses a primary threat to either public sector or private sector institutions in the policy network. It undermines either the economic interests of private institutions, or the political capacities of state institutions. In the context of this study, for example, global financial integration has generated two distinct challenges to the U.S. financial policy network. One challenge involves a threat to the market position of U.S. commercial banks; another involves a threat to the regulatory authority of financial policymakers and the respective government institutions.

b. Challenges which threaten the economic interests of private sector institutions tend to generate a different set of responses, and a different political agenda, than challenges which threaten the political capacities of state institutions. Private sector institutions typically respond to threats to their economic interests with demands for state action to protect and/or restore their market power and profits. For example, private commercial banks reacted to a threat to their market position by pressuring policymakers to deregulate the domestic financial market, thereby allowing them to offer a more competitive range of services.[16] By contrast, public sector institutions typically respond to threats to their political capacity through initiatives designed to restore their own authority. For example, U.S. regulatory authorities reacted to declining capital reserve ratios by attempting to reassert regulatory authority over banks' capital standards.

c. Because each separate challenge mobilizes a different initial group of institutions and generates a different set of proposed policy changes, each challenge activates a different segment of the policy network in response to those proposed changes. For example, the proposed policy changes arising from the challenge to the market position of commercial banks affected the economic interests of a wide array of other private sector institutions and involved the regulatory authority of a large number of public sector institutions. By contrast, the proposed policy changes arising from the challenge to the political capacity of state institutions affected the interests of a more limited number of private and public sector institutions.

To summarize, the mobilization phase sets the stage for the process of formulating responses to external challenges. During this phase, the challenge activates a certain group of public or private sector institutions to seek compensatory policy changes, which in turn engages other segments of the policy network and initiates debates on policy responses. But what are the mechanisms through which such debates are resolved and by which policy responses are generated to meet these external challenges? Furthermore, if policy responses do in fact change over time, what are the causes of change and how does it proceed? In order to answer these questions it is necessary to analyse the conflict phase.

Conflict

As noted above, the redistribution of political and economic power caused by each external challenge sets off a process of conflict among the different private and public sector institutions in the policy network. The subsequent evolution of this process, and of the changing stream of policy responses which it generates, provides the analytical focus of this phase. The nature and form of conflict are shaped by three sets of factors. The first two sets of factors are, in a sense, inherited from the initial mobilization phase of the response process. In other words, the evolution of domestic conflicts and responses to an external economic shock is influenced by the initial conditions under which the shock penetrated the policy network.

One set of factors inherited from the mobilization phase involves the identity and interests of the institutions who initially reacted to the challenge. By setting the policy agenda for the response process, those institutions shape the terms of debate on how to respond to the challenge. They determine what type of policy changes will be debated, and influence the direction in which the debate on policy responses evolves. In other words, the identity and interests of the initially-mobilized institutions set the parameters of subsequent conflict within the policy network, predisposing the policy network to consider certain policy proposals while ruling out others.

While the first set of factors inherited from the mobilization phase determines *what* is debated, the second set of factors influences *how* those issues will be debated. This second set of factors defines the extent to which the policy network is activated by the challenge, and the degree of dissension over how to respond to that challenge. As noted above, each challenge activates certain segments of the policy network and generates a particular range of diverging interests among the institutions involved. As a result, each challenge sets up the institutional framework within which debate takes place, and also determines the array of interests involved in that debate.

More precisely, the process of formulating responses to external challenges cannot be predicted simply by examining the 'structural possibility' of dissension and fragmentation in the U.S. policy network. The U.S. financial policy network has often been characterized as fragmented and prone to conflict because it encompasses a multiplicity of public and private institutions linked together through decentralized channels of authority and decisionmaking. It would be misleading to predict policy responses based on the structure of the entire domestic financial policy network, however, because only certain segments of that network are activated by any one particular challenge.[17] Only if the challenge activates a wide array of public and private sector institutions, and only if both the public authorities and private institutions in the network are divided by internal conflicts of interest, will the structural possibility of dissension and fragmentation be fully realized. If on the other hand the challenge mobilizes only a small segment of the decentralized U.S. financial policy network, and if that segment expresses broad agreement over how to resolve the challenge, that network will respond in a manner typical of a more centralized system.

The main impetus to change arises from the third set of factors, which involves the changing character of the challenge itself. Rather than regarding an external shock as a single, discrete event, it is more accurate to view the shock as an evolving set of continuous pressures. As external economic pressures intensify or lessen, so do the challenges that confront the policy network. And as the challenges change, so do the perceived interests of the institutions in the policy network, as well as the patterns of conflict and coalition-building among the institutions. For example, the intensification of the external pressure can strengthen the position of those institutions which call for major policy changes in response to the particular challenge they face. As a result, the intensification of the challenge can accelerate the speed at which the policy network moves towards resolution of the challenge, and broaden the scope of the proposed policy changes. Policy networks are thus in a constant state of change as interests and coalitions adapt to an evolving external pressure and its respective challenges.

The three sets of factors discussed above not only influence changes in policy responses within a single case, they also provide the basis for comparing divergence in policy responses across cases. In assessing divergence during the conflict phase, it is clear that the two challenges posed by global financial integration generated two very different processes of debate and conflict within the policy network. In terms of the first set of factors, the policy agendas and terms of debate over these two challenges diverged widely. While the challenge to the economic interests of commercial banks gave rise to debates which revolved around deregulation, the challenge to the political capacities of state institutions generated debates which centred around reregulation. Therefore, the entire thrust of the debates involved two very different goals: one, the replacement of political control and state intervention with the free play of market forces; the other, the constraint and limitation of the operation of those market forces.

In terms of the second set of factors, the two challenges activated very different segments of the policy network and generated different degrees of dissension and conflict among the institutions involved. As a result, the challenges created two very different institutional and procedural contexts within which debate was to take place. For example, the challenge to the economic interests of private banks fully realized the structural possibility of fragmentation and dissension in the policy network by activating a wide array of institutions with sharply conflicting interests. The multiple and opposing coalitions among these institutions obstructed progress towards policy resolution and resulted in a series of policy gridlocks. In contrast, the challenge to the political capacity of state institutions activated a narrower, less fragmented set of institutions characterized by a greater degree of convergence of interests. The greater centralization of the policy network and the higher level of internal institutional consensus facilitated the relatively rapid and coherent formulation of policy responses to the challenge generated by the external economic pressure.

In terms of the third set of factors, the shift in the intensity of the external pressures influenced the domestic conflict over policy responses in different ways. As global financial integration progressed, the external policy pressures intensified in both cases, thereby generating growing pressures for policy resolution and leading to realignments of institutional interests and coalitions within the policy network. However, the extent of such realignments, and the time frame within which they took place, differed significantly in the two cases.

Resolution

The final phase of domestic response to external pressures is that of resolution. Resolution is achieved when the institutions initially disadvantaged by the external economic shock succeed in introducing policy responses which redress their loss in economic and/or political power. Through the analysis of policy resolution, it is possible to assess the outcome of the process of change in the context of each separate challenge, while also comparing the degree of divergence in policy outcomes across cases.

Policy resolutions differ along two basic dimensions: *content* and *level*.

Content refers to the substantive details of policy decisions. For example, the content of policy outcomes can range from state-led to market-led, or deregulatory to reregulatory. The content of the policy resolution reflects the nature of the original challenge, the way in which the policy network was mobilized, and the process of conflict over how to respond to the challenge. As noted previously, each challenge mobilizes a particular set of institutions with a particular set of policy goals. Over time, the process of conflict among these institutions gives rise to a changing set of policy responses which ultimately culminates in a policy resolution.

The level of the policy resolution, whether it takes place at the national or the international level, also reflects the nature of the original challenge. For example, the challenge to the economic interests of commercial banks could only be resolved through *domestic-level regulatory reform*. Because the competitiveness of U.S. commercial banks could only be restored through adjusting domestic regulatory structures to the standards prevailing in other major financial markets, the level of the policy resolution was by definition domestic. By contrast, the challenge to the political authority of state institutions generated pressures not only for domestic adjustment but also for *international-level regulatory coordination*. The regulatory authority of U.S. policymakers could only be restored if domestic regulatory reforms were coupled with an international agreement to coordinate financial regulation and thus broaden the political reach of national regulatory authorities in an increasingly integrated global financial market.

Finally, the resolution phase also reveals the extent of institutional change that occurs in response to the challenge and that is required in order to adjust to the challenge. First, as will become evident, institutions are not only the object of the process of change that is induced by an external challenge. Rather, institutions themselves become the agents of their own change and induce change in other institutions. Secondly, institutions do not always break down in a series of crises after periods of resistance to change. On the contrary, they are remarkably flexible, adapting to changing circumstances in order to survive the external challenge, and sometimes even confronting the external challenge itself and emerging from it with renewed strength.

The three phase adjustment model is summarized in Figure 2.1. External economic pressure leads to an increasing integration of financial markets among the advanced industrial nations. This process of international financial integration creates multiple challenges to the domestic policy network. In this particular case, one challenge is directed at the private sector, the other at the public sector. Responding to each challenge, the policy network mobilizes (phase 1). In the case of Glass-Steagall the nature of the challenge leads to the complete mobilization of all the institutions in

Figure 2.1 The Three Phase Adjustment Model

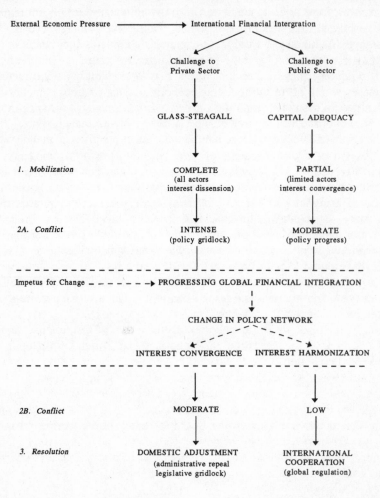

the policy network. The case of capital adequacy, on the other hand, results only in a partial mobilization. Moreover, while the challenge in the case of Glass-Steagall exemplifies strong interest dissension among both private and public sector institutions, there is considerable interest convergence among the institutions in the case of capital adequacy. As a result, the conflicts also differ across the two cases (phase 2A). While the Glass-Steagall debate generates an intense conflict that quickly deteriorates into a policy gridlock, facilitated by the fragmented regulatory structure, the issue of capital adequacy only generates moderate conflicts allowing for some progress towards a policy resolution.

However, the circumstances external to the policy network do not remain constant over time. External pressures change over time and so do the challenges that emanate from them, creating the impetus for change in the policy network. In the case of this particular study, global financial integration continues to accelerate during the 1980s. This alters the interests of some central actors in the policy network, leading to realignment of the opposing coalitions in the policy network. In both cases the change in the policy network also leads to a change in the degree of conflict (phase 2B). In the case of Glass-Steagall the conflict decreases from intense to moderate. In the case of capital adequacy, where conflict was already moderate, it more or less subsides. These changes facilitate the achievement of a policy resolution. With regard to the Glass-Steagall debate, the partial resolution results in domestic adjustment of the regulatory structure despite the fact that some elements of the policy network remain opposed to its repeal. In the case of capital adequacy, the resolution is achieved by forging an international regulatory agreement recognizing the existence of a fully integrated global financial market.

The following two chapters will provide the empirical and theoretical background for the case studies. Chapter 3 will discuss the historical development and the contemporary structure of the U.S. banking and financial system. Subsequently, Chapter 4 will examine the global integration of financial markets, paying particular attention to developments in the United States.

NOTES

1. Katzenstein (1978); Zysman (1983); Hall (1986).
2. For example, Katzenstein emphasizes the stability of domestic policy networks and the continuity in the policies those networks generate in the face of major changes in the external economic environment: 'Both [Austria and Switzerland] have been able politically to absorb very large economic changes without...a fundamental questioning of existing political institutions and practices. Groups that might have benefited from other policies were politically contained within existing domestic structures.' Katzenstein (1984).
3. As Katzenstein points out, 'The contemporary structures of advanced industrial states are rooted in some of the major historical transformations of the past: the elimination of feudalism, the unfolding of the Industrial Revolution, and the building of the modern state. Except in the most extreme circumstances, negotiations on current issues in the international political economy will probably reflect, rather than reshape, these historically-evolved domestic structures.' Katzenstein (1978).
4. Some of the literature does acknowledge the possibility of *cross-sectoral* variations in the effectiveness of the adjustment process within a single country but they do not consider divergence in policy response within the same sector. Zysman (1978).

5. More recently, Katzenstein has acknowledged the importance of change as an element that shapes the policy network and its institutions. In his discussion of recent political and economic developments in West Germany during the 1980s, he identifies 'three prominent changes that are transforming the context in which the West German polity now operates: new production technologies in industrial plants, new social movements in national politics, and new political currents in the international economy.' All three developments are acknowledged as having some influence on the policy network in West Germany, even though it is not quite obvious how deeply these pressures will transform the policy network and its institutional setting in the Federal Republic. Katzenstein (1989).

6. For the seminal article that led to the renewal of interest in the role of institutions in shaping the political process, see March and Olsen (1984); for a more recent and detailed discussion, see March and Olsen (1989).

7. Ikenberry (1988).

8. Lowi (1964); Gowa (1988); Zimmermann (1973).

9. This theory has been most clearly explicated by Stephen Krasner (1984). The cause of the sudden and explosive character of change is thought to lie within the constraints and the resistance of the institutional organization (its structure as well as its individuals) to adapt to changing external circumstances. Kaufman (1971); Wilson (1973); Skowronek (1982).

10. Ikenberry (1988).

11. Hall (1986).

12. It should be noted that Hall does mention that 'the dynamic component of the polity should also be **described** [my emphasis] here' and acknowledges that '...incremental structural change is a familiar feature of politics....' However, he does not provide us with the analytical framework necessary to analyse change, nor does he provide us with any hypotheses as to the sources of change. Hall (1986).

13. Ikenberry (1988).

14. This perspective must not be confused with a situation where institutions have not changed themselves, although their function or utility has changed as a consequence of changes in the external environment. For example, in the case of financial markets, John Zysman has shown how the British financial system, while perfectly suitable to industrial investment in the 1950s and 1960s, has become an obstacle to industrial adjustment in the 1980s. Zysman, however, does not examine how the British financial system itself has adjusted during the 1980s in response to its contemporary inadequacies. Zysman (1983).

15. For the purpose of clarity, a policy network is the overarching concept that is being examined here. The policy network consists of a set of institutions whose interests and relationships to each other define the network (e.g. centralized vs. decentralized). Institutions in this perspective are thus actors that shape policy outcomes. This does not mean that single individuals cannot have a major influence on policy outcomes. When this is the case, the analysis will draw specific attention to it in order to distinguish between actors as individuals and actors as institutions.

16. Another possible means of protecting an industrial sector from intensive international competition, even though it is unlikely to restore its market power, is protectionism. However, given the degree of integration of the U.S. financial markets in international markets, this is no longer a realistic possibility and would not even be in the interest of U.S. banks.

17. Moreover, as this study will show, some challenges require the activation of another country's policy networks, providing an additional dimension to the policymaking process.

3. The U.S. Banking System: Structure and Regulation

THE STRUCTURE OF COMMERCIAL BANK REGULATION IN THE UNITED STATES

The regulations that govern the American banking system are implemented in the context of a decentralized banking and regulatory structure which originated in the nineteenth and twentieth centuries. One of the principal characteristics of the U.S. regulatory structure is the dual banking system. This allows banks to seek a charter at either the federal or the state level. As a result, there are 50 state legislatures that have decisionmaking authority with regard to bank regulation. Similarly, supervisory responsibility and the implementation of bank regulations rest with 50 state regulatory authorities.[1] The state regulatory authorities are represented in Washington by the Conference of State Bank Supervisors, which monitors all federal regulatory activity that could in any way impinge on their regulatory power. This decentralization of regulatory power and authority is replicated within the federal regulatory structure, where the regulation and supervision of commercial banks is divided among three separate agencies: the Office of the Comptroller of the Currency (OCC); the Federal Reserve (Fed); and the Federal Deposit Insurance Corporation (FDIC).[2]

The OCC, an arm of the Treasury Department, oversees all national banks with regard to charters, mergers, branching, consumer-law compliance, prudential limits, soundness examination and international matters. By comparison, the Federal Reserve is an autonomous body whose board members are appointed by the President for 14-year terms. The Fed is the sole supervisory authority with regard to acquisitions and bank-related financial activities of bank holding companies (BHCs).[3] In addition, the Fed shares regulatory authority with the OCC over all national banks, and over any state banks which choose to become members of the Federal Reserve System (FRS).

Finally, the FDIC is a quasi-autonomous organization governed by a five member board composed of the Comptroller of the Currency, the Director of the Office of Thrift Supervision (OTS), and three members appointed by the President for six-year terms. The FDIC is primarily responsible for administering the deposit insurance program, arranging mergers to forestall bank failures, and conducting bankruptcy proceedings. All national banks are required to belong to the FDIC, whose membership also includes all state banks choosing federal insurance.[4]

Together, the dual banking system and the multiple regulators have led to the creation of the four different types of commercial banks, defined by the level at which they are chartered and whether they are insured by the FDIC and/or are members of the Federal Reserve System: national banks, state member banks, insured non-member banks, non-insured banks (Table 3.1). This has resulted in a complex and often confusing web of bank regulation where a single commercial bank is under the jurisdiction of at least two different regulatory regimes and supervised by several regulators (Figure 3.1).[5]

The Securities and Exchange Commission (SEC) is the federal agency that regulates the activities of investment banks. The SEC played an important role in the debate over the repeal of the Glass-Steagall Act, which took place at the interface between commercial and investment banking and thus impinged on the SEC's institutional role in the financial policy network.

Legislative responsibility and primary decisionmaking power over banking and securities matters rest with Congress and the various legislative committees which share jurisdiction over banking and securities regulation. In the Senate, the Committee on Banking, Housing and Urban Affairs legislates on financial regulatory issues. In the House of Representatives, legislative oversight is divided between the Committee on Banking, Finance and Urban Affairs, which is responsible for depository industry regulation (including commercial banks), and the Committee on Energy and Commerce, which deals with all regulatory issues related to the securities industry. In matters relating to antitrust actions or bankruptcy, both the Senate and House Judiciary Committees also have jurisdiction over financial legislation.

In addition to the public sector institutions listed above, the U.S. financial policy network is characterized by numerous well-organized and politically powerful financial lobbies representing the various financial service industries. Within the commercial banking industry alone, one can distinguish between at least three different categories of institutions. First are the large money centre banks, usually organized as holding companies; for the most part, they engage in wholesale banking and international operations. These banks hold the majority of bank assets in the U.S. but represent a small minority of all commercial banks. A second tier of banks operate in major regional banking markets such as Boston, Houston and Atlanta. Finally, there are the thousands of banks in small communities serving the needs of local businesses and farmers.

Table 3.1 The Structure of Commercial Bank Regulation in the United States

BANK CATEGORY

	National bank	State member bank	State non-member bank	State non-insured bank
Chartering authority	Comptroller of Currency	State banking agency	State banking agency	State banking agency
Fed membership	Mandatory	By choice	Non-member	Non-member
FDIC insurance	Mandatory	Mandatory	By choice	Not covered (may be covered by state)

Source: Adapted from Raymond Natter, *Formation and Powers of National Banks — A Legal Primer*, U.S. Government Printing Office (Washington: 1983).

Figure 3.1 The Complex System of U.S. Bank Regulation

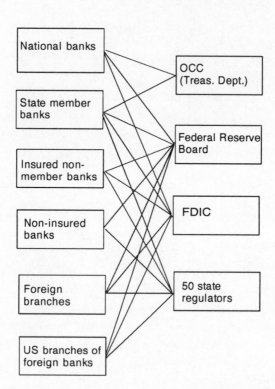

Part of the conflict that is the focus of this inquiry is a result of the diversity in size and client base among commercial banks; this generates considerable differences in banks' economic interests and their resultant political strategies.[6] These diverse interests have led to the existence of a variety of lobbies representing commercial banks on Capitol Hill. Large banks often represent their interests through their own offices in Washington, D.C., as well as through the American Bankers Association

(ABA) and the Association of Bank Holding Companies (ABHC). The actual clientele of the ABA includes commercial banks of all sizes, and the lobby organization has often been split internally over its appropriate position towards various regulatory issues. On one occasion the ABA sent two separate representatives to testify on Capitol Hill, one representing the interests of the small banks, the other those of the large banks. In general, however, the ABA has favoured the positions of the large banks, which has often led to bitter controversies within the organization. The regional banks have their own lobbying organization as well, known as the Coalition of Regional Banking and Economic Development. Small banks are represented by the Independent Bankers Association of America (IBAA). The IBAA has a long tradition of fighting the powerful interests of the larger banks on Capitol Hill. It sees its primary role as the preservation of the dual banking system as well as the safeguarding of all regulations that protect the small rural banks.

Just as in the public sector, where securities regulation is located in a single federal agency, the securities industry lobby is also more centralized than its banking counterpart. The Securities Industry Association (SIA) is the primary representative of investment banks in Washington. Similar to the ABA, it is a powerful and well-funded lobby with close contacts to the relevant banking committees. Another lobby which has become an important voice in some of the conflicts over bank regulation is the Investment Company Institute (ICI), which represents the mutual fund industry.

Viewed in its entirety, the structure of the U.S. financial policy network is comprised of a complex and decentralized array of public and private sector institutions and their interests. As Figure 3.1 shows, this leads to overlapping jurisdictions among the various state and federal regulators with the likelihood of conflict arising among the various regulators if they do not share the same regulatory philosophies towards commercial banks. In addition to this fragmented and decentralized structure, the commercial banking system is governed by a complex array of rules and regulations. One set of regulations geared towards the commercial banks' ability to interact with the real sectors of the economy has restricted, and in many cases continues to restrict, the operations of banks. Price regulation used to control the amount of interest banks were allowed to pay their depositors; geographic regulations place restrictions upon the ability of commercial banks to branch within individual states or across state lines; and product regulation delineates the kind of financial services that commercial banks can and cannot provide. The rationale of these regulations varies. For the most part they are designed to avoid excessive competition and risk-taking among the banks.

A second set of regulations applies less to the broader conditions under which commercial banks interact with other sectors of the economy; rather, it is designed to safeguard the financial and economic stability of the individual institution. Such regulations include: specific requirements that must be met before one can charter a bank; reserve requirements that banks as members of the Federal Reserve System have to maintain; and capital that banks must hold in order to meet sudden and unanticipated losses in their operations.

HISTORY AND DEVELOPMENT OF FINANCIAL PRODUCT REGULATION IN THE UNITED STATES

The history of the American banking system is one of expansion interspersed with recurrent breakdowns and crises. Since the early nineteenth century, periods of rapid growth in the banking sector have culminated in unsustainable expansions of lending, uncontrolled speculation, and eventual financial collapse. As the banking system has experienced cycles of growth and crisis, the regulation of financial products that commercial banks are permitted to provide has undergone parallel cycles of decontrol and restriction. Periods of rapid banking growth have typically coincided with and been fuelled by deregulation with regard to financial product restrictions, while financial crises have led to the reimposition of regulatory controls that separate various banking activities from each other.[7]

Glass-Steagall as a Regulatory Tool

One such cycle of unregulated growth, crisis and reregulation played itself out in the first third of the twentieth century. Rapid banking expansion in the decade following World War I culminated in a sudden and dramatic deterioration in the soundness of the banking system after 1929. Between 1930 and 1933, nearly 9,000 of the nation's 25,000 commercial banks failed. The banking crisis created an environment ripe for radical revision of the legal framework governing depository institutions.[8]

After coming to office in March 1933, President Franklin Roosevelt launched the most far-reaching regulatory reform of the financial services industry in U.S. history. After almost a century of free banking, the pendulum could not have moved more dramatically towards reregulation. The centrepiece of reform was the Banking Act of 1933, which placed a large share of the responsibility for the Depression on the securities activities of commercial banks.[9] According to Congress, banks made 'one of the greatest contributions to the unprecedented disaster which has caused this almost incurable depression'.[10]   This legislation included four key sections known as the Glass-Steagall Act, which was designed to divorce commercial from investment banking.[11] The Glass-Steagall Act prohibited commercial banks from underwriting, purchasing, or selling corporate securities. Conversely, securities firms were prohibited from accepting deposits that were subject to withdrawal by checking, passbook, or certificates.[12]

Congress intended the Glass-Steagall Act to achieve three primary objectives: to restore public confidence in the banking system; to ensure economic stability by prohibiting imprudent bank investment; and to forestall potential conflicts of interest between commercial and investment banking operations.[13]   This set of objectives reflected Congress's conviction that too much competition among banks had resulted in the 'speculative' banking practices of the 1920s, that it was particularly the banks' activities as investors, underwriters, and distributors of securities that had caused the banking panics and the resultant depression.[14]

The Regulation of Financial Products Before the 1980s

The principles of the Glass-Steagall Act were not significantly challenged in the first three decades following its passage. Finding sufficient room for expansion in other areas, commercial banks felt little need to press for repeal of the ban on securities activities.[15] The separate markets that had been carved out for commercial and investment banks in the wake of the New Deal legislation provided sufficient capital for each member of the cartel of financial institutions during the rest of the 1930s and the 1940s.[16]

Subsequently, contrary to what many policymakers and economists feared, the U.S. post-World War II economy experienced a remarkable period of growth and expansion. Following this general trend of the economy, financial intermediaries also experienced a remarkable degree of growth in the quarter century after World War II. Total assets of financial institutions grew from approximately $125 billion in 1940 to over $1 trillion in 1967, surpassing any other growth index. By 1965, financial institutions were supplying 85 per cent of all funds raised in the credit markets compared to about 75 per cent of the much smaller credit pool in the 1950s.[17]

While all benefited from the sustained economic expansion, the growth patterns of individual financial institutions varied. In 1940, commercial banks, life insurance companies, and mutual savings banks were the giants in the financial markets. S&Ls and general insurance companies, about equal in asset size, lagged far behind. And other financial intermediaries, such as investment companies and credit unions, were almost non-existent.

By 1955 this had changed. The assets of pension funds had multiplied 70 times, those of investment companies 45 times, and those of credit unions 40 times.[18] Thus, despite the overall market growth, commercial banks' share of all intermediary assets had fallen from almost 60 per cent in 1950 to 45 per cent by 1960.[19]

The regulatory restrictions placed on commercial banks became increasingly binding in light of the expanding markets of the 1950s and 1960s. To satisfy the rising demand for loans and to finance their growing investment activities, banks required new sources of capital. This need for funds led banks to mount their first serious challenges to the restrictions placed on their activities by the Glass-Steagall Act.[20] Although the Glass-Steagall Act prohibited affiliations between bank holding companies and securities firms, the act placed no other restrictions on the products and services provided by BHCs.[21] And although the BHC Act of 1956 prohibited *multibank* holding companies (MBHCs) from engaging in most non-banking activities, these restrictions did not apply to holding companies that controlled only a single bank.[22] Large commercial banks found that so called unitary or one bank holding companies (OBHCs) provided attractive vehicles for raising capital and diversifying into a wide range of non-bank activities.[23] Of the 1,300 OBHCs that were registered with the Fed by the end of 1970, 891 had been formed between 1966 and 1970. Of those 891, the Fed determined that 455 were engaged in activities other than banking, such as insurance, securities and real estate operations, as well as manufacturing and retailing activities.[24]

Commercial banks' efforts to circumvent regulatory restrictions and to diversify their operations through OBHCs received, for the most part, a negative reception from the regulators, Congress and the Nixon Administration. Regulators warned that '[A] decade marked by great permissiveness, the 1920s, brought almost unrestrained expansion followed by collapse and a depression that caused untold suffering....[W]e appear to be drifting toward a repetition of serious errors that the banking industry fell into in the 1920s.'[25] The Administration, too, was alarmed by the banks' attempt to invade forbidden territories. In March of 1969, President Nixon stated that if left unchecked, the disturbing erosion of the traditional separation of powers between the banks and commerce could eventually result in the formation of a few power centres dominating the American economy.[26] Congress was quick to respond. Led by Wright Patman, Chairman of the House Banking Committee, legislation was introduced which culminated in the passage of the 1970 Amendments to the Bank Holding Company Act of 1956, forcing OBHCs under the same rules and regulations as multibank holding companies.[27] The Administration fully supported the legislation. As a representative of the Nixon Administration explained to the Senate Banking Committee in 1970, the BHC restrictions were necessary to prevent the U.S. from copying the 'zaibatsu' arrangements in Japan.[28]

While Congress and the Fed were closing off attempts by BHCs to diversify their activities, the courts were blocking similar efforts by national banks. During the 1960s, Comptroller of the Currency James J. Saxon, who had sympathized with the banks' drive to expand into the securities area, authorized national banks to engage in various activities that were generally considered to be prohibited by the Glass-Steagall Act. These rulings were challenged by the other regulators and the securities industry, and a series of other judicial decisions eventually rejected each one of the Comptroller's rulings.[29]

In general, therefore, commercial banks had little success in eroding the barriers of Glass-Steagall during the 1960s and 1970s. In their efforts to expand into other markets that were prohibited by the Glass-Steagall Act, they were confronted by a public sector that, with the exception of the Comptroller, had in the early 1960s arrived at a consensus on maintaining the separation between commercial and investment banking under any circumstances.

HISTORY AND DEVELOPMENT OF CAPITAL ADEQUACY REGULATION IN THE UNITED STATES

Bank Capital as a Regulatory Tool

The responsibility of mediating between a nation's lenders and borrowers has placed banks in a position in which the soundness of the industry is a matter of public interest. There exists widespread agreement among policymakers and academics that definite advantages accrue to the public welfare if depositors and borrowers can be assured that individual financial institutions and the financial system at large are safe and sound. In addition, regulation of the financial services industry aims at halting excessive instability in the money supply. In the past, such instability led to severe contractions in jobs, production, and general economic activity. This clearly sets banking apart from other industries and provides a unique and compelling rationale for regulation and close supervision.[30]

Assurance of a sound and stable banking system can be provided in various ways, such as deposit insurance, restrictions on the risks assumed by financial institutions, or requiring financial institutions to hold adequate capital to absorb potential losses. Because of the integral link between a bank's capital base and the soundness of each individual bank and the banking system at large, the periodic evaluation of the adequacy of bank capital is in fact one of the main tools of regulators.[31] The regulatory function of capital stems from its ability to absorb *temporary* and *unanticipated* losses. Temporary and unanticipated are emphasized because no reasonable amount of capital will protect a bank from collapse for a longer time period. Also, banks usually set aside special reserves for anticipated losses so that capital does not have to absorb those losses as well.[32] In addition, capital is not held against losses that might arise from difficulties in the overall economy. Under these circumstances, the country's central bank, as the lender of last resort, will step in and protect the bank from failure.

The temporary and unanticipated losses which are covered by a bank's capital base arise from a variety of risks, including credit and investment risk.[33] Credit risk refers to the possibility that borrowers may default on interest and principal payments. Investment risk is the result of rising interest rates and disintermediation, which leads to the liquidation of securities. Both of these risks are always present and must be considered a permanent feature of banking. Another form of risk arises from unanticipated liquidity shortages.[34] Finally, losses can arise from faulty operating procedures and outright fraud.

In addition to serving as a cushion against the risks inherent in the business of banking, capital also serves several other functions. For example, it protects uninsured depositors and creditors and allows policymakers to constrain the growth of individual banks when it is considered too rapid.[35]

Given these attributes, bank capital has long been an important regulatory instrument. Its ability to absorb losses is instrumental in avoiding bank failure; in addition, it ensures that the owners of the institution are playing with their own money.[36] With deposit insurance, an institution with negligible net worth has great incentives to take risks. However, the potential losses are borne by the insurance system, and ultimately the taxpayer, if the government must come to the rescue. By implementing a capital requirement, the bank has to share the possible loss. Furthermore, the need to raise capital can subject an institution to market discipline. A risk-prone bank will have to pay more to obtain capital than a risk-averse one. This helps to minimize the possibility of failure from excessive risk-taking.

Commercial banks' positions towards capital regulation have historically been quite different from those of regulators. While the regulators have been mainly concerned with ensuring the managerial prudence of individual banks and the soundness of the banking system at large, commercial bankers have been more concerned with safeguarding the competitiveness and profitability of the individual bank. The banks' arguments against capital supervision stem from their desire to maximize profits. For commercial banks, capital represents a cost that inhibits their ability to offer attractive terms and compete with other providers of financial services. They reject the regulators' implicit assumption that banks are quasi-public utilities which must be subjected to capital adequacy supervision in order to ensure the smooth functioning of the national payments system. In fact, banks contend that capital regulations hamper rather than enhance the efficient functioning of the financial system by creating pressure for all banks to capitalize to the lowest standard of competence and the highest standard of risk. Banks argue that if regulations require them to have more capital than they would in the absence of regulations, banks will compensate for that by taking greater risks.[37]

According to banks, the marketplace should determine the extent to which they should be capitalized.[38] The market mechanism, banks argue, exerts discipline upon banks that are becoming too leveraged by making it difficult for them to float debt or equity issues, and by subjecting them to the scrutiny of creditors who will avoid undercapitalized banks.[39]

Regulators have responded to banks' arguments for market regulation of bank capital by pointing out two primary reasons why the market — the principal alternative mechanism — fails to evaluate and establish adequate bank capital standards. The first is the lack of perfect information.[40] The nature of banking is such that adequate information cannot be made available for the market to discipline the banking industry.[41] A large number of small, uninformed depositors face great difficulty and expense in policing each institution's risk level.

The second cause of market imperfections arises from banking's long history of regulation. This has led to an environment where investors have been relatively unconcerned with the soundness of the banking industry. The most obvious example of this is, of course, the fact that small depositors are insured and thus fully protected. But even large depositors have, on the basis of historical experience, little reason to worry ('too big to fail'). Therefore the market has neither the reason nor the experience to evaluate the risk position of banks and is thus not very concerned with bank capital and how much of it is adequate.[42]

While the basic philosophy of regulating capital is shared by the three regulators, there are differences in implementation which stem from their varying roles in the regulatory system. The OCC is generally interested in maintaining competitive and viable institutions, and places an emphasis on individual banks when setting capital standards. Because of its experience in supervising the more stable banks, the Comptroller's office is generally considered the least conservative. The FDIC has a different constituency, as it deals with many small individual banks chartered at the state level. Due to the proclivity of state non-member banks to fail and to put the deposit insurance fund in jeopardy, the FDIC focuses much more on bank failure and depositor protection than the Comptroller. The Fed, on the other hand, is more often identified with monetary policy rather than bank regulation and its policies reflect this position. Emphasis is placed on the well-being of the entire banking system and special consideration is given to aspects of growth, as they pertain to banking, and the BHC movement, which enlarges the relative share of liquid assets over which the central bank can exercise control.[43]

The Regulation of Bank Capital Before the 1980s

Before the Great Depression of the 1930s, federal bank regulatory agencies measured capital adequacy through a capital-to-deposit ratio which focused on bank liquidity.[44] During the depression, the emphasis shifted to measures of solvency, centred around the capital-to-asset ratio. One reason for this shift was that the capital-to-deposit ratio was inappropriate for evaluating a bank's capability to absorb losses, since losses are incurred on assets rather than on deposits.

During World War II, banks expanded rapidly, primarily as a result of investment in U.S. government bonds. The Federal Reserve, in seeking a way to avoid penalizing banks for investing in these low-yield and 'riskless' assets, devised a new ratio of capital-to-risk assets. For this purpose, risk assets were defined as total assets excluding cash, balances due from other banks, and U.S. government securities. Initially, a 20 per cent standard for this ratio was established as 'sufficient' capital. It was at this time that the concept of capital adequacy first became associated with the risks inherent in the earning asset portfolio. Then in 1952, the Federal Reserve adopted an adjusted risk asset approach to measuring capital. All assets were categorized according to risk, with separate capital requirements assigned to each category. The minimum total capital required was the sum of the capital requirements of each category. Banks that exceeded this minimum by 25 per cent rarely had their level of capital questioned.[45]

Throughout this period, the FDIC and the OCC had followed the lead of the Federal Reserve, adopting its principle for measuring capital. In 1962, however, Comptroller of the Currency James J. Saxon, pressured by commercial banks, decided to abandon the risk asset standard on the grounds that it was arbitrary and did not consider factors such as management, liquidity, asset quality, or earnings trends.[46] In addition, there was mounting disagreement between the three regulatory agencies over what constituted capital.[47]

Thus in the early 1960s, regulatory opinion on capital adequacy became divided and the agencies began to apply different standards to their respective client banks. For the remainder of the 1960s and the 1970s, the federal bank regulators continued to use different definitions of capital and methods of measuring capital adequacy. Furthermore, none of these agencies established a firm minimum capital ratio; instead, they assessed the capital positions of banking institutions on the basis of ad hoc, bank-specific evaluations of capital adequacy.[48]

None of the regulatory agencies had the direct legal authority to enforce practices concerning capital. Requests for additional capital were supported by persuasion rather than the threat of legal sanctions.[49] Of course, persuasion could go as far as denying branch and acquisition applications and, in extreme cases, invoking cease and desist orders.[50]

In sum, since the early 1960s the regulatory structure in the area of capital reserves has been fragmented, and the supervision of capital standards has been conducted in an ad hoc manner.[51] This decentralized policy network was little challenged during the 1960s and much of the 1970s. Banking crises were small and isolated and the respective regulatory agencies had little trouble in handling their resolution on an ad hoc and individual basis.

Yet when the challenge of declining capital ratios and the associated systemic risks erupted in the late 1970s, commentators quickly pointed to the difficulties that such a dispersed regulatory structure would encounter in responding to the challenge. They argued that a concerted and coherent effort to resolve the problem of declining capital ratios was unlikely, given the structural separation and the varying institutional responsibilities of the three regulatory agencies, as well as the history of conflicts over capital adequacy supervision.[52]

Coordinated effort was not expected from the legislature either. Throughout the 1960s and 1970s, the legislature had not been involved in any policy debates with respect to capital adequacy. Given the dispersed and individualistic format that was used to evaluate the capital adequacy of commercial banks, there was little room for a more nationwide approach, initiated by the legislature, to the issue of capital adequacy. Moreover, in weighing the chances of congressional action one commentator suggested, '[C]ongress seldom ranks reforms with such a time profile of costs and benefits high on its agenda.'[53] Finally, regulatory agencies were likely to resist if Congress encroached upon their turf and attempted to restrict the freedom of examining banks according to principles internal to the individual organization.

As a result of this complicated institutional structure and the divergent interests, no concerted action was expected to emerge from the policy network.

NOTES

1. Hackley (1966); Scott (1977).
2. Carron (1983).
3. Since 1965, the number of BHCs has grown from 53 MBHCs with 8.3 per cent of all commercial bank deposits to 6,425 BHCs holding 94 per cent of assets of all insured commercial banks. Board of Governors of the Federal Reserve (1990).
4. Silverberg (1976).
5. Reinicke (1983).
6. Keller (1982).
7. For a history of banking in the U.S. before 1933, see: Klebaner (1974); Krooss and Blyn (1971); Polakoff (1970); Goldsmith (1958); Redlich (1946-51); Shull (1983); Hammond (1957); McCarthy (1984); Carosso (1970); White (1983).
8. Kennedy (1973).
9. Senate Report No. 77 (1933).
10. Senator Glass in *Congressional Record*, Vol. 75. In conjunction with the debate to repeal the Glass-Steagall Act, this interpretation has been questioned. According to this revisionist school, the act was designed to benefit both commercial banks and investment banks by restricting competition in both industries. Macey (1984); Benston (1990).
11. The main sponsor was Carter Glass, one of the original sponsors of the Federal Reserve Act of 1913 and Republican Chairman of the Senate Banking Committee's subcommittee to review national banking. In arguing for a separation of commercial from investment banking, Glass adhered strongly to real bills doctrine, which stated that intertwining of commercial and investment banking in the 1920s contributed to the stock market crash and to the wave of bank failures. Congress rejected these views in the early years of the Depression by consistently voting down Glass's proposals to divorce commercial from investment banking. However, the political climate began to change in 1932 in favour of Carter Glass. Perkins (1971); *Hearings on the Operation of the National and Federal Reserve Banking Systems* (1931). Other important provisions of the National Banking Act were a revision and tightening of branching restrictions, the creation of the FDIC, the imposition of interest rate dealings on deposits, and the strengthening of the Fed as regulator of banking activities. Preston (1933). For a text of the act, see *Federal Reserve Bulletin*, June 1933.
12. Public Law 66-48, Stat. 162 (1933). Kelly (1985).
13. Plotkin (1978).
14. After a series of hearings, which later became known as the Precora Hearings, many executives from the nation's largest banks and investment houses admitted to practices that ranged from negligence to outrageousness. By the winter of 1933, the financial community had been totally discredited. Kennedy (1973); Carosso (1970); Saunders (1985). In fact, by the time President Roosevelt declared the bank holiday, the new chairman of the Chase Manhattan Bank, Winthrop Aldrich, endorsed the separation of commercial and investment banking, as did National City Bank. Kelly (1985); Flannery (1985); *Stock Exchange Practices*, 1933.
15. During the World War II years, for example, commercial banks took advantage of the opportunities offered by the federal government's rapidly expanding debt by entering the market for government securities. By the end of the war, banks held almost 50 per cent of outstanding public debt.
16. Huertas (1983).
17. Krooss and Blyn (1971).
18. Ibid.
19. Gerston, Farleigh and Schwab (1988).
20. Eisenbeis (1983); Jesse and Selig (1977).
21. Savage (1978).

22. The Bank Holding Company Act of 1956 was designed to limit MBHCs from product expansion not so much to protect the safety and soundness of the banking system as to prevent undue concentration of banking resources and to preserve fair credit allocation. *Bank Holding Company Act Amendments* (1966); Symons (1957 and 1983).
23. Citicorp was the first bank to form an OBHC in 1968. For a private sector perspective on the one bank holding company movement, see 'One Bank Holding Companies: A Banker's View' (1969); Eglert (1970).
24. 'One-bank Holding Companies Before the 1970 Amendments' (1972); House Committee on Banking and Currency (1969).
25. J.L. Robertson, Vice Chairman of the Board of Governors of the Federal Reserve System, 'An Inside Look at Federal Bank Regulation', address before the State Bank Division meeting of the ABA's 94th Annual Convention, 30 September 1968.
26. Statement of Richard Nixon, 24 March 1969, reprinted in House of Representatives, Conference Report No. 1747, 1970.
27. Public Law 91-607, 1970; for more, see Halpert (1988).
28. Litan (1987).
29. Dunn (1982); Scott (1977); Hackley (1969); Fischer, Gram, Kaufman and Mote (1984); Macey (1984).
30. Orgler and Wolkowitz (1976); Merton (1979); Edwards and Scott (1979).
31. For an excellent discussion of the role of capital as a regulatory tool, see Bhala (1989), especially Chapter 2.
32. The most common example is, of course, the reserves set aside by large commercial banks for the anticipated losses which arise from loans to developing countries.
33. Orgler and Wolkowitz (1976).
34. The incidence of such shortages rose throughout the 1970s and 1980s as banks increased their reliance on liability management; as interest rate volatility increased (along with the likelihood of a mismatch in the term structure of interest rates); and as financial markets became internationalized, leaving the supply of liquid funds not entirely under the control of a national banking system.
35. By raising the ratio of capital to assets a bank is required to maintain, regulators can influence individual banks and the industry and force them into a go-slow policy with regard to bank development and expansion.
36. Horvitz (1987).
37. During the 1970s, bankers charged that the regulatory system was partly to blame for the poor record of the economy in saving and capital investment. Banks claimed that their efficiency, proper choice of investments, and decision making were seriously hampered by the arbitrary imposition of capital requirements by regulators who were ignorant of the facts and who lacked an adequate understanding of how financial institutions control risk. For a refutation of this argument, see Heggestad (1982).
38. *American Banker*, 2 December 1980.
39. It is not fully established that the market actually can do that. Earlier studies in fact concluded that leverage has no impact on stock prices. Pettway (1976); Heggestad (1982).
40. Isaac (1982).
41. Banks are not legally required to routinely provide information on the quality of loans and investments, volatility of liabilities and other aspects of a bank's portfolio. Only about 20 per cent of commercial banks have a sufficient number of stockholders (over 500) to have to disclose financial information under Regulation F of the Federal Reserve Board.
42. Another strong argument often made by banks is that it can be shown empirically that banks do not fail due to inadequate capital. Regulators agree that lack of capital does not cause failure. Failure is more often due to massive real or prospective losses on earning assets or the loss of liquidity, which itself is usually related to perception of prospective losses. However, if the equity were sufficient to absorb the prospective losses, liquidity would not

be threatened. After a bank has collapsed there is seldom residual equity for distribution to stockholders. Thus while inadequate equity does not precipitate failure it is the inevitable result of failure. Accordingly, regulators maintain that banks are less likely to fail if capital is in fact adequate. Gehlen (1983).

43. Demand deposits still represent the largest element of the nation's money supply. Failure of a bank or its parent holding company could weaken public confidence in the safety of their deposits from other banks; this in turn could lead to a significant decline in the nation's money supply and subsequently to the disruption of financial markets. Clarke (1976).

44. Smith (1974).

45. In 1956 the Fed further refined its capital standard by coupling the adjusted risk asset approach with a liquidity test. This test required more capital from less liquid banks. It also considered some off-balance sheet items. The new standard assigned different percentages of capital to the various categories of assets and liabilities. These percentages were used to derive the total amount of capital needed to protect banks from losses on investments and from reductions in deposits and other liabilities. A ratio of actual capital to required capital was calculated; if the ratio was less than 80 per cent, a bank was generally considered undercapitalized.

46. For a detailed list of these factors, see Office of the Comptroller of the Currency, *The Comptroller's Manual*, various years. Until 1971 the manual opened with a statement that disclaimed the reliance on capital ratios in assessing the capital adequacy of national banks.

47. The Federal Reserve preferred to continue to define capital as equity plus reserves for loan losses. By contrast, the FDIC and the OCC wanted to allow somewhat less stringent standards and permit banks to count some forms of debt as capital. As to the ratio, the FDIC relied on a capital-to-average total asset ratio, excluding fixed and substandard assets. The Fed continued to use risk assets as the denominator in its capital ratios, although it frequently revised its definition of risk assets. Orgler and Wolkowitz (1976).

48. Before the 1980s, subjective capital standards based on the results of the regulatory agencies' examinations of individual banks were the main form of capital regulation. Typically, regulators compared capital-to-asset ratios for bank peer groups (banks grouped by common characteristics such as asset size) and tried to ensure that banks that were below the group's average raised their ratio. Particular attention was directed towards smaller banks, whose loan portfolios were not as diversified and whose shareholders were fewer in number than those of larger institutions. For more on the different methods to measure capital, see Mayne (1974).

49. Keeton (1989).

50. This is usually not done. Part of the reason is attributed to the experience of the Fed in 1959 when it attempted to remove a bank from its membership due to inadequate capital. The trial examiner dismissed the case and recommended that the Board clarify its capital evaluation procedure, since the examiner could not judge the capital adequacy from financial ratios.

51. One commentator compared the dynamics among the regulators, as well as the banks, to a poker game. Kane (1981).

52. Kane (1981).

53. Ibid.

4. The Global Integration of Financial Markets

The roots of the trend towards international financial integration in the post-World War II era can be traced back to several developments during the late 1950s and early 1960s which contributed to the evolution of the Eurodollar market.[1] The sterling crisis of 1957 led to restrictions being imposed on the use of sterling bills in international trade between non-British residents. The London bill, a traditional vehicle behind much of world trade, thus abruptly ceased to play a major role. The London merchant banks, determined to maintain their dominant position in international trade, were forced to seek an alternative vehicle to sustain their position. At the same time, the deterioration in U.S.-Soviet relations led Eastern bloc countries to deposit dollar revenues in the more politically secure banks in Western Europe rather than in the U.S. Thus, the initial impetus to the Eurodollar market came from a financing need on the part of the British merchant banks and from an inflow of Eastern bloc dollar deposits.[2]

The Eurodollar market received a strong boost throughout the 1960s, as U.S. financial institutions themselves increasingly went overseas to seek and lend out funds. Two factors were responsible for this development: U.S. regulatory restrictions in financial markets and restrictive monetary policy by the Federal Reserve. Regulation Q, which was imposed by Congress in the early 1930s, placed ceilings on interest rates paid by commercial banks on time and savings deposits; this led investors to seek higher returns abroad and financial institutions to seek business in the Euromarkets where interest rates were not regulated.[3] Similarly, the Interest Equalization Tax, which was imposed in 1963, gave U.S. corporations further incentives not to repatriate their profits and thus further strengthened the Eurodollar market.[4] In addition, restrictive monetary policy, which resulted in the credit crunches of 1966 and 1969, drove U.S. commercial banks to seek more funds abroad in order to be able to meet the demands of a strongly growing U.S. economy.[5]

The expansion of U.S. commercial banks abroad and the growth of the Euromarket were further stimulated by continued economic recovery in Europe and Japan, as well as by the rapid growth of international trade and the internationalization of production through U.S. multinational corporations. The completion of postwar reconstruction in Europe and Japan, the restoration of external convertibility in Europe and the liberalization of capital movements generated a favourable environment for the expansion of trade flows and the ensuing needs for financial support from private banking channels. Concurrently, the internationalization of corporate activity stimulated the broadening of financial services connected with the internationalization of production and international direct investment operations. This expansion of foreign involvement of U.S. banks was most clearly reflected in the increasing presence of U.S. banking institutions abroad (see Table 4.1).[6] International banking was dominated by U.S. banks. In 1960, six of the ten largest banks and 20 of the 50 largest banks were from the United States.[7]

However, the data also show that the number of U.S. banks operating foreign branches began to decline in the second half of the 1980s, as did the share of assets that U.S. banks held abroad. This trend reflected increasing competition both at home, from other financial service providers, as well as abroad, in particular from Japanese and European banks.

Table 4.1   U.S. Banks Abroad, 1960-1990

	1960	1965	1970	1975	1980	1985	1990
No. of US banks operating foreign branches	8	13	79	126	159	163	126
No. of foreign branches of US banks	124	211	532	762	799	967	819
Total assets of branches abroad (bn)	n.a.	8.9	46.5	176.5	397.5	458	557
Total assets of all US banks (bn)	257.6	377.3	576.2	965.2	1703.7	2483.8	3399.9
% of assets held abroad	--	2.4	8.1	18.3	23.3	18.4	16.4

Sources: Rows 1-3: Feileke (1977); *67th Annual Report of the Board of Governors of the Federal Reserve System* (1980); *Federal Reserve Bulletin*, June 1981; *72nd Annual Report of the Board of Governors of the Federal Reserve System* (1985); *Federal Reserve Bulletin*, May 1986; *77th Annual Report of the Board of Governors of the Federal Reserve System* (1990); *Federal Reserve Bulletin*, November 1993. Row 4: *Banking and Monetary Statistics, 1941-70*; *Federal Reserve Bulletin*, June 1976; *Federal Reserve Bulletin*, June 1981; *Federal Reserve Bulletin*, August 1986; *Federal Reserve Bulletin*, June 1991.

Still, with the exception of this strong expansion by U.S. multinational banks, financial markets in the major industrial countries remained relatively separate and insulated during the 1960s.[8] National regulatory structures differed considerably, reflecting distinctive political, legal and administrative traditions, heterogeneous financial systems, and different practical and philosophical approaches to prudential supervision of financial institutions. To a large extent these differences in institutional structure can be traced to variations in the role each national financial system played during the period of the Industrial Revolution.[9]

For most banks, with the exception of U.S. financial institutions, communications and transportation expenses made it too costly to set up financial operations in different national markets. In addition, capital and exchange controls on external financial transactions discouraged the integration of international markets with domestic markets, as well as integration between national financial markets.[10] Therefore, each nation's financial markets developed largely independently of others, and the structure of domestic financial institutions, and the attendant regulatory arrangements, primarily reflected *domestic* concerns.

It was only during the 1970s and, especially, the 1980s that international and domestic markets evolved towards increasing integration. This internationalization emerged as a result of two important trends: the increasing international activities of national financial institutions, and the growing interpenetration and consequent integration of individual national financial markets and their institutions. The root causes of both trends can be traced to a period of macroeconomic instability.[11]

Beginning in the early 1970s, a series of large unanticipated shocks to the international economy contributed to a sharp increase in macroeconomic instability in the advanced industrial nations. The two most important shocks were the breakdown of the Bretton Woods system of fixed exchange rates and the two oil crises of that decade. The abandonment of the system of fixed exchange rates was accompanied by the increased variability of nominal and real exchange rates. Macroeconomic instability also manifested itself in the form of a sharp rise in inflation and an increased volatility of interest rates. Both interest and inflation rates in the major industrial countries started to move sharply higher in 1973, receded temporarily later in the decade, then surged to new peaks around 1980 before falling back again in the mid- to late 1980s. The average rate of inflation in the industrial countries in the 1960s was 3.1 per cent but rose to 7.9 per cent in the 1970s before declining to about 4.5 per cent by the end of the decade. The variance of inflation also increased from 0.6 per cent in the 1960s to 6.7 per cent in the 1970s before declining to 5.5 per cent in the 1980s (Figure 4.1).[12]

Figure 4.1 OECD 1960-1991: Interest, Inflation and Exchange Rates

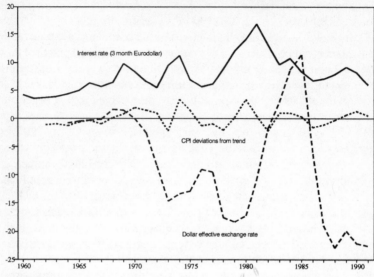

Source: **OECD**

Furthermore, macroeconomic instability contributed to the process of securitization of assets, which in turn played a major role in fostering the internationalization of financial markets.[13]   In its broadest sense, securitization is the process whereby borrowers obtain funds more or less directly from investors, through the sale of publicly-traded, open-market securities.[14] The major difference between tradable securities and the more traditional commercial loan as a form of investment and source of funding is that securities are more flexible and adaptable to changing circumstances in financial markets. Given the macroeconomic instability, securitization became one of the major responses by financial markets and institutions to the increased demand from both savers and investors for financial products that could protect them from the economic uncertainty engendered by high and variable rates of inflation as well as volatile interest rates and exchange rates.[15]

At the domestic level, securitization shifted the centre of financial activity away from more traditional forms of investment, such as commercial bank loans, towards underwriting debt and equity, which is executed by investment banks. In 1980, for example, domestic business borrowing was evenly split between bank loans and securities. By 1990, however, corporate borrowing looked dramatically different. Commercial bank loans were down to 10 per cent while corporate bonds and commercial paper had posted big gains. ABS issuers' loans, a new form of security, amounted to 5 per cent (Figure 4.2).

Many financial institutions, however, were unable to adapt to these changing market circumstances. Domestic regulations either prevented them from engaging in underwriting debt and equity or did not permit the trading of new financial instruments that accommodated the increased risk. Since financial institutions faced a considerably more permissive regulatory environment in international financial markets than in domestic ones, they circumvented domestic regulations that restricted their ability to offer securities by broadening their international activities.[16]

This shift towards securities in international financial markets is remarkable. Between 1981 and 1990, international bond and note issues rose by a factor of seven from \$45 billion to about \$312 billion. In 1985, new international lending facilities in the form of securities peaked at 92.4 per cent as compared to 7.6 per cent for syndicated bank loans. This percentage share has remained above 65 per cent ever since, despite recent gains by the syndicated loan market (Table 4.2).[17]

In sum, the process of securitization contributed significantly to the internationalization of finance by encouraging financial institutions to shift an increasing share of their activities to the international marketplace. Furthermore, this increased international activity associated with the process of securitization fostered the innovation of a series of new financial instruments that were traded in global markets, thereby reinforcing the process of internationalization.[18]

The breakdown of the Bretton Woods system of fixed exchange rates, the two oil crises, and the ensuing world economic instability also contributed in a more immediate way to the process of internationalization and subsequent integration of financial markets. First, the move to flexible exchange rates enhanced the international activities of banks, which had to finance the emerging imbalances in current and capital accounts of the balance of payments, and led to large fluctuations in the banks' net external positions and in their gross asset and liability positions vis-à-vis foreigners. Many public and private institutions shifted their reserve currencies away from the U.S. dollar into such currencies as the Swiss franc, the Deutschmark, and the Japanese yen, which broadened the geographic pool of internationally held money.

Similarly, the share of international borrowing denominated in U.S. dollars declined, as shown by comparing newly announced international bond issues which make up a large portion of world borrowing. In 1982, for example, over 61 per cent of announced international bond issues were denominated

Figure 4.2   Trends in Business Borrowing (by instrument)

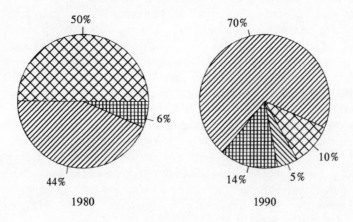

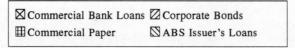

Note: Securities and commercial bank loans made up roughly 55 per cent of total business borrowing.   In 1990, foreign loans were the largest alternative source of business borrowing (37 per cent).

Source: Board of Governors of the Federal Reserve, Flow of Funds Accounts (F.101-F.103) 1991.

Table 4.2 International Financial Market Activity By Sector

($ billions)

	1981	1982	1983	1984	1985	1986	1987	1988	1989	1990
1. International bond issues	44.0	74.3	73.8	108.4	161.9	220.9	180.5	221.6	264.7	239.8
2. Euro-note facilities	1.0	2.4	3.3	18.8	50.3	71.1	73.4	83.2	72.5	72.8
3. All securities	45.0	76.7	77.1	127.2	212.2	292	253.9	304.8	337.2	312.6
4. Syndicated bank loans	131.5	99.4	51.8	36.6	21.1	37.8	87.9	99.3	152.0	157.0
5. (3 + 4)	176.5	173.4	126.6	161.0	232.5	328.2	333.7	404.1	489.2	469.6
6. % share of securities	25.5	44.2	60.9	79.0	92.4	89.1	73.7	75.4	68.9	66.6

Sources: Bank for International Settlements, *Annual Reports*, various years; Bank of England, *Quarterly Bulletin*, May Issue, various years.

in U.S. dollars. By the early 1990s that share had declined to 36 per cent. By comparison, the combined volume of international bond issues denominated in yen, Swiss francs, pounds sterling, ECUs, and Deutschmarks had risen to over 40 per cent by 1990.[19] In addition, the advent of floating rates and the possibility of currency arbitrage also broadened the participation of banks in both spot and forward foreign exchange markets of the major financial centres. Finally, the increased volatility in exchange rates led to an increase in the spread of international assets by investors.[20]

Second, the oil crisis and the central role of banks in recycling the petrodollars provided another formidable boost to the expansion of banks' international activities, which was encouraged by governments unwilling to institute official alternatives for recycling the oil revenues.[21] For one thing, the emergence of large payment imbalances between the OPEC countries and the industrialized nations required financial intermediation on a worldwide scale and brought about a massive increase in both the supply of funds to the international banking system and the demand for balance of payments finance.[22] The international financial industry became the chief beneficiary of this development. International bond financing grew dramatically as governments sought to finance their current account deficits. Moreover, as the large inflow of OPEC surplus capital into the industrial countries exceeded the absorptive capacity of their domestic public and private sectors, banks began lending out the excess capacity to industrializing countries.[23]

Third, in addition to the surge of balance of payments disequilibria, the two oil price shocks of the 1970s subjected the world economy to a deflationary impact that led budget deficits to rise to unprecedented levels in most OECD countries. In a large number of countries the financing of a significant portion of such deficits was carried out by borrowing on international credit markets.[24]

Finally, the growing disassociation between international centres of savings and investment contributed to a further widening of world payments imbalances in the mid- and late 1980s. Of particular significance is the transformation of the United States from a net creditor to a net debtor. The increased involvement of both Japanese and European investors in the financing of the twin deficits in the United States provided another impetus to the growth of international financial intermediation.[25]

The above was reflected in the sharp rise in the growth of the international banking market. For example, the volume of international banking during the last 25 years grew at a compound rate of 24.2 per cent per year. The comparable growth rates for trade and output were 12.6 per cent and 10.4 per cent respectively (Table 4.3).[26]

Table 4.3 World Output, World Exports of Goods and Services, and
International Banking

a. Billions of US dollars
(current prices and exchange rates)

	1964	1972	1980	1983	1985	1988	1990
International Banking							
BIS series for net international bank credit (a)	12	122	810	1240	1485	2390	3350
Morgan Guaranty series for gross size of international banking market (b)	20	208	1559	2253	2833	(#)	(#)
International Trade (c) World trade excluding Eastern bloc countries	188	463	2150	1986	2190	3245	4111
Gross World Product (d) World GDP excluding Eastern bloc countries	1391*	3446	10491	10663	11467	17426	18319*

b. Compound Annual Growth Rates
(per cent)

	1964-72	1972-80	1980-85	1985-90	1964-90
International Banking BIS series for net international bank credit	33.6	26.7	12.9	17.7	24.2
Morgan Guaranty series for gross size of international banking markets	34.0	28.6	10.8	n.a.	n.a.
International Trade World trade excluding Eastern bloc countries	12.0	21.2	0.4	13.4	12.6
Gross Domestic Product World GDP excluding Eastern bloc countries	9.6	15.0	4.7	9.8	10.4

= Discontinued
* = As of December of previous year

Sources: (a) Ralph Bryant, *International Financial Intermediation*, op.cit.; Bank for International Settlements, *Annual Report*, 1988 and 1989. This series nets out interbank redepositing among the banks in the reporting area; (b) Bryant, ibid.; Morgan Guaranty Trust Company of New York, *World Financial Markets*, various years; (c) IMF, *International Financial Statistics Yearbook 1989*, Washington, D.C.: IMF, August; *GATT International Trade report 1988-89, 1990-91* and *IMF Yearbook 1992*; (d) *United Nations Yearbook of National Accounts Statistics 1974*, vol.III, New York: UN, 1975; United Nations, *Trends in International Distribution of Gross World Product*, New York: UN, 1993.

The rising international activities of national financial institutions, however, is only one way to demonstrate the increasing internationalization of financial markets. A second, equally important process was the growing interpenetration and consequent integration of individual national financial markets and their institutions. While there have only recently been attempts made to measure the degree of linkage among these markets, and data are still scant, several economic and institutional indicators can be used to demonstrate this increasing integration.

With respect to economic indicators, for example, there was a considerable convergence of domestic and Euromarket interest rates, as well as of real interest rates, among the major industrial countries, leading to a narrowing of real returns on financial assets across countries.[27] While some have challenged this notion that financial market integration did in fact lead to a reduction in interest rate differentials, they do acknowledge that integration has nevertheless reduced one important source of interest rate divergence: the institutional barriers separating national financial markets.[28]

Another indication of the high degree of international financial integration was the decreasing importance of crowding out private sector investment by the public sector. Given the high mobility of capital among the industrialized countries, the possibility of public sector borrowing crowding out private sector investment declined substantially, since a potential reduction in private sector investment could be easily reversed by the inflow of foreign capital under conditions of an increasingly integrated global financial market.[29]

Finally, in the securities markets the worldwide collapse of national stock markets in October 1987 gave rise to a series of studies that have examined the degree of linkage among these national markets. For example, in its discussion of the 1987 collapse, the report by the Presidential Task Force on Market Mechanisms notes that '[w]hat may have appeared strictly as a "Wall Street" collapse was the result of the cumulative impact of several developments occurring simultaneously in several other financial centers.'[30] Another study reported similar results, concluding that 'stock price movements in major markets have become increasingly similar in the 1980s compared to the 1970s and before. This development appears generally consistent with the ongoing strengthening of cross-border trading, listings, and investment activities.'[31] Other studies pointed less to the international linkages caused by large international investors; rather, they emphasized an 'unobservable and indirect linkage between national stock markets when sharp price declines in overseas markets contribute to a panicky market psychology.'[32]

Turning to the institutional indicators of international financial integration, one of the foremost was the growing importance of external financial transactions for domestic banks. This was reflected in the rise in the proportion of total bank business accounted for by foreign loans or foreign security purchases. For example, the average ratio of foreign business by the banking sector in the OECD countries rose on the asset side from 13.1 per cent in 1970 to 21.3 per cent in 1986. On the liability side it rose from 13.0 per cent to 25.4 per cent during the same time period.[33] Table 4.4 shows the development of foreign business in the banking sector in the G-10 countries. Only Switzerland shows a steady decline on both the asset and liability side, notwithstanding the fact that in a few other cases it has fluctuated.

Table 4.4 Foreign Business of the Banking Sector in the G-10 Countries

(% of balance sheet)

	Assets			Liabilities		
	1970	1980	1990	1970	1980	1990
Belgium	36.6	52.7	55.9	42.6	63.3	69.7
Canada	19.8	21.0	13.4	14.3	24.5	19.3
France	15.8	22.7	24.9	17.0	20.8	28.3
Germany	8.7	9.7	16.3	5.6	8.2	9.3
Italy	12.6	8.5	10.6	12.6	12.7	16.4
Japan	3.7	4.3	13.9	3.1	7.3	19.4
Netherlands	27.0	33.0	36.2	25.9	33.9	29.9
Sweden	4.9	9.6	17.7	3.8	15.0	45.0
Switzerland	37.6	34.7	26.2	32.2	25.1	22.9
United Kingdom	46.1	64.7	45.1	49.7	67.5	48.8
United States	2.9	13.1	8.4	6.2	9.9	11.8

Sources: International Monetary Fund, *International Financial Statistics*, various years, Washington, D.C.: IMF.

Another transformation that indicates the growing integration of national financial markets was the increase in acquisitions of securities by non-resident individuals in different national markets and the rise in foreign securities purchases by individual investors (Table 4.5). Greater participation by foreign financial institutions in domestic markets was also pronounced in most major financial markets and thus also contributed significantly to increasing integration. This was most evidenced by the number of foreign banking firms in industrial countries, which increased sharply and accounted for a considerably greater share of total bank assets (see Table 4.6). Yet another process of change that indicates the degree to which international financial integration increased was the amount of interest which foreign banks held in a national banking system. For example, in 1990 foreign banks in the U.S. held a 25 per cent or greater interest in 90 commercial banks. Together, the foreign banks present in the U.S., and the interest they held in U.S. commercial banks, controlled approximately 22 per cent of all U.S. banking assets.[34]

Another impetus that fostered the integration of financial markets was the rapidly growing number of institutionally managed funds (pension funds, insurance companies, endowments and mutual funds). In 1980, $1.9 trillion in assets were held by institutions. This figure rose to $6.3 trillion by 1990.[35] Seen from a different perspective, in 1955 institutional investors made up 23 per cent of the total value of stocks traded in the U.S. By 1990, this figure had risen to about 50 per cent.[36] By the mid-1980s, these funds began to pursue a policy of diversifying their portfolios internationally and entered into active programmes for investing in international equities. As a result, the international pool of funds participating in equities greatly increased. One major form of such an investment was pension funds. Not only did total pension assets grow; the percentage of total assets invested in foreign securities also increased substantially. In 1980, foreign investment of private sector pension assets was $19.4 billion. This figure had risen to $84.6 billion by 1985 and reached $280 billion by the end of 1990.[37] Finally, there was a growing number of cross-national mergers, strategic alliances and acquisitions among financial firms in the major industrial countries.[38]

The process of securitization and international financial integration, however, could not have progressed with such speed and intensity had it not been for two additional factors. The first is the technological innovations in telecommunications and data processing which enabled financial institutions to adjust to the changes in macroeconomic conditions.[39] These innovations permitted faster, less costly transmission of information and completion of financial transactions. From 1960 to 1985, communications and data processing costs declined annually on the order of 15 per cent and

($ billions)

	1986	1987	1988	1989	1990
A. Trading in Foreign Equities by Investors from:					
France	36.8	76.2	57.2	65.2	58.0
Germany	49.3	61.1	42.9	56.3	41.6
Japan	42.4	134.2	150.0	176.2	147.3
Netherlands	23.1	35.0	23.3	30.0	29.7
United Kingdom	201.9	262.2	232.1	342.0	333.0
United States	123.1	225.2	184.6	276.4	296.9
TOTAL	476.6	793.9	690.1	946.1	906.5
B. Trading by Foreign Investors in Equities from:					
France	33.6	56.5	55.7	86.2	78.5
Germany	77.9	76.8	63.7	105.9	164.6
Japan	189.6	354.5	328.6	432.9	268.6
Netherlands	37.4	50.7	40.2	64.3	63.7
United Kingdom	80.1	141.7	116.7	139.8	145.2
United States	277.5	482.0	364.4	420.7	363.1
TOTAL	696.1	1162.2	969.3	1249.8	1083.7

Source: Baring Securities Limited

Table 4.6 Expansion of International Banking Networks [a]

	1970	1980	1986	1990
Host Country:		Foreign banking presence		
Australia	3	2	18 (6/88)	18
Austria	--	17	22	18
Belgium	26	51	57 (6/85)	65
Canada	0	0	57 (6/85)	58
Denmark	0	5	8	6
France	58	122	152	171
Germany	77	213	283 (6/85)	n.a.
Italy	4	25	36	50
Japan: banks	38	85	115	130
Japan: securities firms	--	5	38	51
Luxembourg	23	99	110	n.a.
Netherlands	23	39	42	47
New Zealand	3	3	12 (1987)	15
Norway	--	--	7	n.a.
Spain	4	25	49	n.a.
Sweden: subsidiaries only	--	--	12	10
Switzerland	97	99	125	n.a.
United Kingdom	95	214	293 (6/85)	358 (2/91)
United States	79 (1975)	153	264 (12/88)	307
Home Country:		Presence of domestic banks abroad		
Australia	--	--	85	75 (1993)
Austria: branches only	--	1	5	9
Belgium	6	14	40 (12/88)	64 (12/92)
Canada	268	290	237	260
Denmark	--	18	56	78
France	--	--	455	500
Germany	8	126	164 (12/85)	n.a.
Italy: branches only	22	44	75	95
Japan: banks	67	139	204	299
Japan: securities firms	--	39	82	145
Netherlands	55	145	170	n.a.
New Zealand	1	1	1	12
Norway	6	16	27	n.a.
Spain: branches only	25	82	136	n.a.
Sweden	--	7	17	29
Switzerland	--	71	79	n.a.
United States [b]	532	787	854 (12/88)	819

[a] Subsidiaries and branches of overseas subsidiaries are generally excluded
[b] Foreign branches of Federal Reserve member banks

Sources: OECD, *Competition in Banking* (1989); Board of Governors of the Federal Reserve System, *Annual Report* (various years); for 1990, individual country submissions.

25 per cent respectively.[40]   This permitted the development of new financial products as well as enlarged the range of geographic and product markets in which financial institutions could provide cost-effective and competitive services.[41] In addition, the greatly reduced costs and expanded scope of telecommunications allowed providers of new financial instruments to match up end users who were previously in isolated markets. Both of these factors contributed significantly to the integration of financial markets.[42] By the early 1990s virtually instantaneous worldwide trading existed in some markets. Technological developments allowed financial exchanges to link themselves together electronically and to list securities or contracts so that these instruments could be traded around the clock in one or another exchange. It is important to note, however, that the increased possibility of linking financial markets electronically does not necessarily result in greater decentralization of the world financial market. To the contrary, as one OECD report notes, the more sophisticated telecommunication becomes, the more it favours established business centres at the expense of the periphery.[43]

The second factor that contributed fundamentally to the international integration of financial markets was a worldwide tendency by national governments to deregulate and to reduce structural rigidities and barriers to competition in domestic financial markets.[44]   The moves towards deregulation (as well as the degree of previous national regulations) varied from country to country, leading to variations in the degree of liberalization across countries.[45] In general, they included the abolition of exchange rate controls; the phasing-out of interest rate ceilings on deposit and lending activities of financial intermediaries; the opening of domestic financial markets to foreign financial institutions; reduction and/or elimination of withholding taxes on interest payments to non-residents; and the relaxation of traditional boundaries, such as those between commercial and investment banking, limiting the types of financial activity in which particular financial institutions could engage.[46]

With respect to the liberalization of capital flows, the most noteworthy measures were taken in the U.S., where restrictions on capital outflows were dismantled in 1974.   Around the same time, some other oil-importing countries also relaxed their controls on capital.   A second wave of deregulation came in 1979 and early 1980 with the elimination of British and Japanese exchange controls.   The Japanese deregulation measures adopted in 1984 and 1985 were a further move in the direction of global integration of financial markets. Likewise in Germany, the opening of financial markets was stimulated by the liberalization of capital flows, which resulted in the 1981 lifting of restrictions on purchases by non-residents of domestic bonds and money market instruments.[47]

The reasons for these deregulatory moves were multiple.[48] First, there was a deliberate commitment to deregulation by the governments of most industrial nations in the OECD area.[49] These governments considered it vital to liberalize domestic financial markets in order to eliminate structural rigidities and thereby improve resource allocation and generate new opportunities for savers and investors.[50]

Second, the macroeconomic instability associated with the external shocks of the 1970s put pressures on national regulatory authorities to relax regulatory controls in order to attract foreign investors to finance growing fiscal and trade deficits. Finally, the desire to avoid sharp shifts in market shares between different sectors of the domestic financial system (disintermediation) and the threat of losing a significant market share of financial activity to less-regulated foreign markets put strong pressures on policymakers to deregulate their national financial systems.[51] These deregulatory moves by most industrial countries, either to avoid a substantial outflow of investment capital or to attract capital in order to finance new investment, led to a process of 'competitive deregulation' across the major financial markets throughout the 1970s and early 1980s.[52]

Together, the increase in international activities by national financial institutions and the growing integration of national financial markets, reinforced by technological advances and liberalizing measures taken by national regulatory authorities, led to a considerable degree of integration among national and international financial markets by the mid-1980s. As one U.S. official stated in a hearing before Congress, 'whether we like it or not, the globalization of financial institutions and markets is a reality... [and] cannot be reversed in any material way by regulation or legislation.'[53]

NOTES

1. Multinational banking is certainly not a new phenomenon. From a longer-term historical perspective, American banks took a leading role in the *re-internationalization* of banking. For a century before World War I, European and especially English banks played a major role in the operation of a world capital market. It was mostly government controls on convertibility and international capital flows that reduced the role of international banking between 1914 and 1960. Feis (1965); Born (1983); Kindleberger (1984).
2. Einzig (1967).
3. Winningham and Hagan (1980).
4. Kelly (1977); Hawley (1987); Brimmer and Dahl (1975); Goldberg and Saunders (1980); Friedman (1975).
5. Friedman (1987).
6. For a detailed analysis of the activities of U.S. banks abroad, see Houpt (1988).
7. Goddin and Weiss (1981).
8. United Nations Center on Transnational Corporations (1989).
9. Goodhardt (1988); Kindleberger (1974 and 1984); Cox (1986).

10. Schott (1983); Benz (1985); Gavin (1985); Walter (1985).
11. Watson, Mathieson, Kincaid and Kalter (1988); Pecchioli (1983 and 1987); OECD (1985).
12. International Monetary Fund (1988).
13. The institutionalization of savings, growing investor sophistication, higher costs of capital, and declines in information and transaction costs in the securities markets also fuelled the process of securitization. Cumming (1987).
14. Booth (1989); Rosenthal and Ocampo (1988); Boemio and Edwards (1989).
15. Bank for International Settlements (1986).
16. Meerschwam (1989). Besides their ability to circumvent national regulations, large international banks also used the process of securitization to move assets off their balance sheet. This allowed the banks to avoid some of the regulatory costs associated with reserve requirements that are measured as a percentage of the balance sheet and other costs associated with regulation of the balance sheet. BIS (1986).
17. These figures actually understate the degree to which net new borrowing from banks in the form of syndicated loans has contracted, because they include loans used to replace outstanding or maturing credits, and make no allowance for the contraction of the conventional kind of bank lending in non-syndicated form. The trend towards securitization has been reflected in many other ways besides the decline in international loan activity. For example, on the liability side, banks have far more important borrowers on the international bond market. They are motivated by the need to strengthen their capital bases, by a desire for closer symmetry between their long-term lending and their funding, and by the new opportunities to benefit in interest rate and long currency swaps. BIS (1986).
18. Four major new financial instruments in international financial markets were note issuance facilities (NIFs), currency and interest rate swaps, foreign currency and interest rate options, and forward rate agreements (FRAs). Interest rate or currency swaps also have an integrating influence on international capital markets by allowing access to portfolios in a financial market independent of the borrower's currency or interest rate preferences, because the borrowers can simultaneously undertake swaps to modify these aspects of the transactions. IMF (1986). For a detailed description of these instruments, see BIS (1986).
19. BIS (1986).
20. Kane (1987).
21. Cohen (1987).
22. United Nations Center on Transnational Corporations (1989).
23. Wellons (1985 and 1987).
24. Watson et al. (1988).
25. United Nations Center on Transnational Corporations (1989).
26. Ibid.
27. Obstfeld (1986); Fukao and Hanazaki (1987); Frankel (1988); Kool and Tatom (1988).
28. Kasman and Pigott (1988).
29. Frankel (1989).
30. Presidential Task Force on Market Mechanisms (1988).
31. Bennett and Kelleher (1988).
32. Aderhood, Cumming and Harwood (1988); Roll (1988); Dwyer, Jr. and Hafer (1988).
33. These averages exclude Luxembourg whose percentages for 1986 were 97.6 per cent and 86.1 per cent respectively. OECD (1989).
34. Federal Reserve Board (1990).
35. Riverside Economic Research (1993).
36. *WP*, 19 August 1990.
37. InterSec Research Corporation, Stamford, Connecticut.
38. United Nations Center on Transnational Corporations (1989); 'Necessity Links U.S., Japanese Firms, Investment Firms Need Local Partners in Both Markets', *American Banker*, 27 March 1989.

39. Revell (1983).
40. Morgan Guaranty Trust Co. (1986).
41. Congress of the United States, Office of Technology Assessment (1987).
42. Saunders and White (1986); Revell (1983).
43. *Science, Technology, Industry Review* (1989); de Jonquières, Guy (1989).
44. Bröcker (1990); OECD (1984 and 1987); Germany and Morton (1985); IMF (1986).
45. For the perspective that, with the exception of the U.S., there has in fact been very little deregulation in the G-7 countries, and that was concentrated mostly on the external sector, see Denning (1986).
46. OECD (1989).
47. Watson et al. (1988); Frankel (1984).
48. Germany and Morton (1985).
49. In financial markets, this period beginning in the mid-1970s, which was characterized by the deregulatory moves of most governments, in a sense marked the end of what John Ruggie has called 'embedded liberalism'. Ruggie (1982).
50. OECD (1987 and 1989).
51. For a detailed analysis of the forces of competitive reregulation, see: Kane (1987); Ogata, Cooper and Schulmann (1989); Folkerts-Landau and Mathieson (1987).
52. Folkerts-Landau and Mathieson (1987); Giddy and Allen (1979).
53. Statement by Gerald Corrigan, 6 May 1987.

5. Glass-Steagall and the Politics of Gridlock

MOBILIZING IN RESPONSE TO EXTERNAL PRESSURE

The failure to achieve any substantive change in Glass-Steagall during the 1960s and early 1970s did not convince commercial banks to abandon their assault on regulatory restrictions. In fact, growing competitive pressures in the 1970s strengthened commercial banks' incentives.[1] As discussed in Chapter 4, the external economic shocks of the 1970s stimulated a process of securitization and disintermediation in financial markets.[2] In addition, the sustained rise in interest rates caused by external shocks catalysed a massive shift in assets out of low-return commercial bank deposits into other financial instruments, as commercial banks' traditional role as intermediaries between investors and lenders was increasingly supplanted by direct markets in securities.[3]

Throughout the 1970s, technological advances and product innovations accelerated the securitization process, as other financial and non-financial institutions began to offer financial products in direct competition with commercial banks. As a result, commercial banks suffered a serious erosion in their market share.[4] Between 1960 and 1981, for example, commercial banks' share of the market for short- and intermediate-term commercial lending declined from 83 per cent to 60 per cent.[5] Similarly, the share of assets of American financial institutions held by commercial banks dropped from 57 per cent to 38 per cent between 1946 and 1980.[6]

During the initial stages of the mobilization phase, the external economic shocks of the mid- and late 1970s and their repercussions on the U.S. economy led banks to renew their pressure for policy changes which would halt their eroding market share and redress their loss of economic, and thus political, power in the U.S. economy. Repeal of Glass-Steagall or some elements of it, commercial banks argued, would allow them to follow lenders and investors into the new markets and eliminate the regulatory disparities which allowed non-bank financial institutions to invade banks' markets.[7] As they had done in the 1960s and 1970s, commercial banks pursued regulatory reform through two major channels. One avenue was through the legislature, as banks lobbied congressional committees for repeal of Glass-Steagall.[8] The other avenue was through administrative and judicial channels, as commercial banks appealed to state and federal regulators to reinterpret that act through administrative rulings with the help of the courts.

The commercial banks' pursuit of regulatory reform through these two avenues mobilized a broad array of institutions in both the public and private sectors. Within the public sector, a multiplicity of legislative and administrative authorities were drawn into the debate on regulatory reform. The first public sector institutions to be mobilized were the federal bank regulatory authorities — the Federal Reserve Board, the FDIC, the OCC, and the SEC — as well as the regulatory commissions and legislatures at the state level. Commercial banks appealed to the regulatory agencies who in turn mobilized those congressional committees with jurisdiction over financial services regulation: the Senate and House Banking Committees and the House Committee on Energy and Commerce. These committees felt compelled to become involved in the debate over regulatory reform because of their growing conviction that the evolution of the regulatory system should be governed by congressional legislation rather than by piecemeal administrative decisionmaking by the agencies.[9]

The mobilization of the agencies and Congress in turn activated those sets of private sector institutions whose interests would be affected by the repeal of Glass-Steagall. These actors comprised a broad range of bank and non-bank financial institutions, including mid-size regional banks, small local banks, investment firms, thrift institutions and insurance firms. Each group of financial institutions was represented by its own lobbying organizations, which, among others, included the American Bankers Association (ABA), the Association of Bank Holding Companies (ABHC), the Independent Bankers Association of America (IBAA), the Securities Industry Association (SIA), and the Investment Company Institute (ICI). All were powerful industry lobbies with large financial resources and strong ties to congressional committees and/or individual senators and representatives.[10]

THE FIRST STAGE OF CONFLICT: THE POLITICS OF REGULATORY GRIDLOCK

As discussed earlier, conflicts over policy responses to external pressures are shaped by three sets of factors. Two sets of factors, involving the policy agenda and the range of interests and institutions participating in the debate over policy response, are inherited from the mobilization phase. Because commercial banks were the first institutions to mobilize in reaction to the challenge of securitization, they set the terms for the subsequent evolution of debate on regulatory reform and also determined the framework within which debate took place. By mobilizing a certain set of institutions with a certain range of interests, the commercial banks' policy proposals defined the institutional and procedural context for debate and conflict over policy responses.

The third set of factors which shapes the process of conflict relates to change in the nature of the external challenge which the policy network confronts. In the case of the challenge to the economic interests of commercial banks, the first two sets of factors dominated the process of conflict during the first half of the 1980s. Then after 1986, the intensification of external financial pressure catalyzed a series of changes in the domestic policy network and in the debate over regulatory reform.

The initial phase of conflict over the repeal of Glass-Steagall took place between 1980 and 1986, when fierce conflicts both among and within the private and public sector broke out over the need to repeal part of, or the entire, Glass-Steagall Act. One aspect that was initially targeted by commercial banks was the underwriting of tax-exempt revenue bonds. At the time Glass-Steagall was written, the market in revenue bonds was insignificant. But this had changed by the late 1970s. Issues in revenue bonds jumped from $6.1 billion in 1970 to $34.3 billion in 1980, while general obligation bonds, which commercial banks were allowed to underwrite, stagnated.[11] Given the increasing importance of revenue bonds, commercial banks argued that restrictions in the revenue bond area should be removed. Their additional sales effort would drum up more customers, hold bond prices down, and save revenue bond issuers money.[12] Bankers were particularly hopeful, since the lower costs of underwriting would primarily benefit state and local governments and thus could be directly linked to benefiting the general public.

Legislation to end this particular prohibition for commercial banks passed twice in the Senate. However, because of the general mistrust of commercial banks' activities during the 1920s, similar proposals did not receive a hearing in the House until 1979.[13] The banks were unable to convince representatives of the potential benefits of allowing them into the business of underwriting revenue bonds.

However, as mentioned above, commercial banks did not rely only on the legislature for a change in the Glass-Steagall Act, but also lobbied the various federal agencies to reconsider the Depression-era legislation. In fact, commercial banks were quite hopeful that some liberalization of the Glass-Steagall Act through administrative rulings by the various independent agencies would be possible. During the late 1970s, all three agencies on several occasions expressed their concern about the eroding market position of commercial banks. As discussed earlier, the Comptroller's Office had, on earlier occasions, demonstrated its favourable disposition towards liberalizing some of the restrictions imposed by Glass-Steagall — this sentiment had increased in the late 1970s.[14] Similarly, the Federal Reserve publicly stated that it supported the banks' drive for underwriting municipal revenue bonds.[15] Moreover, in the fall of 1980, in what turned out to have far-reaching consequences, the Fed Board ruled that commercial banks could compete directly with securities firms in selling commercial paper.[16]

But while there were some indications that regulators were sympathetic to the banks' cause, the relationship between banks and their regulators could not always be characterized as a close public-private alliance with matching interests. For example, the Fed had to balance its support for a liberalization of Glass-Steagall against its interest in the stability of the entire financial system. More importantly, allowing commercial banks to enter a whole series of new activities was likely to undermine the primary function of the Fed — the control of the supply of money. On the other hand, bank holding companies, which were regulated by the Fed and were most aggressive in the pursuit to breach Glass-Steagall, felt that the Fed did not express sufficient support for their cause. As one banker described it, '[T]here's a new militancy as a result of competitive pressures. The ever-so-slow grinding movement of the Federal Reserve must be challenged by initiatives from our side.'[17]

Encouraged by the Fed's rulings on commercial paper and the support from other regulators, bankers and their lobbyists mounted their most concerted effort ever to change the 48-year-old act.[18] But while the large commercial banks constituted one of Washington's most powerful lobbies, the investment banking industry was equally well represented on Capitol Hill and was determined 'to fight to the end to keep the banks out of the securities business.'[19] In fact, the securities industry was so adamantly opposed to banks getting into jealously-guarded securities activities, such as revenue bond underwriting and corporate finance, that the smaller members of the SIA were arguing to impose some limits on its own members.[20] Moreover, those commercial banks wanting to enter the securities field were challenged from within their own industry by smaller rural banks. According to the IBAA, small banks were 'philosophically opposed to any erosion of the separation of depository banking activities from other forms of commerce such as securities underwriting.'[21] Whichever way the legislature would eventually decide, it was clear any change in the current banking law would only come about through a long and protracted struggle among the public and private sector interests that had a stake in its outcome.

1981

Clearly one important factor determining the likelihood of the large banks' success on Capitol Hill was the new Republican Administration's attitude towards deregulation of the financial industry. Commercial banks were hopeful that the White House and newly appointed Secretary of the Treasury Donald Regan would be sympathetic to their cause. When Regan testified for the first time on Capitol Hill he confirmed those hopes: 'Glass-Steagall definitely should be revisited....I am not saying it is outmoded, but I certainly think it needs an updating.'[22]

The Administration had a chance to outline a more detailed plan during a series of hearings that Senator Jake Garn, the new Republican Chairman of the Senate Banking Committee, scheduled for the fall. In his opening statement, Garn himself took a position. He argued that commercial banks did indeed have a competitive disadvantage relative to other financial institutions and that some legislative action had to be taken to deal with that issue.[23] To the surprise of many observers, Senator Garn stated that he was willing to consider allowing banks to engage in currently prohibited lines of business, such as underwriting municipal revenue bonds and managing their own mutual funds. As a reason for the sudden change, Garn cited the fact that 'events have happened much more rapidly than I had thought possible.'[24]

Garn was supported by the Administration, which became more specific and called for a reconsideration of the Glass-Steagall Act. In September 1981, for example, a Justice Department official suggested that the act may have become unnecessary, since various securities regulations adopted since 1933 had lessened the potential for abuses in commercial banking and securities activities. In a speech at Georgetown University Law School, Treasury Secretary Regan complained that '...we're still governing the financial system with a law that was passed almost 50 years ago.' He questioned whether it was not time to relax the barriers between the banking and securities industries and recommended that Congress take a close look at the Glass-Steagall Act.[25]

Developments continued to move at a rapid pace and bankers were confident that for the first time in two decades some action with respect to Glass-Steagall would be taken.[26] Within a month, citing the 'revolution that is taking place in the financial services industry,' Garn introduced a bill to deregulate the financial services industry. Among other things, the bill would authorize commercial banks to underwrite municipal revenue bonds and to operate, manage, and sell interests in mutual funds.[27]

During the hearings on the Garn bill, the Administration announced its own proposal, endorsing Garn's plan to allow commercial banks to offer money market funds and underwrite municipal revenue bonds. But contrary to Garn, who would allow banks to undertake the new powers with the same corporate entity, Regan suggested that banks that wanted to offer these products should do so through separate affiliates within a holding company structure. Regan argued that these new and higher-risk activities should be distinct from the more traditional banking operations, which are federally insured. In addition, the Secretary suggested that the new powers conducted by the separate affiliate should be regulated by the SEC.[28]

Bank holding companies, though enthusiastic about the possibility of being granted new powers, complained that it would require big investments to set up the separate securities affiliates. Small banks were even more opposed to this particular aspect of the proposal. Since many of the banks were not organized as holding companies, they would have to alter their corporate structure to account for this, which would amount to a very costly enterprise. Calling the Regan proposal 'a provincial New York City idea,' the IBAA charged that many of the small banks would not be able to compete.[29] Garn, who despite his differences with the Administration saw a real opportunity to pass a bill in the Senate, charged that the banks' pleas were characteristic of the 'selfishness and greed of the individual parts of the [financial services] industry.' The senator told the bankers that if they persisted they would lose an historic opportunity to gain some new competitive powers, and that without 'some consensus within the depository institutions you are not going to have any legislation.'[30] Clearly, Senator Garn's remarks were in anticipation of strong and vigorous opposition from the securities industry and possibly from the House, which only a united banking lobby could hope to outbid on Capitol Hill.

The Administration also pleaded with the banks to accept its proposal despite their reservations. To gain the support of the industry, the Treasury made some concessions to the smaller banks. In a proposal sent to the Senate Banking Committee in late November, the Treasury suggested that banks with assets of $100 million or less would not need to convert to a BHC to establish or acquire a bank securities affiliate.[31] But commercial banks, small and large, remained opposed to the bill.[32]

Even if the banks had been willing to agree to the proposal, the House Banking Committee was unlikely to have considered any such comprehensive legislation during 1981.[33] In fact, the House was adamantly opposed to new securities powers for commercial banks and refused to broaden its own legislative agenda, which was a narrow emergency bill to help the S&L industry.[34] During a floor debate on the bill, Committee Chairman Fernand St. Germain assured his fellow representatives that he would not allow the House bill to become a 'Christmas tree' on which the Senate and the Administration could hang their more far-reaching banking provisions. 'If this bill comes back with anything extra on it, it goes to the committee and it dies right there, period, nothing. I do not care what happens,' St. Germain stated on the floor.[35] Garn retaliated and refused to act on the House bill.

Commercial banks had little to lose by refusing to negotiate a bill, nor did they take St. Germain's threats very seriously. In fact, they expressed great confidence that within the not-too-distant future, they would be allowed to enter the securities business to an even greater extent than currently envisioned by the Senate Banking Committee.[36] Banks knew that pressure from the Administration would continue to take even broader steps towards reconsidering the separation between the two sectors of the financial industry.[37] Moreover, large commercial banks once again turned to their regulators to press for change in the rules that governed the policymaking network.

Commercial banks were dealt a temporary setback in July of 1981 when a federal judge ruled that commercial paper is a security, thus overturning the Fed's ruling of 1980. The immediate impact of the decision was not quite clear since the court did not determine whether Bankers Trust (the New York money centre bank) was also acting as an underwriter.[38] More importantly, the court indicated that it was well aware of the changing conditions in financial markets. This dispute was 'only the proverbial tip of the iceberg as to debates currently raging in the houses of Congress concerning the proper functions of commercial banks, especially in light of a more active "banking" role taken by securities dealers,' according to the judge. But the court also stated that it did not agree with the attempt by regulators and the banks to shift the centre of policymaking authority away from Congress toward the regulators, which in this particular instance was the Fed. '[T]he realignment of our nation's financial industries is for the elected representatives of our nation to bring to fruition by comprehensive legislation' and should not be the result of 'fiat by judicial decree or by administrative policymaking.'[39]

This did not prevent the banks from trying to find other legal-administrative loopholes in the Glass-Steagall Act that would somehow allow them to offer those products that both borrowers and lenders preferred. In late November, Bank America Corporation, one of the nation's largest banks, announced that it intended to acquire Charles Schwab & Co., the largest discount brokerage firm in the U.S.[40] Both the bank and the discount broker were confident that it could convince regulators that its move would not violate the Glass-Steagall provisions.[41] Other commercial banks were surprised by the boldness of the move, but praised the leadership shown by one of the biggest banks in a firm response to brokerage firms' incursion on the banks' turf.[42]

1982-1983

The commercial banks' faith in the Administration's determination to deregulate the financial system was reconfirmed in early 1982 when the Administration introduced a new bill during further hearings on the financial system.[43]   However, in response to pressure from the SEC, the Administration's bill also contained provisions that would limit the Fed's ability to decide independently which expanded financial services BHCs would be allowed to offer. In essence, it would have removed the new activities conducted in the holding company's affiliate from the Fed's jurisdiction and placed them under the jurisdiction of the SEC, which endorsed the Administration's proposal. According to John Shad, Chairman of the SEC, 'the advantages of the Treasury proposal [as opposed to that of Senator Garn] are that the new securities and banking affiliates would be subject to the same tax treatment, rules and regulations as all other concerns engaged in the same activities.'[44] In other words, the SEC in principle did not object to expansion of bank powers as long as it took place within the holding company framework and the SEC was granted supervisory authority over the securities subsidiary.[45]

Initially the Fed tried to fight the SEC's potential intrusion on its regulatory turf by rejecting the notion that banks had to engage in securities activities through a separate affiliate in a holding. According to one of its members, the 'Board does not see the need to require that the proposed activities be done in a separate affiliate within the corporate structure.'[46] But the Fed also realized that some compromise among the various institutions was necessary in order for legislation to advance. Thus it stepped away from its original position and agreed with the Treasury — as long as the agency could maintain a regulatory monopoly over BHCs, including the securities affiliates.

> From a regulatory perspective we want to apply the same basic set of rules...and the Board sees advantages in utilizing the supervisory apparatus already in place for banks and thrifts. Therefore, we would urge that, if Congress accepts the Treasury's concept of separate affiliates, such affiliates continue to be subjected to regulatory oversight by the bank regulatory authorities....[47]

The Administration's bill added to the already-existing conflict over commercial bank powers by pitting the Fed against the SEC in a turf battle over regulatory jurisdiction.

The Fed was also opposed to giving banks the power to start money market funds, another element of the Administration's bill. For the purpose of monetary policy, money market funds lie outside the definition of the money base. Given that the Fed's institutional identity was most closely associated with control of the money supply, the agency saw its ability to execute that goal undermined if banks were permitted to start those funds.[48]

The hearings held in early 1982, therefore, only further exacerbated the various conflicts that were becoming increasingly pronounced as both public and private sector institutions were defining their different economic and political interests. A standoff also continued between the House and the Senate over the extent of the banking legislation, leaving little hope that a bill could pass in Congress if the policy gridlock continued.[49] In Garn's own committee, some senators also voiced their opposition to outright deregulation as envisioned by the Administration or Garn. For example, Alfonse D'Amato, Chairman of the Subcommittee on Securities and a longtime supporter of the large Wall Street investment banks, voiced strong scepticism.

When Garn realized that he did not have the support of his own fellow Republicans on the committee, he decided to introduce less sweeping legislation. Rather than authorizing banks to offer Money Market Mutual Fund accounts (MMMF), the bill authorized commercial banks to set up so-called Money Market Deposit accounts (MMDA), which were short-term interest-bearing accounts that would be able to compete with money market funds. The authority for commercial banks to underwrite revenue bonds was also taken off the bill.[50] The Senate Banking Committee passed the proposed legislation and it was approved by the Senate in late September.[51] Within a few days, House and Senate conferees came to an agreement and Congress passed the bill. With the exception of the MMDAs, the bill addressed issues unrelated to the bank powers issue. For the large banks, their ability to offer MMDAs was considered a small success but unlikely to slow down their declining market share.[52]

Given the unwillingness of Congress, especially the House, to reconsider any fundamental overhaul of the regulations governing the U.S. financial system, large banks turned to the regulators. Both the FDIC and the OCC had expressed their support for a considerable expansion of bank powers during the hearings held in 1981 and 1982. In early September, the OCC authorized a national bank to establish a discount brokerage subsidiary.[53] Just as in the case of the Bank of America, the OCC's decision would allow the bank to act only as a passive agent in buying and selling securities for its customers. However, in order to avoid the regulatory reach of the Fed, the Comptroller did not require the bank to change its corporate structure into a holding company, but allowed the bank to offer discount brokerage services within the same bank.

Shortly after, in a landmark decision, the FDIC gave permission to so-called insured state non-member banks (banks that are chartered at the state level and do not belong to the Federal Reserve System) to open securities subsidiaries.[54] The FDIC argued that the Glass-Steagall prohibition — a federal law — does not apply to banks that are solely regulated by state authorities.[55] Moreover, the FDIC did not just allow discount brokerage services, it allowed subsidiaries to engage in issuing, underwriting, selling, and distributing any kind of securities. The securities industry vehemently opposed the FDIC's interpretation of the bank regulatory framework and filed a suit against the agency.[56]

Shortly afterward, commercial banks were handed another major victory when a federal appeals court ruled that the Glass-Steagall Act does not prohibit commercial banks from dealing in commercial paper. The court also reversed the judge's earlier contention that the Fed did not have authority to determine what is and what is not permissible for banks and argued that the lower court had given 'insufficient weight to the expertise of the Federal Reserve Board as the agency responsible for the provisions of the Glass-Steagall Act,'[57] shifting the distributional power away from the legislature to the regulatory agencies.

But while the administrative avenue proved to be a rather promising way for commercial banks to enlarge their powers, it also created pressure and even conflict among the regulators, due to their different regulatory philosophies and due to the fact that regulators were competing for the charters of the banks. In other words, given the dispersed regulatory structure and the ability of banks to switch their charters among the regulators, a liberal interpretation of a bank statute by one regulator would clearly influence other regulators in their attitude towards deregulation, since banks might decide to switch their charter to the more permissive regulatory environment.[58] For example, the FDIC's policy statement on allowing state banks to open securities subsidiaries was issued only a few days before the Fed was scheduled to hold hearings on the proposed acquisition of Charles Schwab by the Bank of America. Clearly, the statement put additional pressure on the Fed to approve the application, because banks regulated by the Fed would be subjected to a competitive inequality if the Fed ruled against them, and therefore they might feel encouraged to switch from a federal to a state charter to enjoy the more liberal regulatory environment created by the FDIC's interpretation of the Glass-Steagall Act. The OCC's decision to allow a national bank to offer discount brokerage services had the same effect.

In January of 1983, the Fed approved Bank of America's application to buy Charles Schwab, the discount broker.[59] The decision followed a year of often bitter hearings and heated debate over the legality of Bank of America's move and whether the Fed should approve it. The pressure on the Fed to act on the issue had increased not only because of the rulings by its fellow regulators. In addition, in the fall of 1982 Bank of America started to offer discount brokerage services through Schwab at six of its offices, and several other large banks announced their intentions to make similar acquisitions.[60]

Commercial bankers considered the Fed's decision a major breakthrough since the central bank was deemed to be a more conservative regulator than either the OCC or the FDIC. In justifying its decision, the Fed argued that it distinguished between firms such as Schwab, which merely execute orders to buy and sell securities, and investment banks, which also underwrite securities and provide other investment banking services. The SIA reacted sharply to the Fed's decision, and stated that the decision 'reflects the Fed's bias in favor of the banking industry, a bias found among most bank regulators.'[61]

The competitive pressures that the decentralized policy network created among regulators did not always lead to rulings that matched across the agencies. It also produced open and protracted conflicts among the regulators. For example, in the fall of 1982 the Dreyfus Corporation, an investment bank dealing mostly in mutual funds, filed an application with the OCC and the FDIC to establish its own national bank and to purchase a state-chartered New Jersey bank, respectively. The Fed strongly opposed both filings on the grounds that they were unlawful under the BHC and Glass-Steagall Acts.[62] The Comptroller and the FDIC ignored the Fed's protests and approved the applications in early 1983.[63]

In addition, despite strong criticism from the Fed, in 1982 the OCC began to allow financial and non-financial companies such as Sears to obtain national banking charters for their so-called non-bank subsidiaries. The companies claimed that these subsidiaries technically were not banks under the BHC Act because they did not offer their customers the ability to make deposits and commercial loans at the same time. By offering only one of these services, the non-bank banks and their parent companies avoided the legal definition of a BHC, thus skirting regulation by the more conservative Fed.

The fragmented and decentralized policy network allowed banks to exploit yet another avenue that was based on the jurisdictional and regulatory competition among regulators. Late in 1982, large commercial banks began to turn to the state legislatures in the drive to enlarge their powers. Encouraged by the FDIC decision that Glass-Steagall does not apply to state-chartered banks, large commercial banks successfully lobbied for a whole series of deregulatory bills that would allow them to enter the investment banking field at the level of individual states.[64] Bankers did not conceal their challenge to the federal level. According to the president of the ABA, 'banks are in a position now where they're going to have to figure out new ways of making money, and if they can't do it on a national basis then it's a fair game to go at it from state to state.'[65]

This strategy soon proved to be successful. Early in 1983, after intense lobbying, Citicorp persuaded the South Dakota legislature to open a path around federal regulations. On March 4, Republican Governor William Janklow passed two laws: the first authorized out-of-state BHCs to acquire or charter a state bank in South Dakota; the second gave any state-chartered South Dakota bank authority to own an insurance firm if the insurance subsidiary operated only out of state.[66] Soon after, Citicorp announced that it would acquire a state-chartered bank to enter the insurance business.

To summarize, by early 1983, most of the major institutions that had an interest in the outcome of the debate over product regulation were mobilized. Congress was deeply divided not just between the House and Senate, but also within the various committees with jurisdiction over bank regulation. For the most part, these divisions reflected the individual members' responsiveness to various private sector pressures. Regulatory agencies were divided as well. While the FDIC and the OCC favoured a fundamental overhaul of Glass-Steagall, the Fed was much more cautious. These differences were not only a reflection of different regulatory philosophies, but also the result of conflicting policy responsibilities, such as in the case of the Fed; most importantly, these differences caused turf battles among the regulators, given the shifting and overlapping boundaries of permitted activities of financial institutions.

The pursuit of interests of individual institutions and/or institutional alliances created a confusing picture of private sector interests trying to exploit, often successfully, the dual and fragmented regulatory structure, and of a legislature that was incapable of developing a coherent long-term strategy that would delineate the structural changes in U.S. financial markets in the years to come. Rather than looking for possible compromises, by the end of 1982 the various factions, both in the public and private sector, were preparing with even greater vigour for renewed legislative and administrative battles in the years to come, vowing to either defend their protected turf or to eliminate the competitive inequalities that were increasingly becoming apparent.

The regulatory turmoil and disorder led Congress to call for a major debate on the future of the U.S. financial system. Regulators were asked to define more clearly their positions on the issue of bank powers — with regard to both the degree of product deregulation as well as the corporate structure such deregulated institutions should operate in. As indicated earlier, the Comptroller's position had been the most liberal throughout this period. For example, by early 1983 the OCC had allowed ten non-financial companies to obtain national banking charters for their so-called non-bank subsidiaries. The Fed reiterated its more cautious position. In an important policy statement that would influence the debate for many years to come, Gerald Corrigan, president of the Federal Reserve Bank of Minneapolis and a close associate of Fed Chairman Paul Volcker, outlined what was generally believed to be the position of the Fed.[67] Corrigan argued that banks, by virtue of their central role in the overall economy, are 'special.' This justified their privileges, including deposit insurance and the right to borrow from the Fed at below market rates. At the same time, however, banks have to accept certain restrictions imposed on them, including a limit on the right to engage in potentially risky activities or to be in any way associated with non-financial companies.

In addition, given the Fed's primary role in the conduct of monetary policy, Corrigan argued that banks provide an important backup source of liquidity for all other institutions and a vehicle for operating monetary policy which gives them unique public responsibilities. This 'special' role of banks in turn justifies the continued separation of banks from other financial institutions and, especially, commercial activities. Corrigan's arguments were thus not only directed at the banks' attempt to enter the securities field, but also at the recent approval by the OCC of Dreyfus's bank acquisition, the ability of securities firms to offer quasi-chequebook accounts such as Merrill Lynch's Cash Management account, and the continued invasion of manufacturing companies such as Sears, Ford, and Gulf & Western into the financial services through non-bank banks.[68]

The FDIC also went on record with its perspective on the future of the financial services industry. The FDIC had little interest in the impact of deregulation on monetary policy, but was much more concerned with its ability to fulfil its primary task as the insurer of banks. Consequently it put less emphasis on what a bank could or could not do. In fact, contrary to the Fed, which was insisting on the traditional definition of a bank, William Isaac, Chairman of the FDIC, proposed 'to redefine the term "bank" and reconsider the activities in which it or its affiliates may engage.'[69] The FDIC, as an insurer of banks, saw as its institutional interest instilling more discipline in the banks and in the financial markets by strengthening its own supervisory power. Increased institutional power would be achieved by improving the FDIC's ability to collect information regarding the financial conditions of banks and making the information public. In addition, the FDIC wanted greater independence in handling the failure of banks through mergers rather than the insurance system. Finally, the FDIC favoured a comprehensive reform of the institutional structure of the regulatory system, which included consolidating the agencies and reorganizing regulation along functional lines. To no one's surprise, the thrust of the proposal was to consolidate all other regulators into a single agency, while the FDIC remained an independent agency with sole supervisory, but no regulatory, responsibility.

Despite the fact that regulators had divergent views with regard to the bank powers debate, they agreed that it was primarily up to Congress to act and to bring to a close the confusion over the future course of financial regulatory policy. In order to allow for an open and extended debate on the future of financial services regulation, the Comptroller, under pressure by Congress and the Fed, agreed to impose a partial moratorium on new bank and non-bank activities till the end of 1983.[70] However, the moratorium applied only to new applications, not to pending ones, and put a halt only to non-financial companies invading banks' turf. It did not prevent banks from continuing to seek ways to circumvent Glass-Steagall, either by exploiting permissive rulings by the OCC or by turning to the state level. According to Comptroller C.T. Conover, the moratorium would thus reduce but not eliminate the 'pressure of escalating marketplace innovation at the national level that could outpace congressional deliberation.'[71]

But the prospects for a legislative solution did not look very promising. Several members of the committees with jurisdiction over bank regulation expressed doubt that congressional action on amending Glass-Steagall was likely during 1983, some because they were responsive to pressure by the investment banks, others such as Fernand St. Germain because he still did not see any pressing need for legislation.[72]

When hearings opened in 1983, both the Administration and the Treasury called on all federal regulators to impose a temporary moratorium.[73] However, the moratorium proposed by the Treasury Secretary was broader, as it put a halt to all financial and non-financial institutions invading each other's turf until a comprehensive solution could be found. In addition, Regan proposed that the federal government should override states that have relaxed restrictions on the services banks may offer and bring to a halt the continued circumvention of federal law by banks. This did not imply that the Administration was against a substantial liberalization of the financial services industry. To the contrary, Regan told the Senate Banking Committee that the Treasury was preparing a new version of its 1982 bill. But according to Regan, the Administration 'would like to see Congress handle this issue rather than have the regulators do it piecemeal.'[74]

The Fed also issued a plea for congressional action, calling for a broad-based *legislative* moratorium much more stringent than those proposed by either the OCC or the Treasury. In addition, the Fed urged immediate action on 'some of the most obvious distortions and loopholes in the present regulatory structure,' referring specifically to the Comptroller's approval of non-bank banks and the ability of banks to circumvent federal law by chartering banks at the state level.[75]

The other regulators were strongly opposed to such a broad-based legislative moratorium. Both the FDIC and the OCC feared that an indefinite congressionally-mandated moratorium would take the pressure off Congress to act. Commercial banks were split in their support for the moratorium. Supporting the position of the larger banks, the ABA argued that the moratorium would only stall congressional action. The IBAA, representing the small banks, supported the Fed on the grounds that more time was needed to study the issues.[76] A moratorium was also favoured by the SIA, which hoped to be able to slow the deregulatory momentum.[77]

On Capitol Hill, support for the moratorium was mixed. In the Senate Banking Committee, there was growing support for legislation that would simply close the loophole in the BHC Act. At the same time, Garn stated that it was unlikely that Congress would impose the moratorium. 'We are not under a lot of pressure at this point to go ahead with one [moratorium],' Garn stated in an interview.[78] This position was not very surprising since Garn had favoured swift congressional action on the Glass-Steagall issue, which was less likely to occur if a moratorium was in place. On the other hand, those that were more reluctant to move on the bank powers issue favoured the moratorium. According to Charles Schumer, a member of the House Banking Committee, '[A] legislated moratorium with a commitment to enact legislation is warranted....'[79]

For most of 1983, therefore, Congress did not make any progress at all on the central issues before the committees. Rather than taking a decisive step forward and legislating if, and to what degree, banks should be allowed to enter the securities industry, the legislature was locked in an endless debate over the correct political environment — a congressional versus an administrative moratorium — in which those issues should be discussed.

This did not prevent those regulators favouring policy progress from moving forward. In mid-May of 1983, the FDIC announced a proposal that many observers considered the most significant breach of the Glass-Steagall Act yet. The FDIC's Board tentatively proposed expanding its previous ruling and authorizing state-chartered non-member banks to also underwrite corporate securities.[80] The FDIC's action presented a major challenge to the other institutions in the policy network. The investment banking community called the action outrageous and pledged to sue the FDIC if it went ahead with its plan.[81] It also presented yet another challenge to the Fed board and Chairman Volcker, who was adamantly opposed to letting banks underwrite corporate securities. If the FDIC's interpretation of the law was upheld, the Fed would be powerless and more banks might switch their charters.[82]

The real intention of the FDIC, however, was to exert further pressure on Congress. Given that the FDIC proposal had the consent of the Comptroller, who sits on the insurer's board, and the Comptroller would be hit hardest if national banks switched their charter, it is correct to assume that the board's real intention with its proposal was to induce congressional action. The FDIC was hopeful that the challenge from the states would have a particularly strong effect on Congress, which was standing by as its institutional authority as the nation's legislative body was rapidly undermined by states and independent agencies.

Initially, the action by the FDIC had its intended effect in both the House and Senate. After the FDIC went public, Senator Garn stated that the issue was bigger than state bank powers and should be decided by Congress. When Senate hearings opened in June, there was a much greater sense of urgency to deal with a policy issue that in the eyes of many senators had got out of control and threatened to undermine congressional authority over bank regulation. For example, according to Senator John Heinz, '[I]t is not the place of self-interested parties, federal regulators, or state legislators to threaten the public with a breakdown of a system that has functioned effectively for 50 years just because Congress will not adopt a timetable suitable to them.'[83]

In the House, the FDIC's action also resulted in outrage. Timothy Wirth, from the House Energy and Commerce Committee, which shared jurisdiction with the House Banking Committee, strongly objected to the FDIC's intrusion into the jurisdictional domain of his committee, calling the action 'an attempt by an individual unelected regulator to usurp congressional legislative powers.'[84] According to Wirth, '[T]his, it seems to us, is a legislative issue, not one to be left to an obscure regulatory institution to fundamentally alter the nature of the way our financial system works....And I find it absolutely astounding that this proposal has been made without congressional input.'[85] Other institutions opposing the FDIC's action also stepped up their activities. On June 23, Volcker sent a letter to Garn renewing his plea for a congressional moratorium until the end of the year.

The Administration was concerned that the FDIC's action would result in an indefinite moratorium and thus put a halt to its deregulatory agenda. To reduce the pressure for a moratorium, the Treasury unveiled a new banking bill on July 8.[86] Significantly, the bill was a carefully crafted compromise between the interests of the Treasury and the Fed, which had opposed the previous year's Administration bill. First, the Treasury had dropped those provisions that would have curbed the regulatory powers of the Fed. Second, the provision that would allow banks to underwrite corporate securities, which had been rejected by the Fed, had also been dropped. Finally, the Treasury proposed to close the loophole by which non-financial companies had acquired banks and circumvented Fed supervision. In sum, the new bill would lead to a net increase in the Fed's regulatory power, which explained Volcker's support when the bill went to Congress.[87]

On introducing the bill, Regan urged the senators, 'If Congress is going to have any impact on the future of the financial services industry, it must act quickly and decisively.' Otherwise, the Treasury Secretary stated, 'banks will go to states that allow the most advantages to them. State legislatures will determine the future of the national banking system of the United States.'[88] Garn stated that he had some reservations about the bill, but indicated that he was willing to compromise and would try to act on new banking legislation as early as September.[89]

But numerous other conflicts remained that made any decisive action unlikely. One issue that seemed especially difficult to resolve, even if bank regulators and the banks had been able to compromise, was the SEC's jurisdictional claim over the securities activities of banks. While agreeing in principle with the Treasury proposal, the SEC made it clear that if such powers as stock brokerage were approved, the SEC would require banks to register with the agency and adhere to its rules for brokers and investment advisers, thus expanding its regulatory authority over the banks. The move was immediately opposed by commercial banks who feared the additional SEC regulations. A spokesman for the ABA said, 'It's our legal view that, clearly, the SEC isn't empowered to regulate the brokerage activities of commercial banks.'[90] Bank regulators also rejected the SEC's proposal. Not only the Fed but also the OCC felt that the SEC was encroaching on its regulatory turf, and announced that they would resist the proposed action by the SEC.[91]

In addition, Garn, who still hoped to pass a bill, failed to anticipate the strong congressional opposition to expanded powers even in his own committee. Strong opposition and heavy lobbying by the securities industry ensured that the Administration's bill would go nowhere. Shortly before Garn wanted to introduce a new bill that was based on the Treasury proposal, Senator Heinz, who already in 1982 had forced Garn to tone down a bank powers bill, announced that he would soon introduce legislation that would extend the moratorium (which had not even been voted on) to the middle of 1984. Heinz argued that bank deregulation had gone far enough, and that there was no consensus in Congress for expanding the powers of commercial banks. Congress was dubious about further deregulation, he stated, because the result would be a greater concentration of financial power in large organizations. In addition, according to Heinz, Garn's bill 'has united nearly every interest in the United States, except the banking lobby, against it.'[92] Heinz's threat to lead a revolt against Garn was particularly credible because he could count on the support of a considerable number of fellow Republicans and Democrats on his committee. His position seemed to be close to that of St. Germain, who continued to show

little interest in the bank powers issue.[93]   St. Germain had promised to
introduce the Administration's bill, but had not yet even decided whether to
hold hearings on the legislation.   Meanwhile, Wirth did hold hearings on
banking issues, which were limited to the FDIC's action regarding state-
chartered non-member banks.

Despite Heinz's announcement, in mid-November Garn introduced his bill
which would allow banks to expand into municipal revenue bond
underwriting and mutual fund sponsorship.   In a concession to the Treasury,
Garn changed his original proposal and thereafter also advocated the holding
company structure.   Since Garn was not up for reelection the following year,
he was willing to push his bill while publicly criticizing his fellow
legislators: 'Somehow they [other senators] think that delaying these
decisions will make them easier.   These aren't Republican or Democratic
decisions — it's simply that they don't want to irritate the realtors, the
bankers, the securities people, *et cetera*.'[94] The Fed and the OCC reacted
favourably to the bill.   The Comptroller responded by extending his
moratorium until March 1984, removing the immediate pressure on
Congress to redefine financial boundaries by administrative fiat and allowing
some time to debate the proposal on Capitol Hill.

1984

Regan and Volcker, who both subscribed to the Garn bill, urged the Senate
to act and rewrite the nation's banking laws so that the increasing overlap
of the once-distinct segments of the financial industry could be sorted out
by the government.   Volcker reiterated the Fed's general position that
'depository institutions continue to perform a unique and critical role in the
financial system and the economy.   This unique role implies continuing
governmental concerns about the stability and impartiality of these
institutions.'[95]

Others, however, were more sceptical.   Despite Garn's commitment to act
on the bill during 1984, they saw little hope for decisive action in Congress
during an election year, given continued strong opposition from the
securities industry and divided committees in both chambers.   In fact, it was
the emerging consensus among the Treasury, the Fed and some key senators
that led to a reaction in the House, which for a long time had even resisted
holding hearings on bank powers.   In addition, in light of the rulings by the
FDIC and the OCC, St. Germain realized that he could not stop the
unravelling of the financial system by simply refusing to address the issue.
But right from the start, St. Germain made it clear that his committee would
take a very different approach to the issue of bank deregulation than some
members of the Senate Banking Committee, the Administration, and the

regulators. '[M]uch of what has been proposed to date in the name of deregulation', St. Germain said, 'is nothing less than a total reworking of the economic fabric of the nation — something that the worker, the consumer, the small business person has as much stake in as the banker and the corporate executive.'

St. Germain's announcement and the subsequent hearings would not bring to a halt the momentum in the Senate. Shortly after St. Germain's speech on the floor, all regulators who testified to the Senate Banking Committee once again reiterated their long-held positions, all of which supported an overhaul of Glass-Steagall. According to the FDIC, '[E]xcept for moratorium legislation, it is hard to imagine the Congress adopting any bill that is worse than the status quo. The marketplace is deregulating, and, try as one might, it cannot be stopped.'[96] Comptroller Conover went even further and told the Committee that he would not renew the moratorium which was due to expire in March.[97] Between 23 March and 30 April 1984 alone, 26 banks filed applications with the Comptroller to open non-bank banks in states other than their own.[98] Only after the Comptroller met with legislators on Capitol Hill did he agree to extend the moratorium one more time until the end of the congressional session.

Those in favour of deregulation were also applying more immediate pressure. State legislatures continued to undermine federal regulatory policy and congressional authority by debating, and in some cases passing, bank regulations that were more liberal than those at the federal level.[99] At the same time, the FDIC announced a slightly revised set of rules that would allow subsidiaries of about 9,000 state-chartered banks to underwrite corporate securities, and reiterated that it was determined to persevere. Regan warned Congress that 'states will shape the financial services industry of the future. And it will be inconsistent, inefficient, costly and less effective in delivering services to the consumer and once again the prices will go to those who are swiftest in finding the loopholes.'[100]

The momentum in the Senate was dealt a serious setback, however, when on 17 May 1984, Continental Illinois National Bank & Trust Co. of Chicago avoided *de jure* failure only after regulators stepped in with a $7.5 billion rescue package for the bank. Garn tried to maintain the momentum, arguing that Continental's plight was irrelevant to his bill and was being exploited by opponents. The regulators sided with Garn, stating that the failure of Continental was not linked to the bank powers issue. Volcker, in a letter to Garn, said, 'we do not believe the problems of the Continental Illinois Bank argue against granting new powers to bank holding companies....'[101] FDIC Chairman Bill Isaac went even further, linking Continental's failure to the bank's inability to compete effectively with other financial institutions.[102]

In general, however, there was a drastic shift on Capitol Hill against any further deregulation of banks. Even supporters of Garn, such as Senator Alan Dixon, admitted that, 'there was a feeling by everyone that we didn't want to go forward when the financial news was dominated by the Continental situation.'[103]   Others on the Senate Banking Committee opposing Garn used the failure of Continental to further their cause: 'People are saying "What are we doing offering powers to these lunatics when they can't handle the powers they've got?"'[104]

On the House side the reaction was even stronger. According to St. Germain, '[W]hen we are asked to endorse the movement of banks into fields even riskier than conventional banking, this type of incident does strongly suggest the need for careful analysis and caution.'[105]   A few days after his statement, with momentum turning away from deregulation after the *de facto* failure of Continental, St. Germain introduced his own bill which, while closing the loophole, did not contain a single new power for the banks.[106] Commenting on the disparity between the House and Senate bills, Chalmers P. Wylie, a Republican from Ohio and co-sponsor of the House bill, said, 'Senator Garn prefers his own bill of course but he recognizes the political reality of the situation — that the bill which the Treasury sent up, and he introduced, is not going anywhere.'[107]   Those members of the House Banking Committee supporting the bill were confident that the Continental affair would strengthen their cause. According to Rep. Charles Schumer, a Democrat from Brooklyn and a strong supporter of the bill, '...Continental has delivered a punch in the gut of those who want quick and simple deregulation.'[108]

The reaction from the other institutions was predictable. A spokesman for the money centre banks immediately rejected the House bill while the SIA welcomed the effort to sort out the confusion in the financial system. The response of the regulators was mixed. Given that the bill did in fact address the non-bank bank loophole and overruled the FDIC's decision regarding non-member state banks, Volcker called it a 'positive step so far as it goes'.[109] The Comptroller, on the other hand, called it 'an attempt to turn back the clock in a way that would weaken the banking industry and be detrimental to consumers.' Similarly, Secretary Regan charged that 'to halt banks' diversification is really protectionist legislation for the securities and insurance industries.'[110] The House was not very impressed by the Administration's statements. Certain of finding sufficient support among their members and the general public in light of the Continental affair, the two committees with jurisdiction over banking and securities in the House committed themselves to voting on their bills before the July 4 recess.

In the Senate, Garn also had to pare down his bill considerably in light of the Continental failure. Persuaded by Senators D'Amato and Heinz that additional bank powers would meet resistance on the Senate floor, Garn deleted many of the securities powers. Of the broad banking deregulation that Garn, with backing from the Administration, had initially proposed, he kept only provisions allowing banks to deal through affiliates in mutual funds, mortgage-backed securities, municipal revenue bonds, and commercial paper. But having taken out some of the most controversial aspects, Garn made clear to the House that he would not support their narrow bill that only closed loopholes without providing new powers for banks. Moreover, anticipating that some of his own committee members might side with the House, he threatened that he would recommend to President Reagan a veto of any bill that limited banks' expansion into new financial services.

When Congress returned in September, Garn's bill was approved by the Senate by a vote of 89 to 5.[111] The passage of the bill, however, did not end the struggle of those in the Senate opposing the bill. Both D'Amato and Heinz pledged to defeat the bill when it went to conference with the House.[112] Supporters of enlarged powers used the passage of the Senate bill to urge similar legislation in the House, reminding the chamber that a loophole closing bill without enlarged powers would not be accepted by the Administration.[113]

If anything, the action in the House went in the opposite direction. Given St. Germain's stronghold over the entire committee, there was little chance that the House Banking Committee would change its position.[114] Within a few days of the Senate vote, St. Germain announced that he did not plan to move on bank legislation before the election recess on October 4, thus avoiding a direct confrontation with the Senate. 'I regret that it is not possible to move on the loophole closing legislation in this session, but it is obvious that the Senate will not consider it unless we buy off on new and greatly expanded powers for banks and other financial institutions.'[115] Garn was infuriated by St. Germain's action and threatened not to seek or support an extension on the Comptroller's moratorium, hoping he could change St. Germain's mind.[116] In reality, however, it meant that the House and Senate had reached an impasse and that any action was likely to be delayed until 1985.

Despite the total failure of Congress to generate some legislative policy outcomes, policy did move forward during 1984. In fact, as Congress appeared increasingly incapable of producing any legislation that would provide some guidance for both the regulators and the banks for the future course of the nation's system, the agencies, in conjunction with the courts, were beginning to fill the policy vacuum that Congress was leaving behind. In late January, the Supreme Court agreed to hear a suit brought by the SIA against the Fed on the grounds that its approval of Bank of America's purchase of Charles Schwab violated both the BHC Act and the Glass-Steagall Act.[117]   The Fed's approval had been upheld earlier by the Second U.S. Court of Appeals in New York in July of 1983.[118]   Clearly, by accepting the Schwab case the judiciary expanded its involvement in the debate over bank regulation. Since it was the Supreme Court that would decide the case, this decision could no longer be challenged unless Congress overturned the ruling by the high court. In addition, only a few weeks earlier the Supreme Court had accepted another appeal by the SIA, challenging a federal court's decision to let banks underwrite commercial paper.[119]

Shortly after that, the banks were handed a significant victory when the Supreme Court unanimously upheld the Fed's regulation permitting bank holding companies to offer discount brokerage.[120]   In fact, the court had preempted policymaking since the House bill did not allow banks to engage in discount brokerage, and Congress would therefore have to overturn the ruling. Significantly, the Supreme Court gave substantial discretionary power to the makers of bank regulatory policy when it stated in its decision that the Fed had spelled out with commendable thoroughness how discount brokerage is indeed closely related to banking, and that the Fed's view is entitled to 'greatest deference.'[121]   In another case, the Supreme Court ruled against the Fed's decision which had given Bankers Trust the right to market commercial paper for its clients.[122]   However, in its decision, the Court returned the case to the federal appeals court to determine whether Bankers Trust's activities in fact constituted underwriting. In the meantime, Bankers Trust continued its activities in the commercial paper market.[123]

The OCC and the FDIC also began to take on the role of policymakers. By the time Congress adjourned, there were more than 300 non-bank applications awaiting approval. According to an aide at the OCC, the Comptroller had 'a wet pen ready' to okay pending applications.[124] Leaders of the banking committees, including Garn, warned the Comptroller that non-bank banks chartered after 1 July 1983 would have to be divested under all bills currently pending in Congress, and they 'emphasized that legislation addressing the competitive and regulatory framework of the financial system will be first priority of the Banking Committees of the House and Senate' as soon as Congress reconvened in 1985.[125]   The IBAA, in a letter to President Reagan, asked the Administration to intervene since the OCC's actions 'would violate the spirit of the laws which are the foundation of our financial system.'[126]

But the Administration refused to act. At a press conference, Secretary Regan told reporters that the failure of Congress to act during an 18-month moratorium indicated that the House believed that there was no emergency. 'It leads me to believe that they want the Comptroller to do his job and uphold the law. And the law permits non-bank banks to exist. We, as loyal government servants, have nothing to do but to uphold the law,' the Secretary said with a smile, according to news accounts.[127]

Shortly after Congress went into recess, the OCC announced that it would not extend its moratorium and would begin to decide on pending applications. In addition, the Comptroller publicly encouraged banks to file applications, thus intensifying the Administration's confrontation with the legislature.[128] On 1 November 1984, Conover approved the first 29 of the 332 pending applications.[129]

The FDIC also reacted to congressional paralysis. In the latter half of November, the FDIC finalized its rules under which the 9,300 state-chartered non-member banks it supervised could enter the securities business. Officials from the FDIC argued that 'since Congress did not finally act, we must.'[130] The FDIC's ruling prompted an immediate reaction from the securities industry, which stated that it would challenge the ruling in the courts.[131]

In another development, which turned out to be the most important test for the regulators, Citicorp, which had been the leader in trying to find ways to breach the investment banking field, filed for permission from the Fed to underwrite corporate bonds, commercial paper, mortgage-related securities, and municipal revenue bonds. Citicorp claimed it had found a loophole in the Glass-Steagall Act that would permit it to engage in securities activities: part of the 1933 act permits bank holding companies to underwrite the normally forbidden securities if they do it through a separate subsidiary and the subsidiary does not make underwriting those securities its principal business.

Looking back, two developments in the financial policy network stand out. In the legislative segment of policymaking, all institutions involved were now actively pursuing their own interests or those of their constituents. While the House committees in earlier years had refused to even consider the issue of bank powers, they were forced to take a position during 1984. This led to complete gridlock in the legislature and began to shift the policymaking process to the administrative/judicial arena, leaving the regulators and the courts with primary responsibility in shaping the future of the banking industry. Given the different interests of the regulators and the time-consuming nature of financial litigation, the result was a policy network characterized by a haphazard, confusing, and often controversial mix of laws and regulations undermining the entire regulatory structure of the U.S. financial system. Unless Congress acted in 1985, the entire structure was likely to break down, threatening 'a progressive unraveling of the basic tenets of public policy.'[132]

1985

Both Garn and St. Germain had stated their intention to address the issue of financial services reform immediately when the 99th Congress opened for session. In a joint statement released on 4 October, they said that 'legislation addressing the competitive and regulatory framework of the financial system will be the first priority' of both committees.[133] But when Congress did open, little changed. St. Germain reintroduced his bill that would close the non-bank bank loophole and added that he intended to frustrate Administration-backed efforts to further deregulate the financial service industry. He denounced deregulation as 'little more than a synonym for industry wish list' and warned that Congress would be 'foolish if it did not demand some quid pro quo for the American consumer, small business, and others often left on the sidelines when the big decisions are made about financial services.'[134] Garn did not change his position either. 'I don't intend to walk away from an 89-5 victory,' he stated, referring to the Senate's 1984 vote.[135] This meant that there had to be some reconciliation between the two chairmen, and at that early stage it was difficult to judge whether that was possible. However, as the term evolved it became apparent that Garn had no intention of changing his position. While he did hold further hearings during 1985, he considered them more of a formality.

> ...[W]e do not need to reinvent the wheel. We've had hundreds of witnesses....Many of these issues were before Congress before I even became a Senator, let alone Chairman of the Committee. I'm getting rather tired of being told year after year we can't do it this year, but next January we will. I've heard that now for 6 or 7 years. So we will hold these relatively brief series of hearings and then I do intend to push as hard as I possibly can for comprehensive banking legislation. The time to act is not this year; it was last year.[136]

The House did not even generate a bill, as St. Germain got involved in a bitter dispute over interstate bank regulation. Banking legislation died in Congress once again in 1985.

Given Congress's continued inaction, regulators and the courts were further forced into policymaking positions. In June of 1985, the Fed ruled in favour of Bankers Trust, spelling out in detail the conditions under which banks may legally sell commercial paper.[137] But in a separate statement, Volcker also urged Congress to grant banks the authority. 'I believe that a more straightforward way of proceeding would be to obtain legislative authorization for banks to deal in and act as agents for the distribution of commercial paper.'[138]

Another important development was Citicorp's decision to file for permission from the Fed to underwrite, through its subsidiary, corporate bonds, commercial paper, mortgage-related securities, and municipal revenue bonds, in what was considered the most serious challenge to the securities industry yet.[139]   Early in the year, Citicorp suddenly withdrew its application after the Fed indicated it would have to reject such a sweeping plan.[140] One of the reasons the board rejected Citicorp's application was that 'the board believes that the Congress is the appropriate forum for resolution of the public policy considerations involved in this proposal, such as that advanced by Citicorp, that would dramatically alter the framework established by Congress in the Glass-Steagall Act for the conduct of the commercial and investment banking businesses.'[141]

But Citicorp did not give up hoping that the Fed would ultimately be willing to take on an active policymaking role. Within a month of the Fed's unofficial rejection, Citicorp submitted another application — this time, however, not seeking to underwrite corporate debt. In what might be considered a partial success, the Federal Reserve announced in mid-May that it would seek public comment on Citicorp's request.[142]   Within a few days, Chemical Bank joined Citicorp, and in the fall J.P. Morgan joined the two banks. According to Morgan, the issue was no longer the permission to engage in some marginal activities in the securities field, but the repeal of the entire Glass-Steagall Act.[143]

Subsequently, an intense battle developed between commercial and investment banks trying to convince the Fed of their causes. The SIA based its campaign on the Fed's own arguments that banks are special and cannot be allowed to enter such activities. The securities industry also claimed that the proper forum to decide these issues was Congress and not the regulators.[144] In addition, if the Fed decided in favour of the banks, the SIA stated that it would go to court, challenging the Fed's policymaking authority.[145]

The large New York money centre banks were quick to counter, matching every argument step by step and mounting a major public relations campaign to convince policymakers of the competitive and public policy benefits if they were allowed to enter the securities field.[146] Initially, the Fed was supposed to make a decision on the Citicorp application before the end of the year, but the decision was postponed until 1986.

Finally, in April of 1985, in yet another major victory for the banks and another sign that the agencies and the courts had taken on the policymaking role, a federal judge let stand the FDIC's ruling that the Glass-Steagall Act does not bar state-chartered non-member banks from underwriting securities.[147] Even though few banks were expected to take advantage of the ruling immediately, the courts had effectively opened a route for banks to circumvent the entire Glass-Steagall Act.[148]

1986

For the most part, 1986 turned out to be an equally disappointing year with regard to comprehensive legislative reform. In Congress, the debate over enlarging the product powers of commercial banks moved increasingly to the background as the worsening state of the S&L industry led the legislature to turn its attention to these more immediate problems. It appeared that the severity of the S&L debacle would create the proper crisis environment and political pressure for Capitol Hill to enact some bank legislation. However, as it turned out, the underlying conflict between the House and the Senate, as well as the Administration and the regulatory agencies, on the issue of enlarged powers was so intense that it was injected into the debate on the ailing thrift industry and threatened to paralyse policymaking in this particular area too.

In separate appearances in early March, the two banking committee chairmen renewed the policy battle that had blocked enactment of any significant banking legislation since 1982. At a hearing in early March, St. Germain strongly criticized the Administration's continued call for an omnibus bill deregulating the financial services industry and indicated that only a limited bill that would close the non-bank loophole and help the S&L industry would pass the House. Garn in return continued to insist on his bill that had passed the Senate in 1984. In addition, Garn for the first time publicly acknowledged that he was willing to relinquish Congress's policymaking authority to other institutions in the policy network. '[F]rankly, I'm content to wait [for St. Germain]. I'd rather see the courts and the states act, if Congress won't. We may never move a bill. If there is no interest on the part of the House to move a[n omnibus] bill, why bother?'[149]

The bank powers issue died again. But this time it did not just stall action dealing with the increasing competitive threat from non-financial corporations entering the traditional banking business through the Glass-Steagall loophole. Due to the link that both the House and the Senate established between the powers issue and other bank legislation — a connection which the Administration and the agencies were willing to put aside in light of the urgency of the S&L bailout and the necessity to enlarge regulators' powers to deal with troubled banks — it led to the complete standstill of *any* bank legislation.[150]

As a result, policymaking was dominated by the regulators and the courts during 1986, and though progress was made in some areas, in general banks received conflicting messages regarding a framework for bank regulation in the years to come. For example, with respect to the conflict over commercial paper, banks were dealt a major setback early in 1986. In February, a U.S.

district judge overruled a 1985 Fed approval and stated that Bankers Trust was engaged in underwriting when it sold commercial paper on behalf of its clients.[151]   Bankers Trust and other banks that were distributing commercial paper reacted angrily. The banks stated that they would appeal the decision and in the meantime continue their activities, despite the efforts of the SIA to seek an injunction in federal court to stop Bankers Trust from continuing its now eight-year-old commercial paper activities.[152] But the decision also had broader implications. There was general agreement among bank analysts that the decision, if it were to stand, would cast severe doubt over other efforts by commercial banks to enter the securities business, specifically the pending applications by the money centre banks to underwrite securities.

Then in April 1986, an appeals court heard from the various industry factions as well as the Fed, which continued to support Bankers Trust's position, and in December 1986 the court reversed the lower court's decision, ruling that Bankers Trust's activities did not amount to underwriting and that the bank could indeed sell commercial paper. But as in many other instances, the final outcome remained uncertain since the SIA immediately responded that it would appeal the decision to the Supreme Court.[153]

In another case, several money centre banks had applied to the Fed during the spring of 1985 to underwrite a variety of securities; large banks were likely to join them if the Fed approved the application. Initially the Fed was to decide on some of the applications during the spring of 1986, but then decided to postpone its decision until after Congress adjourned in October.[154] Commercial banks interpreted this as a positive sign and were confident. Money centre banks were also hopeful because two recent appointees to the Fed board by the Reagan Administration — Wayne D. Agnell and Manuel H. Johnson — strongly favoured additional powers for commercial banks.[155] Bank analysts suggested that the Fed had indeed decided to approve at least some of the securities activities contained in the application. But the agency wanted to stall the approval in order to avoid a congressional backlash and the enactment of legislation that would ban such powers. Also, the Fed was afraid that an approval of additional powers while Congress was still in session could jeopardize other bills on Capitol Hill that the Fed had an interest in seeing passed.

To the great disappointment of the banks, the Fed did not act on the applications during 1986. Late in December, the agency announced that it would hold hearings in February 1987 to consider the request by Citicorp, J.P. Morgan, and Bankers Trust to underwrite some securities in subsidiaries that were separate from their banking operations. A final decision would be made in April. Just as in the courts, the Fed in announcing its decision issued a plea to Congress to enact comprehensive legislation that would enable the agency to implement the regulatory policies rather than making policy itself. 'I fully realize that these are hotly contested issues, with large private economic interests at stake,' said Volcker in announcing the decision. 'Although the legislative process has hitherto been paralyzed by this conflict, a new Congress provides new opportunity for prompt action in the public interest.'[156]   But even if the Fed had decided on the applications, little actual policy progress would have been achieved. Both private sector factions declared in advance of the decisions that if the Fed decided to their disadvantage, they would sue the agency, thus delaying any final decision on the issue.

1986 turned out to be a disappointing year for banks. They failed to enter the securities field in any major way. The successes that they scored with the regulators or the courts were limited in scope and uncertain in their ability to survive, as most of the decisions were appealed by the securities industry. In addition, the constant appeals by the regulators to Congress to enact comprehensive legislation indicated that they were not yet willing to take on the sole responsibility and burden of making federal bank regulatory policy.

But there was little indication that Congress would act in 1987. While one might argue that by the end of 1985 Congress was more or less split on the issue of bank powers, the situation had changed by the end of 1986. First, the mounting difficulties in the banking industry strengthened those forces in the House and especially in the Senate that opposed further deregulation of banking.   Second, the congressional elections in the fall of 1986 generated a Democrat majority in the Senate in addition to the House. William Proxmire, a Democrat from Wisconsin, returned to power as Chairman of the Senate Banking Committee. Proxmire's return was likely to mark a fundamental change in banking policy. His record in the committee was one of a pro-consumer who was in favour of preserving the legal barriers that separated banking from commerce and restricting interstate banking.   He had also been critical of the concentration of financial power in large money centre banks.[157] Proxmire was unlikely to push for an omnibus banking bill, but would probably attempt to pass more restrictive bills, especially with regard to the loophole issue. Indeed, it was Proxmire's reluctance to compromise that contributed to the failure of Garn's omnibus bill in the last Congress. In an interview shortly after his victory, Proxmire said, 'We've got to do everything we can to maintain the banking system we have. I think it's worked very well.'[158]

The change in the Senate majority did improve the likelihood that Congress might finally enact some legislation, but not in the area of bank powers. As House Banking Committee Chairman St. Germain commented on Proxmire's return, '[I]t's obvious he and I are very much in synch. We'll be able to accomplish a lot more.... I'm looking forward to a very productive session.'[159] However, this was of little interest to the large commercial banks. To the contrary, the closure of the loophole, which had allowed the banks to expand across states as well as into some securities activities without any enlarged powers, would be the worst possible scenario for the banks.

GRIDLOCK

In conclusion, the legislative gridlock over Glass-Steagall, and the banks' resultant recourse to piecemeal, ad hoc administrative loopholes, reflected the way in which the debate over Glass-Steagall mobilized the financial policy network. This debate involved a wide array of institutions in the policy network, and generated deep conflicts of interest among those institutions. Therefore, the structural possibility of gridlock was fully realized. Disputes among private financial institutions, between regulatory agencies, and within Congress meant that neither the public nor the private sector institutions could articulate a unified position on regulatory reform, or undertake a concerted effort to achieve change. The fact that the regulatory authorities were divided by conflicting interests and by competing alliances with various private sector institutions led to a gridlock of opposing forces and generated a political impasse over the repeal of Glass-Steagall.

In Congress, clearly one of the main causes of the gridlock was the fact that committees were politically responsive to various private sector interest groups with very different positions on financial deregulation. Divisions within the banking industry itself, and between commercial banks and other financial institutions, put opposing pressures on congressional committees and impeded the creation of consensus on regulatory reform.

The confusing and often contradictory signals emanating from the federal regulatory agencies also contributed to the policy gridlock. Although the main regulatory agencies were unanimous in calling for congressional action to bring about regulatory reform, they disagreed sharply over its extent. The federal regulators' clashing and sometimes internally contradictory positions on Glass-Steagall clearly impeded the progress of regulatory reform. The fact that Congress received confusing and conflicting signals from the regulatory agencies, rather than clear-cut and unanimous statements, added another element of fragmentation and discord to an already deadlocked situation.

In the first half of the 1980s, therefore, U.S. responses to the financial pressures arising from the external shocks of the 1970s conformed to prevailing notions of a weak, fragmented American state. Just as conventional wisdom would predict, the decentralization of the U.S. policy network fostered piecemeal, ad hoc policy responses which failed to achieve structural adjustment to external shocks.[160] Rather than formulating a comprehensive reform of the U.S. financial regulatory system, the policy network was paralysed by struggles between conflicting interests and competing jurisdictions. And it was hard to see how it could ever change.

Yet in the second half of the 1980s, the structural and procedural factors inherited from the mobilizational phase, which had previously set the terms of debate on Glass-Steagall, were gradually reshaped by a process of change. This process of change reflected the progressing global integration of financial markets, a trend which subjected U.S. banks to increasing competitive challenges from foreign financial institutions. As will be shown, the acceleration of financial integration affected the perceived interests of the main institutions in the policy network, the patterns of political alliance and conflict among them, and therefore the nature of the debate on regulatory reform.

NOTES

1.   Vietor (1987); Cargill and Garcia (1983).
2.   Hammond and Knott (1988); Litan (1987); Kaufman, Mote and Rosenblum (1983-84).
3.   Cooper and Fraser (1986); Rosenthal and Ocampo (1988).
4.   Pavel and Rosenblum (1984 and 1985); *Harvard Law Review*, 1985.
5.   Appendices to the statement by Paul Volcker before the Subcommittee on Commerce, Consumer and Monetary Affairs of the House Committee on Government Operations, 1986.
6.   McCall and Saulsbury (1986).
7.   Bennett (1980).
8.   *NYT*, 9 February 1979.
9.   For a discussion of the early developments see the report from the Subcommittee on Telecommunications, Consumer Protection and Finance of the House Committee on Energy and Commerce, July 1986.
10. *CQ*, 6 February 1982.
11. *Federal Reserve Bulletin*, February 1973 and 1983. By 1990, revenue bonds had increased to $81.3 billion.
12. Kessel (1971); Cagan (1978).
13. *NYT*, 27 June 1979.
14. Dunn (1982).
15. For the revenue bonds, see *NYT*, 29 June 1981; for the other rulings, see *Banking Law Journal*, 1980; *NYT*, 20 February 1980.
16. *NYT*, 30 September 1980. However, within a few weeks the SIA and A.G. Becker, one of the largest underwriters of commercial paper, filed suit against the ruling of the Fed Board. *NYT*, 16 October 1980; *WP*, 29 October 1980.
17. *NYT*, 14 June 1981.
18. *American Banker*, 27 March 1981.

19. *WSJ*, 1981; *American Banker*: 30 April 1981 and 25 September 1981; Goldberg and White (1979); Sametz (1981). For a more extensive presentation of the arguments, see the statements by Edward O'Brien, President of SIA, and David Silver, ICI, in *Competition and Conditions in the Financial System*, 13 May 1981.

20. With the acquisition of Prudential Insurance of the Bache Group and American Express's acquisition of Shearson Loeb Rhoades, they feared commercial banks would find it much easier to pressure their regulators, as well as Congress to liberalize, some aspects of Glass-Steagall.

21. *NYT*, 3 March 1981; *WSJ*, 11 March 1981; *American Banker*: 27 April 1981 and 7 May 1981.

22. Statement by Donald Regan, *Competition and Conditions in the Financial System, Part I*, 28 April 1981.

23. Senator Jake Garn in *Competition and Conditions in the Financial System, Part I*, 28 April 1981.

24. *WSJ*, 15 September 1981.

25. *American Banker*, 23 September 1981.

26. *United States Banker*, **92** (8), 1981.

27. *NYT*, 8 October 1981; *WSJ*, 8 October 1981.

28. *WSJ*, 16 October 1981 and 20 October 1981; *NYT*, 20 October 1981; *WP*, 23 October 1981.

29. *WSJ*, 20 October 1981; *American Banker*, 20 October 1981.

30. *WSJ*, 21 October 1981.

31. *WSJ*, 16 November 1981; *NYT*, 23 November 1981.

32. *American Banker*, 17 November 1981; *WSJ*, 30 November 1981 and 18 November 1982.

33. *American Banker*, 18 March 1981 and 16 July 1981.

34. The House had approved a much narrower bill that did not address any of the Glass-Steagall issues, see *WSJ*, 30 November 1981.

35. *CQ*, 31 October 1981.

36. *American Banker*, 2 September 1981 and 30 September 1981.

37. *WSJ*, 4 December 1981.

38. *NYT*, 29 July 1981.

39. *WSJ*, 29 April 1981.

40. *American Banker*, 25 November 1981; *The Economist*, 28 November 1981.

41. *NYT*, 25 November 1981; *American Banker*, 27 November 1981.

42. *NYT*, 27 November 1981.

43. *WP*, 4 February 1982.

44. Statement of John S.R. Shad, Chairman, Securities and Exchange Commission, *Securities Activities of Depository Institutions*, 4 February 1982.

45. *WSJ*, 19 March 1981; *American Banker*, 24 February 1983.

46. Statement of J. Charles Partee, Member of Governors of the Federal Reserve System, *Securities Activities of Depository Institutions*, 4 February 1982.

47. Ibid.

48. *WP*, 5 February 1982.

49. *CQ*: 6 February 1982, 15 May 1982, 22 May 1982; *NYT*: 11 February 1982 and 25 February 1982; *WSJ*: 9 March 1982 and 29 March 1982.

50. *United States Banker*, September 1982; *WP*, 6 August 1982.

51. *CQ*, 28 August 1982; *WP*, 25 September 1982.

52. *WP*, 30 September 1982.

53. The SIA planned to sue the OCC, see *NYT*, 14 September 1982.

54. *WSJ*, 2 September 1982; *WP*, 2 September 1982.

55. *Bankers Monthly Magazine*, 15 September 1982.

56. *WP*, 22 May 1982.

57. *NYT*, 3 November 1982; *WP*, 3 November 1982.

58. Statement by Wolfgang Reinicke, *Strengthening the Supervision and Regulation of the Depository Institutions, Part 2*, 11 April 1991.
59. *NYT*: 8 January 1983 and 19 April 1983.
60. *WSJ*, 21 October 1982; *NYT*: April 1982 and 22 July 1982.
61. Edward O'Brien, president of the SIA, as quoted in *NYT*, 8 January 1983.
62. *Deregulation*, **3** (3), 1983.
63. *American Banker*, 8 February 1983; *NYT*, 14 December 1982.
64. These states include California, Arkansas, South Dakota, Delaware, Washington, New York and Connecticut.
65. *NYT*, 26 March 1983.
66. The out-of-state clause was necessary to appease the South Dakota insurance lobby.
67. Corrigan (1982).
68. *WSJ*, 22 March 1983.
69. Isaac (1983).
70. *WP*, 4 May 1983.
71. *WSJ*, 6 April 1983.
72. See for example the statements by Senator Paul Sarbanes during an address to the SIA in January 1983, *American Banker*, 21 January 1983.
73. Statement by Donald Regan, *Financial Institutions Oversight, Part I*, 6 April 1983.
74. Ibid.
75. *NYT*, 27 April 1983; Wallich (1983).
76. *NYT*, 4 May 1983.
77. Linton (1983).
78. *NYT*, 10 May 1983.
79. Schumer (1983).
80. *WSJ*, 18 May 1983.
81. *WP*, 19 May 1983.
82. This is not the first time that this would happen. Up until the 1920s, federal law prohibited national banks from underwriting corporate securities. Since many states did not impose such restrictions many banks began to switch to state charters. To stem the sharp decline of national banks the federal government dropped its restrictions in 1927.
83. Opening Statement by Senator Heinz, *FDIC Securities Proposal and Related Issues*, 16 June 1983.
84. *NYT*, 21 May 1983.
85. Opening Statement by Timothy E. Wirth, *FDIC Securities Proposal and Related Issues*, 16 and 28 June 1983.
86. The proposal envisioned a substantial liberalization of the industry. It would allow bank and thrift institution holding companies or their subsidiaries to deal in and underwrite U.S. government and municipal revenue bonds. They could also sponsor, manage, advise and control investment companies or mutual funds and underwrite their securities. In addition, they could engage in securities brokerage transactions, conduct insurance underwriting and brokerage activities, and take part in real estate development and brokerage activities (limited to 5 per cent of capital in the case of a BHC). *WSJ*, 8 July 1983.
87. *WSJ*, 25 July 1983. The Fed called it 'a constructive attempt at permanent legislation', but added that the agency might still seek some changes. The Fed continued to press Congress for a moratorium until the end of the year. *WP*, 4 July 1983; *NYT*: 18 July 1983 and 14 September 1983.
88. *CQ*, 23 July 1983; *WP*, 19 July 1983.
89. *NYT*, 19 July 1983.
90. *NYT*, 28 October 1983.
91. *WSJ*, 20 October 1983.
92. *Business Week*, 28 November 1983.

93. *WP*, 3 November 1983; *WSJ*, 3 November 1983.

94. *CQ*, 5 May 1984.

95. Statement by Paul Volcker, *Competitive Equity in the Financial Services Industry*, 16 January 1984.

96. Statement by William M. Isaac, *Competitive Equity in the Financial Services Industry*, 21 March 1984.

97. Statement by C. Todd Conover, *Competitive Equity in the Financial Services Industry*, 21 March 1984.

98. *CQ*, 5 May 1984.

99. *WSJ*, 16 February 1984; *NYT*, 24 April 1984.

100. *WP*, 10 April 1984.

101. *NYT*, 16 August 1984.

102. Isaac (1984).

103. *NYT*, 7 June 1984.

104. *CQ*, 2 June 1984.

105. Ibid.

106. *WSJ*, 26 May 1984.

107. *CQ*, 26 May 1984.

108. *NYT*, 7 June 1984.

109. *NYT*, 13 June 1984.

110. *Non-bank Loophole Legislation*, 12 June 1984.

111. *CQ*, 15 September 1984.

112. *WP*, 14 September 1984; *Washington Financial Reports*, **43**, 17 September 1984.

113. Ibid.

114. *CQ*: 8 September 1984.

115. *Washington Financial Reports*, **43**, 24 September 1984. St. Germain's announcement coincided with hearings by the House Banking Committee on the Continental failure, where both regulators and banks were charged with imprudent behaviour. See for example, *CQ*, 15 September 1984; *WSJ*, 19 September 1984.

116. *Washington Financial Reports*, **43**, 1 October 1984.

117. *American Banker*, 24 January 1984.

118. *American Banker*: 23 May 1983 and 25 May 1983; *NYT*, 11 August 1983.

119. *WSJ*, 4 October 1983.

120. For earlier developments in the discount brokerage case, see *American Banker*: 25 April 1984, 18 May 1984, 1 June 1984; *WSJ*, 18 June 1984.

121. *WSJ*, 29 June 1984; *Washington Financial Reports*, **43** (2), 1984.

122. The Fed had argued that commercial paper did not constitute a security. The court disagreed, stating that 'we cannot endorse the board's departure from the literal meaning of the Act' in its interpretation of the term 'security'. As quoted in *NYT*, 29 June 1984.

123. *American Banker*, 6 July 1984.

124. *Washington Financial Reports*, 8 October 1984.

125. *Washington Financial Reports*, 15 October 1984.

126. *Washington Financial Reports*, 10 October 1984.

127. *WP*, 30 October 1984.

128. *WSJ*, 25 October 1984.

129. *CQ*, 3 November 1984. In various legal manoeuvres the Fed tried to challenge the Comptroller but was not successful, see *Washington Financial Reports*: 1 October 1984 and 29 October 1984.

130. *NYT*, 20 November 1984.

131. *American Banker*, 29 November 1984.

132. See for example *American Banker*, 21 December 1984; see also *WSJ*, 31 December 1984. The quote comes from a letter by Volcker to Congress on 1 November 1984, cited in *CQ*, 2 February 1985.
133. *CQ*, 2 February 1985.
134. *American Banker*, 8 January 1985.
135. *WP*, 13 January 1985.
136. Opening Statement of Chairman Garn, *Comprehensive Reform in the Financial Services Industry*, 8 May 1985.
137. *WSJ*, 5 June 1985. For more background, see *American Banker*, 22 April 1985.
138. *American Banker*, 5 June 1985.
139. *American Banker*: 4 January 1985, 7 January 1985, 9 January 1985.
140. *American Banker*, 27 February 1985.
141. The other reason given by the Fed was that the 'board's preliminary analysis indicated that the application would be inconsistent with the Glass-Steagall Act.' For a copy of the original text, see *American Banker*, 1 March 1985.
142. *American Banker*, 15 May 1985.
143. *WSJ*: 16 May 1985 and 10 October 1985; *NYT*, 11 October 1985; *Euromoney*, October 1985.
144. *American Banker*, 25 July 1985.
145. *American Banker*, 9 December 1985.
146. *American Banker*, 22 August 1985.
147. *WSJ*, 24 April 1985.
148. The SIA responded that it would appeal the decision in the Supreme Court. *ABA Bankers News Weekly*, 5 November 1985.
149. *CQ*, 8 March 1986.
150. *WP*, 22 October 1986.
151. *WP*, 5 February 1986.
152. *American Banker*, 7 February 1986.
153. *American Banker*, 24 December 1986.
154. *American Banker*, 28 March 1986.
155. *American Banker*, 31 January 1986.
156. *WP*, 25 December 1986.
157. *CQ*, 8 November 1986.
158. *WP*, 23 November 1986; *American Banker*, 30 December 1986.
159. *CQ* 15 November 1986.
160. Krasner (1978).

6. Glass-Steagall and the Politics of Change

THE SECOND STAGE OF CONFLICT: THE POLITICS OF DOMESTIC ADJUSTMENT

By the second half of the 1980s, international financial integration and technological innovation had proceeded to the point where foreign commercial banks were able to attract U.S. businesses away from domestic commercial banks. Given the more liberal regulations under which most continental European banks were operating, they were able to offer American customers full underwriting of corporate debt and equity at competitive prices.

The role of competition from foreign financial markets, as well as foreign institutions located in the United States, had influenced U.S. financial policymaking for some time. One prominent case during the 1970s dealt with the pressure that foreign markets, and especially the London Euromarkets, exerted on Regulation Q, which imposed interest rate ceilings on deposit and time accounts in the United States. Similarly, the institutional presence of foreign banks in the U.S. market also helped shape regulatory policy. For example, in 1978 the International Banking Act attempted to create a level playing field among all commercial banks in the U.S., independent of the origin of their headquarters. However, it did grandfather the activities of 17 foreign banks, including those not permitted under the Glass-Steagall Act to U.S. commercial banks.[1]

As early as 1980, commercial banks not only complained about increasing competition from other domestic financial institutions, but also warned of the increasing threat of foreign competition. Indeed, during the 1970s foreign institutions comprised the fastest growing segment of American banking. By 1980, for example, foreign banks accounted for 40 per cent of banking business in New York, and granted between one-sixth and one-fifth of all the business loans in the U.S., double their market share from the early 1970s.[2] On an international scale, U.S. commercial banks had also lost their once predominant position. In 1970, six of the world's largest banks were from the U.S. By 1980, only Citibank and Bank of America remained among the top ten. Finally, the incidence of takeovers of U.S.

91

institutions by foreign banks began to increase.[3] Banks continued to complain about the foreign threat throughout the first half of the 1980s, but for the most part their warnings got little recognition among policymakers.[4]

This situation, however, began to change during 1986. Several events attracted widespread attention in the U.S., including that of policymakers. For example, in the spring of that year U.K. financial markets completed the most sweeping deregulatory programme in the history of British financial markets. The major impetus for this move, often referred to as the 'Big Bang', was the fear that the city of London would lose its predominant position as the world's financial capital to other financial centres. Many of the regulatory changes were related to the London stock market, but the 'Big Bang' also eliminated all remaining barriers for commercial banks, including foreign ones, to underwrite securities. This not only increased the attractiveness of London as a financial marketplace, but also allowed U.S. commercial banks, which were not restricted by U.S. regulations abroad, to undertake extensive underwriting operations and demonstrate that they were perfectly capable of doing so.[5]

Another sign of the increasing globalization of financial markets was the rising institutional presence of foreign financial organizations in the U.S. Thus far, this foreign presence had been established through mergers between U.S. and foreign banks or the acquisition of a U.S. bank by a foreign bank. This changed in the summer of 1986, when Goldman, Sachs & Co. announced that it had made an offer to Sumitomo Bank of Japan for a special limited partnership in exchange for a $500 million investment in its operations.[6] Within a few months, the Fed approved the deal. Even though it involved a foreign bank, the Fed's action set a precedent for U.S. banks as well. Sumitomo owned a bank in California and was thus subject to the same rules and regulations regarding its U.S. operations as U.S. bank holding companies.[7]

U.S. banks reacted by calling for similar allowances.

> There's nothing wrong with the marriage [between Goldman Sachs and Sumitomo]. But American banking laws prohibit Sumitomo's American competitors from buying into such investment houses as Goldman Sachs. The two make a very powerful combination: the lending resources of a big bank, allied to the great flexibility of an investment house to underwrite all sorts of securities, participate in mergers and acquisitions, and to deal on its own account as well as its customers'. If it's proper for a Japanese bank to make this kind of a connection, it ought to be proper for American banks to do the same thing.[8]

The Fed's decision was significant because it indicated the beginning of a shift in its attitude towards the separation of commercial and investment banking. The source of the change in the Fed's position, however, was not domestic in origin, but international. In essence, the Fed did not want to put a halt to the increasing internationalization of financial markets, as it would lead to a slowdown of the infusion of foreign capital, a development considered detrimental to the U.S. economy. This international orientation was especially strong in the New York Fed, which was in charge of most of the international operations of the central bank and thus more aware of developments in international financial markets. For example, noting the declining profitability of U.S. commercial banks, a study by the New York Fed concluded that internationalization trends 'in evidence of the past several years are a cause for concern. The trends are most significant for large U.S. banking organizations which compete more directly with foreign banks, large security firms and diversified non-bank financial companies.'[9]

Similarly, New York Fed president Gerald Corrigan, who only two years before had defended the Glass-Steagall Act by arguing that 'Banks Are Special', now linked the need to reform the domestic regulatory structure to the emerging global capital markets. According to Corrigan,

> Money is now truly international in character, operating in enormous size, around the clock and around the world....[I]t is now increasingly evident that the distinction between commercial banking and investment banking is also being eroded....What is needed is a broad-based and progressive overhaul of our Federal banking and related statutes....[10]

Even at the Federal Reserve Board in Washington, there was an increasing sensitivity to the competitiveness of U.S. banks. This was partly due to the fact that some new board members were more receptive to the globalization argument.[11] More importantly, however, those banks that were advancing the arguments of international competitiveness most strongly — Chase Manhattan, J.P. Morgan, Citicorp and Bankers Trust — had announced that they were considering giving up their banking charter unless they were given more securities powers in order to compete.[12] This was a direct threat to the Fed, which would face a substantial drop in income due to a considerable decline in the non-interest bearing reserves that banks hold with the central bank. In addition, such an action by the banks would make the execution of monetary policy less effective, since the money base would become an increasingly smaller part of the liquid assets circulating in the economy.

While the FDIC and OCC did not have to change their basic position regarding Glass-Steagall, they began to use the threat of foreign competition to press for reform. According to Comptroller Robert Clarke,

> U.S. banks operate under laws that contradict the end of the laws themselves. That end — that purpose — is the enhancement of the strength and stability of our banking

system. Instead of making our banking system stronger these laws make it weaker. These laws constrain U.S. banks in the face of world competition, and thus they are a misapplication and abuse of our reason. For American banking to be preserved these laws must be changed. I am concerned when only one U.S. bank is among the world's largest ten. I am concerned that our banking structure is not equipped to meet the competition when a major Japanese bank can propose to become a partner in a major American securities firm — while American banks are severely limited in the types of securities activities in which they can engage here. I am concerned that our banking system is not equipped to meet the competition when an American bank can do things in London or Tokyo that it is prohibited from doing in the United States.[13]

On Capitol Hill as well, 1986 marked the year the globalization of financial markets and its competitive consequences for American banks entered the debate over banking reform. In the spring of 1986, the Senate Banking Committee held hearings on the internationalization of capital markets. As Chairman Garn explained in his opening statement,

[A]mong the issues the hearings will address are...the international role and competitiveness of United States financial institutions; and the effect of liberalized regulatory schemes in other countries, particularly in the United Kingdom....The testimony in these hearings will show that internationalization is accelerating and affecting virtually every aspect of the banking and securities industry. It is, therefore, important for this committee to stay abreast of these developments in these markets and recognize their impact on any legislation this committee considers.[14]

The senators would only hear testimony from the private sector and not from the Administration or the regulators. For the first time, the large commercial banks were given the opportunity to present their arguments. In the course of these hearings, it became obvious that the globalization of financial markets allowed the large commercial banks to develop a new political strategy in their effort to shift the balance of power among the institutions in the policy network in favour of a repeal of Glass-Steagall. Banks argued that the declining vitality and strength of the American economy was directly linked to the regulatory restrictions which prevented the U.S. financial system from raising and allocating capital in the most efficient way. This allowed them to shift the terms of debate away from a focus on private profits to one on national interest. Rather than serving the narrow economic motives of private commercial banks, deregulation was now presented as a necessary reform to defend the U.S. financial system against foreign competition, and to arrest the competitive decline of the U.S. economy in global markets. It even changed the language that was used to denote the general effort to repeal Glass-Steagall. Giving banks securities powers was no longer considered *deregulation*, but a necessary *reform* to stabilize the U.S. financial system and the economy as a whole.

In his testimony to the Senate, Dennis Weatherstone, chairman of J.P. Morgan, outlined the banks' three part line of reasoning. First, Weatherstone argued that international financial integration had caused sweeping and irreversible changes in the operation of financial markets and the way in which corporations raised funds. In 1974, corporations with assets of more than $1 billion satisfied 59 per cent of their short-term funding needs with bank loans while turning to commercial paper for only 33 per cent of such needs. By 1985, these percentages had reversed. Only 26 per cent of short-term corporate borrowing was done through bank loans and 52 per cent through commercial paper. Since investors and borrowers increasingly bypassed banks by exchanging funds directly in international capital markets, commercial banks could only remain competitive if they were free to better serve their clients' needs through underwriting and distributing securities. Weatherstone also stated that the problem was compounded by the fact that more than a dozen major international competitors of U.S. banks were permitted by the International Banking Act to conduct both commercial and investment banking in the U.S.

Secondly, the chairman argued that other major financial centres — including Great Britain, Japan, Canada and France — were already adapting to the realities of the new global marketplace and bolstering the competitive position of their financial systems by allowing their banks to offer the widest possible range of services. Given the integrated nature of financial markets, the fact that other major economic powers were deregulating their financial systems meant that U.S. financial institutions were placed at a severe competitive disadvantage.

Thirdly, and most importantly, Weatherstone argued that these trends boded ill not only for the American financial services industry, but for the U.S. economy and the country as a whole.

> We believe that the internationalization of the capital markets — particularly in light of the [successful] Eurobond experience [of commercial banks] calls for a major revision of the Glass-Steagall Act, which is an increasingly serious impediment to capital market efficiency in the United States. As a nation, we have a vast need for capital to support economic growth and to foster new industries and jobs. Future improvements in productivity and industrial competitiveness depend in a very tangible way on the capacity of our financial markets to raise large amounts of capital cheaply and to allocate capital efficiently.[15]

In essence, money centre banks established a direct link between the decline in America's industrial competitiveness and the decline in its financial might.

Initially, the securities industry rejected the need for any changes in the laws that separate commercial from investment banking. According to Robert Hormats, Vice President of Goldman Sachs, the industry 'certainly understands the reasons behind Glass-Steagall. As people in our industry have testified, we don't see a need to change that.'[16] But even to a few members of the SIA the threat of foreign competition presented a compelling argument for financial market reform. For example, during the SIA's 1986 annual meeting one speaker told his audience that the Glass-Steagall Act was 'the regulatory version of the Maginot Line. It offers no real protection against invaders who have the capacity to outflank the defense.'[17] He attacked the SIA for pursuing partisan interests that 'inhibit the competitiveness of U.S. players in today's global marketplace' in order to protect their own turf.[18]

1987

In January of 1987, a group of 45 banks, thrifts, insurance companies, brokerage houses and non-bank banks formed a private sector coalition to press Congress to deregulate the financial industry. Pointing to the increasing threat from financial institutions and markets, a statement issued by the group read, '[W]e can't let financial services get into the same predicament as steel, autos and textiles.'[19] The mandate the group had set for itself was immediately endorsed by the Administration. George Gould, an Undersecretary at the Treasury and the Administration's new pointman on Glass-Steagall, quickly endorsed the group's orientation, saying that the nation needs 'comprehensive, pro-competitive financial services legislation that will enable American firms to take on their foreign competitors.'[20]

Turning to specific legislation, in the first half of 1987 Congress passed a bill that dealt primarily with the worsening state of the S&L industry. However, the bill contained two provisions that were immediately relevant to the Glass-Steagall debate. The bill outlawed the creation of any new non-bank banks after 5 March 1985. In other words, the grandfather date for non-bank banks had been moved up from mid-1983, giving a total of 168 non-financial corporations the ability to remain in the financial services field. Secondly, the bill imposed a moratorium lasting until 1 March 1988 on bank entry into securities, insurance and real estate even with the approval of the regulators.[21] This compromise between the House and Senate had become possible because both St. Germain and Proxmire strongly opposed the continued proliferation of non-bank banks. With regard to the moratorium, both were determined not to allow the regulatory agencies to continue their role as shadow policymakers. But the passage of a bill that called for yet another moratorium was deceiving. It was more the immediate result of the crisis situation in the thrift industry than a reflection of the actual interests and political forces in the policy network.

Despite the change of leadership in the Senate Banking Committee, bankers were optimistic in early 1987 that legislation to repeal provisions of the Glass-Steagall Act would finally succeed in that year.[22] By linking the repeal of Glass-Steagall to the restoration of America's economic health and its role in global leadership, the large commercial banks were hoping to catalyse significant shifts in the positions of some of the key institutions in the financial policy network.[23] When hearings opened before the Senate Banking Committee, Treasury Undersecretary Gould reiterated the close policy linkage the Administration had established between external pressure and domestic policymaking.

> International competition and the globalization of financial markets underscore the need to reevaluate restrictions on U.S. financial institutions.... Yet the opposite seems to be occurring in a segment of our financial industry. Outdated and unfair restrictions on the U.S. banking industry are hindering its ability to compete in global markets.[24]

Even the very cautious Paul Volcker endorsed some of the banks' arguments. In testimony before the House, Volcker warned that the international competitive position and long-term strength of the U.S. financial services industry were being inexorably undermined by restrictive regulation.

> I cannot emphasize enough...that a strong, stable, and competitive banking and financial system is an indispensable ingredient of a healthy and growing economy. Plainly, inescapable forces of change — technological, economic, and competitive — at work on an international scale require appropriate and effective response if the broader public interests at stake are to be served.[25]

As mentioned earlier, the central bank's leading advocate to adjust regulatory policymaking to the external pressures was the Federal Reserve Bank of New York. In early 1987, the New York Fed published a proposal by its president to restructure the U.S. financial system.[26] The proposal contained two central elements: first, the increasing integration of national financial markets highlighted longstanding differences in supervisory, tax, accounting, and regulatory treatment of classes of institutions at home and abroad. This in turn further sharpened the competitive differences among commercial and investment banks and thus increased incentives for financial institutions to exploit loopholes and circumvent supervisory policies. Second, the technological and competitive forces now operating in a global context were simply too powerful to be overcome by a regulatory or legislative regime based on the past. Corrigan's proposal did not make any specific recommendations, but defined a bank holding company as an institution that 'could, in time, engage in a broad range of "financial" services including banking, insurance and securities activities....'[27] As mentioned previously, the other two federal regulatory institutions, though long advocates of wholesale deregulation, had also internalized the idea of globalization and its consequences for the U.S. financial industry into their line of reasoning and used it now to pressure Congress to act.[28]

Not a single hearing went by without a warning from large commercial banks of the negative consequences of the globalization of financial markets for the U.S. financial services industry and the nation's economy at large.[29] Coinciding with those hearings was the release of a report by the Office of Technology Assessment, entitled 'International Competition in Services', that had been requested by several Senate committees. One conclusion of the study states:

> The maze of U.S. banking regulations — implemented by the states as well as by the Federal Agencies — exerts wide-ranging implications on the international competitiveness of the U.S. financial services industry. Rapid expansion of international banking makes these impacts much more important than just a few years ago, but policymakers have given them little consideration. OTA's analysis indicates *a need for the policymaking process to reflect, on a routine rather than exceptional basis, the impacts of Federal policies on the international competitiveness of the U.S. financial services industry* [OTA's emphasis].[30]

The Congressional Research Service also released several studies examining the role of Glass-Steagall in light of increasing competition at home and abroad. While not in a position to make any specific policy recommendations, the study stated that '[B]anks are losing historical market shares of their major activities to domestic and foreign competitors that are less restricted.'[31]

Members of Congress simply could no longer ignore the growing debate. Those senators that had long advocated deregulation internalized the new set of arguments provided by the money centre banks, while others rejected it as a baseless exaggeration of reality.[32] But whatever the particular reaction, money centre banks had succeeded in injecting the notion of the internationalization of financial markets and its domestic implications into the congressional debate over financial reform.

By the fall of 1987, the effectiveness of the globalization argument showed its first signs of success. Probably the most dramatic shift occurred in the Senate, where Senator Proxmire reversed his long-standing resistance to the repeal of Glass-Steagall. In September, reports surfaced that Proxmire was considering introducing legislation that would abolish the Glass-Steagall Act. According to his staff director, Kenneth McLean, one of the major reasons for this dramatic turnaround was Proxmire's conviction that the globalization of financial markets made such a move necessary in order to preserve the vitality of the American banking industry.[33] How much the international dimension had influenced Proxmire's thinking and how much he had internalized the banks' arguments became clear when he held hearings with the sole purpose of examining the extent to which the globalization of finance had affected the U.S. domestic economy and its financial institutions. Proxmire opened the hearings with the following statement:

> When the Glass-Steagall Act was passed in 1933, capital markets were overwhelmingly domestic....We live now in a global market....The question before this committee is whether this has undermined Glass-Steagall. U.S. banks have underwritten a wide range of securities overseas without major incident. Fifteen foreign banks underwrite securities in the United States pursuant to grandfathered rights under the International Banking Act....Repealing the Glass-Steagall Act would increase competition in investment banking....[34]

Even the commercial banks were stunned by the change in the Senator's attitude. When Proxmire announced that he would not seek another term in the next Congress, the ABA's spokesperson stated: 'There were a lot of bankers who were worried sick about Senator Proxmire [when his tenure began] who are going to be sorry to see him go.'[35]

During the hearings, the money centre banks, represented by Morgan Guaranty, presented a newly revised, enlarged and even more compelling set of arguments linking the repeal of Glass-Steagall to such issues that would have to find a positive reception in Congress. For example, the banks now linked the repeal of Glass-Steagall to the overall position of the U.S. in the international political economy, including the ever-worsening trade deficit. According to the representative from Morgan Guaranty:

> [G]iven the interdependence of financial and political forces, the strength and influence of the Nation's financial firms is a matter of considerable national interest....In addition, as the United States strives to redress its international trade deficit, it will need to look in greater part to the services sector. Strong, competitive capital markets in this country can make a significant contribution to our ability to export financial services.[36]

In a strategic move, Proxmire invited former Comptroller of the Currency John Heimann, who during the time of his tenure strongly supported the cause of the banks, to testify. Heimann now held the position of Vice Chairman at Merrill Lynch Capital Markets Group and was thus considered a representative of the securities industry. Although Heimann did not endorse any change in the Glass-Steagall Act, he clearly spelled out his perspective on the effects of globalization for the U.S. domestic financial structure. According to Heimann:

[A] new cycle of market capitalism, global rather than national, is being launched....[G]lobal markets have created global competition, and global competition is reshuffling the world's largest banks into a new environment and a new class of participation.... Banks faced with the loss of their best and highest-quality customers, have had to alter their strategies... and it is not surprising that they are pushing, in the U.S., for an end to Glass-Steagall, so that they can recapture the financial activities of their own prime customers.[37]

Proxmire's shift in position reflected a broader and more fundamental realignment going on within the Senate. Congressmen, Republican and Democrat alike, became increasingly responsive to the concerns about foreign financial competition raised by the commercial banks. These new concerns also transformed the nature of the debate on Glass-Steagall within the Senate. As one senator stated, 'I am dismayed by those who continue to see this as a selfish turf battle. The issue is the future of our Nation's financial system...and its ability to compete abroad.'[38] Most members of the Senate Banking Committee came to agree that foreign financial competition was seriously threatening the viability of the U.S. financial industry and the strength of the U.S. economy. As one senator remarked, 'it is a sad irony that the Glass-Steagall Act, which was passed to promote the safety and soundness of the banking system, is today having exactly the opposite effect. U.S. commercial banks are being tested by global competition just as our auto makers, steel factories and other manufacturers are.' If Congress failed to repeal Glass-Steagall, he predicted, 'the Japanese, German, Swiss, and British institutions will elbow our banks out of the marketplace altogether.'[39]

Even staunch opponents of the banks' cause on the Senate Banking Committee began to realize that globalization could indeed be used to generate political capital. During the same hearing mentioned above, Senator Alfonse D'Amato flatly rejected the link between globalization and the competitiveness of the U.S. financial services industry. 'This morning's pretense for reform or restructuring', D'Amato opened his statement at the beginning of the hearings, 'is that unless America changes its laws we are doomed to become a second-class player in the financial world.'[40]

But only seven weeks later, D'Amato introduced his own bill that envisioned even more sweeping powers for banks than the current proposal before the committee had envisioned. In justifying the legislation, the bill stated: 'Congress hereby finds that current laws inhibit the ability of domestic financial markets and intermediaries to respond to the serious competitive challenges presented by foreign intermediaries and the globalization of markets.'[41]

By pointing to the far-reaching implications that the globalization of financial markets held for the nation's economy, the advocates of reform also found a more receptive audience in the House. While still refusing to hold hearings in the full committee on the specifics of globalization, St. Germain could not avoid advocates of regulatory reform within and outside his committee using other hearings on international financial and economic matters to bring up the issue of Glass-Steagall reform. For example, during his last appearance before Congress, Paul Volcker presented his perspective on the relationship between developments in international and domestic banking. 'I don't think you can separate these days international banking from domestic banking in any significant way, and I hope the review that you intend to conduct on the international side...will proceed apace with the next stage of domestic legislation because I think they are inextricably linked.'[42]

House members favouring a reform of Glass-Steagall tried to get an official endorsement from the chairman of the Federal Reserve. For example, Stan Parris (R-Va.) asked Volcker, '...[D]oes it make any sense that banks can engage in underwriting in Europe but not in the United States?' Volcker answered, 'I think that, broadly speaking, the answer is no....' Doug Barnard (D-Ga.), who had long advocated a radical reform of Glass-Steagall and pressured St. Germain to hold hearings on the topic, raised the issue directly by asking Volcker's opinion regarding the reform of Glass-Steagall. And Volcker, though still cautious, responded positively, 'We have been arguing for relaxation of Glass-Steagall...and I wish you would get on with it.'[43]

A similar strategy was used in the Committee on Energy and Commerce, whose consent was needed in order to reform Glass-Steagall. During hearings on the globalization of the securities markets, the Administration used the opportunity to emphasize the fact that different financial institutions could no longer be dealt with in isolation. Rather, globalization should force a reevaluation of all restrictions on U.S. financial institutions so that their competitive advantage could be preserved.[44]

Advocates of reform in the House went even further by circumventing St. Germain's staunch refusal to hold hearings on the issue. In the fall of 1987, Doug Barnard, chairman of the Subcommittee on Consumer and Monetary Affairs of the Government Operations Committee, released a widely publicized report on the need to reform the U.S. financial system. One of the major conclusions of the report was that 'these legal barriers [the Glass-Steagall Act and the BHC Act] to the redeployment of corporate capital by banking firms, which have no counterpart in other industries, have serious adverse consequences for the financial soundness of banks and the efficiency and competitiveness of the entire U.S. financial sector.'[45] The report was based on an extensive series of hearings that Barnard, in his capacity as the chairman of the subcommittee, with the support of his Republican colleague Stan Parris — also a member of both the Banking Committee and Consumer and Monetary Affairs Subcommittee — had held throughout 1986.[46]

In the fall of 1987, St. Germain finally succumbed to the pressure of several of his senior colleagues and held hearings. St. Germain realized that the committee could no longer ignore the issue without being accused of boycotting the debate over reform. 'Globalization of the markets, the interdependence between our national and international economies and the impact our current financial structure has on the abilities of our financial institutions to compete in today's domestic and international markets will be explored thoroughly', St. Germain opened the hearings.[47] But this in no way implied that he was ready to furnish the banks with securities powers. '[H]owever, in our efforts to find the solutions to problems embodied in our financial system as it is currently structured, we must never forget the hard lessons this country has learned from the past.'[48] This view was still shared by some influential members of the House Banking Committee, who remained unimpressed with the banks' new arguments.[49] Moreover, those sectors of the financial services industry that had long opposed a change in the Glass-Steagall Act — smaller banks and the securities industry — did not alter their position either, maintaining their pressure on the House not to concede to the banks.[50]

Thus, even though there was considerable change in the legislature, it was not yet sufficient to decisively turn the balance of power in Congress in favour of a repeal of Glass-Steagall. Regulators were fully aware of this and continued to chip away individual segments of the act in conjunction with the courts, because they considered the repeal of Glass-Steagall a necessary condition for U.S. banks and the economy at large to regain competitiveness and they knew that their actions would exert strong pressure on Congress to act. Money centre banks and regulators scored three important victories that year — two of them in the Supreme Court. Early in January 1987, the Supreme Court backed the Fed's ruling that banks were allowed to set up discount brokerage services wherever they wanted — including across state lines.[51] In April, a federal appeals court unanimously upheld the 1984 FDIC regulation that state-chartered banks that are not members of the Federal Reserve System may own securities subsidiaries, giving a boost to the FDIC's institutional standing as not only an insurer but also a regulator.[52] Finally, in the summer of 1987, the Supreme Court refused to hear an appeal by the SIA that would have prevented Bankers Trust from selling commercial paper, letting stand the earlier decision by a federal appeals court which had decided in favour of the Fed and Bankers Trust.[53]

But the development in the administrative realm that presented the biggest challenge to Congress was the historic decision by the Federal Reserve to approve, by a 3-2 vote, the applications of several money centre banks to underwrite securities in separate affiliates. The board allowed Citicorp, Bankers Trust, and J.P. Morgan to underwrite commercial paper, mortgage-backed securities, and municipal revenue bonds.[54] In order to comply with Glass-Steagall, the Fed limited the securities activities of the subsidiaries to 5 per cent of their total gross revenue and limited each of them to 5 per cent of the domestic market share. In determining what would qualify as securities activities, three governors agreed that government securities should not count when calculating the 5 per cent limit; Paul Volcker and Wayne Agnell disagreed and voted against the ruling.[55] This narrow vote did not necessarily reflect a disagreement over the fundamental issues. Rather, both Volcker and Agnell, who had been the more conservative members on the board, wanted to slow down the entry of the banks into the securities business. The majority of business undertakings by affiliates was indeed the underwriting of government securities, whose inclusion would have severely limited the volume of new securities activities.

Despite the narrow ruling, the decision by the Fed reflected a considerable shift in the agency's position. On earlier occasions, as in the case of commercial paper, the Fed argued that the instrument under consideration was not a security and thus Glass-Steagall would not apply. This was not the case any more; by accepting the banks' reasoning of the not-principally-engaged clause, the Fed disregarded the nature of the activity as long as it was executed in a separate subsidiary and limited in volume.

In essence, the Fed had taken over as the policymaking body with regard to regulatory reform of the financial system. Throughout the spring, the Federal Reserve Board heard arguments from supporters and opponents of the applications.[56] This was only the third time in its history that the Fed heard public testimony on applications. Ironically, while a member of the Board would usually travel to Capitol Hill to testify before Congress, a representative of the House Banking Committee, Rep. Charles Schumer, now appeared before the Board. The Fed's blatant challenge to the legislative authority of Congress not only infuriated the House Banking Committee but also its colleagues in the Senate. For example, in a letter to Volcker, Proxmire strongly objected to the Fed's action.

> The Congress adopted the Act on the assumption — then universally accepted — that the Glass-Steagall Act prohibits affiliates of members from underwriting securities. The Congress never intended to give the Board authority to permit such underwriting....[U]ntil Congress changes the law, the Board lacks the authority to permit the activities in question.[57]

But the Fed ignored Proxmire's warning. In July, the Board, again by a 3-2 margin, approved applications from six money centre banks to underwrite so-called consumer-related receivables.[58]

A second development that would change the Fed's position even more dramatically was the resignation of Chairman Volcker in July of 1987. Although Volcker had changed his position towards reform of the Glass-Steagall Act considerably since the early 1980s, he was still considered a conservative among the board members. While Volcker endorsed the contention that the integration of national financial markets would expose the U.S. financial system to other less-regulated financial markets, raising the question of competitive inequality, he cautioned policymakers not to overreact to the globalization argument.

This would change drastically with his successor, Alan Greenspan.[59] Those institutions that favoured a repeal of Glass-Steagall were hopeful. '[M]aybe the emphasis will change, permitting the banking industry to respond to international markets', said one representative of a money centre bank.[60] Moreover, although previous Fed decisions had already favoured the large banks' cause, their weight in the legislature as well as the judiciary was sometimes in doubt since the chairman of the Board had voted against them. With Greenspan at the head of the central bank, this would change, transforming the already powerful Fed into a body that spoke with one voice and thus making its decisions more influential in the larger policy network.[61]

When Greenspan testified for the first time on Capitol Hill, he described himself as a 'strong deregulator' and argued that the development of new technologies and the increasing internationalization of financial markets had resulted in a highly competitive environment for banking, while at the same time 'banking has been frozen within a regulatory structure fashioned some fifty years ago.'[62]   Shortly after that, the Fed chairman outlined the official position of the entire Board. In testimony to a subcommittee of the House Banking Committee that St. Germain had called to appease pro-reform forces in the House, Greenspan called for the repeal of the Glass-Steagall Act. According to Greenspan, repeal of the act 'would respond effectively to the marked changes that have taken place in the financial marketplace here and abroad and would permit banks to operate in areas where they have already considerable expertise', referring to U.S. banks' securities activities in foreign financial markets.[63]   Questioned by St. Germain, Greenspan elaborated.

The important point, however, is that allowing American banking organizations to engage in expanded securities activities will make them more effective competitors in financial markets, both at home and overseas, with real benefits to consumers....[I]f American banking organizations are permitted to engage in securities activities there is substantial potential that some financial transactions that now take place overseas would take place instead in the United States. This, of course, should bring direct benefits in terms of expanded job opportunities in this country.[64]

To avoid any spillover of the risks of securities activities into the commercial banks, the Fed proposed two elements that would insulate the two activities. First, the holding company structure would be used to institutionalize the separation between a bank and a securities affiliate as two separately capitalized entities. Second, the resulting institutional barrier, often referred to as a firewall, would be strengthened by limiting personal and financial interconnections, particularly credit transactions, between the banks and securities affiliates.

During his testimony, Greenspan indicated that he personally would favour even broader deregulation, but that such a proposal would be unlikely to pass in Congress at the present time, and thus he was endorsing Proxmire's bill. In a series of private meetings in the week before the hearing, Greenspan and Proxmire agreed that a more limited bill had the best chances of passing in the near future.[65] Those meetings also included representatives from the Administration, who had even more radical plans with regard to banking reform but decided to considerably scale down their ambitious plans as well.[66]

To get sufficient support for his bill, Proxmire also needed the backing of his colleague, Senate Minority Leader Jake Garn. Garn initially opposed Proxmire's plan because by forcing banks to conduct their securities activities in the holding company structure, the Fed — the sole regulator of holding companies — would acquire much more authority.[67] This enlargement of regulatory turf by the Fed was also opposed by the FDIC and the Comptroller. The two regulators argued that establishing a holding company would be an unnecessary expense for small banks; they should be able to conduct securities activities through their own subsidiaries.

The Fed showed willingness to compromise. After Greenspan indicated that banks with assets of less than $500 million could be exempted, the Comptroller and the FDIC reluctantly agreed. In addition, both Greenspan and Proxmire suggested they would defer to the SEC in regulating the securities affiliates, although the Fed would retain some oversight. Garn and the SEC also agreed to the bill.[68] Even the large money centre banks were exhibiting a more cooperative attitude toward the lawmakers and toned down some of their more extreme demands. Given the real possibility of substantial change, they did not want to give those still opposing reform the opportunity to sabotage legislation once again. On 20 November, Proxmire introduced a bill, cosponsored by Garn, that would repeal large parts of the Glass-Steagall Act.

As discussed previously, the primary reason for the conversion of Proxmire, who only six months earlier had refused to even consider a repeal of Glass-Steagall, was that the globalization of financial markets had dramatically altered the effect of restrictive regulations on U.S. commercial banks. Rather than preventing commercial banks from entering risky financial activities and ensuring a safe and stable financial system, Glass-Steagall by the fall of 1987 was perceived as promoting instability in the financial system and hurting the U.S. economy, as U.S. banks were either moving their operations abroad to less restrictive regulatory environments or were losing business to foreign banks subject to less stringent regulations. Despite minor differences over the exact details of regulatory reform, the subsequent hearings confirmed that all the major federal regulatory agencies agreed with Proxmire and were willing to suppress their differences in light of the urgent need to adjust the regulations in the U.S. financial system.[69]

In retrospect, 1987 marked an important shift in the distribution of power in the policy network in favour of those political and economic forces that wanted a repeal of the Glass-Steagall Act. Globalization of financial markets had allowed large commercial banks to move the focus of the debate away from the pursuit of individual profits and toward the collective fate of the U.S. banking industry and, ultimately, the nation's economy. This line of argument not only convinced many members of Congress that drastic reform of financial services regulation was indeed necessary, but it also furnished them with a convincing set of arguments for their constituents, many of whom had not forgotten the 1930s and rejected large and powerful financial institutions. This was especially the case in the House, where the populist tradition for rejecting large financial power was much more prevalent than in the Senate. But as discussed above, by the end of 1987, even in the House some members did see the rationale of the globalization argument. Moreover, given that the notion of globalization and the threat of foreign banks to the American economy could be used to embed the repeal of Glass-Steagall in the traditional populist rhetoric that had been used on earlier occasions in the case of the steel and automotive industries, it had a very appealing element to members of the House.[70]

Indeed, the momentum in the House for a repeal of Glass-Steagall was so great, with support from an increasing number of his colleagues on the Banking Committee, that St. Germain felt compelled to act. In mid-December he released a statement that he had ordered his staff to draft a bill that would let banks engage in real estate development, insurance and securities activities.[71]

The other central change of course was the shift in the Fed's position towards the Glass-Steagall repeal. With Greenspan's confirmation by the Senate, all Fed Board members had been appointed by President Reagan and advocated substantial deregulation. On earlier occasions, individual Board members had pointed out their concerns about the effect of restrictive regulations on U.S. commercial banks in a global financial market. However, the Board was now unanimous in its position, best summarized by Chairman Greenspan. Upon learning that Proxmire and Garn had introduced the bill, he said, 'In our view, we now have an historic opportunity to put the financial system on a sounder footing — perhaps a unique opportunity to make it more responsive to consumer needs, more efficient, more competitive in the world economy, and equally important, more stable.'[72]   With the Fed's change in its policy, as well as its concession of some regulatory power to the SEC, the four federal regulators that had long quarrelled over the nature and extent of deregulation were now united in their overall policy and in their pleas to Congress to repeal Glass-Steagall.

Indeed, in the Senate the tide had changed so much in favour of repealing Glass-Steagall that even the stock market collapse in October 1987, an otherwise powerful reminder of 1929, did not change the position of either the regulators or those members of Congress that advocated a repeal of the act.[73]   To the contrary, the reaction by all other major stock markets around the world was proof of how integrated national financial markets had become. Moreover, large commercial banks with securities activities in London and other European financial centres pointed to the fact that U.S. banks had easily mastered the crisis there. It appeared that 1987 had turned out to be the crucial year in which the political foundation was laid for a repeal of Glass-Steagall before the end of the decade.[74]

1988

And indeed, the momentum toward banking reform continued in early 1988. On 2 March 1988, only one day after the congressional moratorium had expired, the Senate Banking Committee approved Proxmire's bill by a wide margin.[75] Proxmire was determined to get the bill through Congress before he retired. Only a few months before, he had threatened to curb the Fed's power if the regulators approved the pending applications by the money centre banks. Now the senator stated that if Congress did not act, '[T]hey [the regulators] can go right ahead. They are free to do it, and I assume they will.'[76]

Within a month, the bill passed the Senate by a vote of 94-2. Many securities activities would become available to bank affiliates immediately upon enactment of the bill. Dealing in mutual funds and corporate bonds was delayed for six months. Bank affiliates could not underwrite or sell corporate stocks unless Congress enacted a separate law granting that power;

the bill established an expedited procedure for such a vote no later than 1 April 1991.[77] While most activities had to be conducted through a separately capitalized affiliate, some activities could be conducted in the same bank. This was a concession to the two federal regulators who feared that banks might convert to the holding company structure, which would give the Fed additional regulatory power. It was also supposed to be a concession to the smaller banks who all along had argued that it would be too expensive to open a separately capitalized subsidiary. But the IBAA rejected the bill. Small banks were especially fearful that they would lose business to larger institutions and they argued that the bill would lead to greater concentration of power in larger banks and securities houses, despite the fact that the bill prohibited banks with assets of $30 billion or more from merging with securities firms of $15 billion or larger.[78]

In the House, St. Germain could no longer ignore the pressure that was mounting within and outside his own committee. The fact that the Senate Banking Committee had approved a repeal of Glass-Steagall by such a wide margin could not be ignored, and there was increasing support for a similar bill among his fellow committee members. In addition, a report commissioned by another House committee advocated the gradual repeal of Glass-Steagall and, with regard to the international dimension, endorsed the banks' argument that

> the Glass-Steagall restrictions are one factor causing U.S. banks to undertake securities activities abroad. Thus business that would have been conducted in the United States, is being carried out abroad. These restrictions are therefore prejudicing the competitiveness of the U.S. capital markets. A similar loss of business occurred in the 1970s when Regulation Q forced financing arrangements to relocate from the United States to the Eurodollar markets. If banks are allowed to underwrite securities in the United States, we anticipate that some business will reenter this country. This process would enhance the competitiveness of the U.S. capital markets.[79]

Commercial banks, sensing that repeal of Glass-Steagall was gaining momentum in Congress, also increased their pressure. Early in the year they started a major advertising campaign that again and again alerted the public to the decline of the U.S. banking industry in international financial markets and its consequences for the U.S. domestic economy.[80] In another effort, bankers managed to assemble about 4,000 community leaders who endorsed a repeal of Glass-Steagall and thus undermined the continued resistance of smaller community banks.[81] To support their argument that the repeal of Glass-Steagall would benefit not only the financial markets but also the real economy, the banks pointed to a statement released by the National Association of Manufacturers that called for a repeal of Glass-Steagall, arguing that 'manufacturers have borne additional costs because of artificial barriers.'[82] This was confirmed by a poll released by the Senate Banking Committee that said that 77 per cent of the chief financial officers of the nation's largest corporations said that the Glass-Steagall Act should be repealed. Sixty-nine per cent believed the costs of raising new funds were likely to drop if banks were allowed to underwrite corporate stock and bonds.[83]

St. Germain responded to the mounting pressure by releasing a draft bill that was much more limited than that passed in the Senate and contained additional consumer service requirements for banks.[84] The banks immediately rejected the bill, calling it 'regressive, anti-consumer and anti-competitive.' Even the IBAA rejected the bill because of the additional provisions for the poor and elderly.

But this was not the only opposition that St. Germain had to contend with. In a sign of how much the tide had changed even in the House, several committee members staged a revolt, openly opposing the bill.[85] Pressure to change the bill also came from all of the regulators. For example, at a conference hosted by the Federal Reserve Bank of Chicago, Greenspan stated that unless banks were given the powers contained in the Proxmire bill, they would be forced to make higher-risk loans and raise interest rates to remain profitable (both of which were actions that few House members wanted to be associated with).[86]

When St. Germain realized that he could not muster enough support, he made a new proposal that contained a considerable number of underwriting powers. However, banks were not allowed to underwrite mutual funds or corporate stock.[87] The changes were sufficient to pass the committee level with a small majority of votes, although many still disapproved of the bill.[88]

But before a bill could be voted on the House floor, it had to be considered by the Energy and Commerce Committee, which has jurisdiction over securities regulation. Chairman John Dingell, whose father was one of the original architects of the Glass-Steagall Act, was flatly opposed to granting banks any new securities powers. 'I don't believe there is a need to change anything [in the current law]', Dingell said, even before the House Banking Committee had voted on the bill. But he said he 'might make some concessions', so as to not impede a bill.[89] Dingell's change of heart was less out of a genuine belief that some compromise was needed to avoid yet another congressional gridlock which would give the Fed another opportunity to expand its policymaking authority; it was rather that the Chairman of the Energy and Commerce Committee saw an opportunity to gain more power over bank legislation. If he made enough concessions on securities activities for commercial banks, he most likely would win several seats on the conference committee that would be established to reconcile the remaining differences between the two chambers.[90]

The version of the House bill reported by the Energy and Commerce Committee accomplished just what Dingell had hoped: a seat for him on the conference committee. In his version, banks would only be allowed to sell mutual funds and underwrite and deal in commercial paper, municipal revenue bonds, and asset-backed securities. This was the minimum set of concessions that Dingell had to make in order to get his committee jurisdiction over bank regulation. In addition, the bill would establish such high firewalls that the new securities activities would be very costly to execute.[91] Opposition to Dingell's move was strong. The Treasury issued a statement condemning the action which 'demonstrates that the House of Representatives is not prepared to move forward into the modern financial world...[and is] retreating into a protectionist, anticompetitive regime left over from the 1930s.'[92] Commercial banks, including the small banks, rejected the bill, though for different reasons, and suggested that Dingell was out to kill banking reform in the 100th Congress.[93] The securities industry, on the other hand, was elated and claimed that Dingell had effectively killed the bill.[94]

The release of Dingell's bill reduced the debate over banking reform in the House to a heated power struggle over jurisdictional turf among two committees.[95] Members of the Banking Committee refused to negotiate. 'I don't see any point in meeting with Energy and Commerce members. It's not their jurisdiction.'[96]

As Congress moved closer to recess with no compromise in sight in the turf battle between St. Germain and Dingell, Greenspan wrote a letter to Speaker of the House Jim Wright, urging him to intervene in the impasse over bank deregulation. Greenspan said that failure to act would be 'unfortunate', and members interpreted the letter to say that the Fed would act if Congress did not. Both Wright and St. Germain wrote Greenspan that the issue was for Congress, not the regulators, to resolve. St. Germain also warned the Fed not to act: 'I will not feel bound to ratify in our legislation decisions made by federal banking regulators and, if necessary, our legislation will be made retroactive to the end of this session.'[97]

In October, after a last effort to save his bill with a parliamentary manoeuvre, Proxmire conceded defeat. 'This means the end of the banking bill', Proxmire stated, adding that Congress may have had its last chance to establish its own guidelines for the reform of the nation's banking system.[98] However, before Proxmire retired, the Senator turned to the Fed and demanded that the agency step in and fill the policymaking vacuum that the House turf battle had created. 'Congress has failed to do the job', the outgoing chairman said. 'Now it's time for the Fed to step in.'[99] Shortly after Congress adjourned, a group of senior House Banking Committee members joined Proxmire and other senators, and called on the Fed to expand bank underwriting powers.[100]

Initially, it was unclear how the Fed would react to these conflicting pressures. The Fed's role as an institution that formulates bank regulatory policy had been strengthened throughout 1988 by important court rulings. Early in 1988, a federal appeals court upheld a lower court decision that seven money centre banks could engage in the securities activities that were granted to them by the Fed in the spring of 1987.[101] The SIA appealed to the Supreme Court, but the court refused to review the case and thus let the Fed's approval and the previous court rulings stand, handing the banks a major victory.[102]

It was the Supreme Court's ruling that led Proxmire and his colleagues in the Senate and House to call on the Fed to permit banks to underwrite corporate debt and equities. Proxmire and Garn noted that the courts had upheld the central bank's authority to permit banks to underwrite otherwise impermissible securities through affiliates not principally engaged in securities underwriting. In a separate letter, Proxmire explained why he had changed his mind. 'In the face of such authority my view of the law stands corrected', Proxmire said. '[M]y belief that structural reform should come through the legislative process has been tempered by observing this Congress squander an historic opportunity to enact comprehensive legislative reform.'[103]

The congressional developments of 1988 shifted the centre of policymaking authority almost entirely towards the administrative and judicial domain. The Fed, while it had the backing of the courts, did not have the institutional legitimacy to grant important new powers but had been encouraged by members of the legislature. More importantly, given the shift in institutional authority to the regulatory agencies and the continued stalemate in Congress, important segments of the policy network opposing bank reform, such as the SIA, had been demobilized. This reduced the number of institutions that were actively engaged in the policymaking process and enhanced the chances of resolving the conflict.

How extensively the Fed would use its newly granted institutional authority, however, remained to be seen. Despite the unique possibility to enlarge its role as bank regulator and to shape the future structure of U.S. financial regulation in a significant way, the Fed's primary interest remained the effective and autonomous execution of monetary policy. For example, if those members of Congress who opposed any further action on the bank power issue threatened to retaliate against further activities by the Fed with regard to bank regulatory policy by venturing into the Fed's institutional prerogative and independence with respect to the execution of monetary policy, the agency might well back down. Such a scenario had become all the more possible since the Democrats expanded their power in both chambers of Congress in the elections of 1988. Moreover, with the retirement of Proxmire, the Fed would lose an important ally among Democrats in the Senate, and the chairmanship in the House Banking Committee was likely to go to Henry Gonzales, who on earlier occasions had led efforts to curb the Fed's power.[104]

Chairman Greenspan, who would ultimately decide on how far the Fed would go, also faced conflicting pressures from within his own institution. Clearly, the governors, all of whom had been appointed by Reagan, favoured as much deregulation as was possible under the current law. But Greenspan also had to contend with his own staff, who approached the issue of bank deregulation much more cautiously. For example, one study by two staff members of the Federal Reserve Bank of Minneapolis concluded that mergers between bank holding companies and securities firms 'are not likely to result in the reduced risk of failure that advocates of such mergers have predicted. If anything, such mergers are likely to increase bank holding company risk.'[105] The study also disagreed that firewalls can insulate banks from securities affiliates' activities, thus directly challenging Greenspan's position.

> Incentives for intercorporate cross-subsidization are very strong, particularly if an affiliate is in financial distress. Resources can be moved among corporations in a myriad of ways, some of which are still waiting to be discovered. The history of Fed supervision in this area suggests that when management is determined and creative, thwarting such inter-affiliate transfers is extremely difficult.[106]

Finally, the Fed was only one of several regulators both at the state as well as the federal level. Although the prospect for congressional action on bank reform had led the different agencies to compromise in order to ensure passage of legislation, regulatory turf battles were still very much alive. With the failure of Congress to act, those turf battles quickly reopened. For example, in a speech to the annual convention of the SIA, David S. Ruder, Chairman of the SEC, reiterated that deregulation would benefit not just the banks but the whole country. '[W]e would be better off as a nation if we had bank entry into the securities industry, because we would be able to compete better in the international capital markets.'[107] But at the same time, the SEC Chairman bitterly attacked bank regulators for encouraging banks to engage in securities activities outside the SEC's jurisdiction. Directing his remarks at the Comptroller of the Currency and the Federal Reserve, Ruder stated that he had consistently supported a repeal of Glass-Steagall, because of the pressing need for capital in the United States, on the condition that his agency would regulate the securities activities of the commercial banks.

Similarly, if the Fed approved additional applications it would instill resentment from the two other federal bank regulatory agencies, which many officials believed had been the Fed's strategy all along: the debate and enactment of bank deregulation as an instrument to enlarge its own regulatory turf.[108]

But the Fed was also under pressure from the money centre banks to expand their powers. Money centre banks had hoped that congressional action would settle once and for all the costly and lengthy legal battles between the two industries. But when it had become clear that once again Congress had failed to enact any legislation, they turned to the Fed. Three days after Congress adjourned, four of the largest banks asked the Federal Reserve for permission to underwrite and deal in corporate securities within the 5 per cent limit adopted by the Fed.[109] The banks were optimistic. According to a spokeswoman for the ABA, '[T]he market is really moving fast. By the time the Congress gets around to officially legislating on some things, the states or the Fed may have already acted.'[110]

Two other developments increased the likelihood that the Fed would make use of its policymaking power in the future. First, in Congress, the outcome of the congressional elections and Proxmire's retirement led to new leadership in both chambers. In the Senate, Donald Riegle took over as chairman of the Banking Committee. Riegle had been closely associated with the securities industry in the past. On the other hand, in 1988 he had leaned toward those members of the Banking Committee that changed their position in order to protect the American banking industry from foreign competition. Still, many observers were unsure what Riegle's position as chairman would be.

Other senators who had supported the banks' cause lost in the elections.[111] The biggest surprise, however, occurred in the House, where St. Germain was not reelected.[112] His successor, Henry Gonzales, stated that he would take a slow approach on the issue of bank powers. According to Gonzales, the bill reported by the House Banking Committee in 1988 should not be a starting point for future legislative action.[113] Also, Congress was unlikely to address the Glass-Steagall Act during 1989 because the crisis in the thrift industry had taken on such enormous proportions that it replaced the Glass-Steagall Act at the top of the congressional agenda for that year.[114]

The above factors that hindered Congress from taking any swift and decisive action with respect to Glass-Steagall did not apply to the regulatory agencies or to the Administration. First, there were no major impediments arising from the new Bush Administration. All three key bank regulators remained in office and all three pledged continuity in their policy positions with regard to bank reform.[115] Secondly, bank regulators, especially the

Fed, were not immediately affected by the crisis in the S&L industry because they did not regulate that industry.[116] At the same time, the Fed, by law, had to decide on those applications the money centre banks had submitted in the fall of 1988, shortly after Congress had adjourned.[117]

RESOLUTION

1989

In January 1989, the Fed moved on the applications and granted the banks the power to underwrite corporate debt, but deferred for a year a decision on whether banks would be allowed to underwrite corporate equities.[118] The ruling preserved the tight restrictions that the Fed had imposed in its 1987 ruling.[119]

Reaction in the private sector was as expected. A spokesman for J.P. Morgan said, '[I]n the long run, it's essential we have the powers to underwrite a full range of corporate debt the same way our competitors do overseas.'[120]   The securities industry protested sharply and called on Congress to intervene.   SIA President Edward O'Brien stated, 'SIA disagrees emphatically, because [the Fed's action] represents piecemeal dismantling of the appropriate separation which exists in the financial services industry.'[121]

The first final approval to underwrite corporate debt was given to J.P. Morgan in June of 1989.[122]   In July, three more banks — Citicorp, Bankers Trust, and Chase Manhattan — were cleared by the Fed to commence underwriting operations.[123]   In September, the Fed announced that it had decided to double the limit on bank affiliates' underwriting activities from 5 per cent to 10 per cent.[124]

As a result, the conflict between the Fed and Congress heightened. According to Dingell, '[T]he Fed is on its way to giving banks an invitation to shoot craps with the taxpayer's money. This is the kind of irresponsible behavior that gave us the savings and loan crisis and brought about the 1929 crash.'[125]   Others went even further and openly threatened the Fed's independence. 'I think you are on a roll in terms of what you want to do and the powers you have. Maybe we have to close some of the loopholes of your powers.'[126]   Gonzales charged that '[t]he Federal Reserve has crossed the line into policymaking clearly reserved for the Congress', and ordered a broad-based congressional investigation of the Fed.[127]   Shortly after that, Lee Hamilton, Chairman of the Joint Economic Committee (JEC), introduced a bill in the House that called for a drastic reduction in the Fed's independence.[128]

But not all members called for restrictions; some came to the defence of the Fed. They referred to the Supreme Court's 1987 decision and argued that the Fed had acted within the law and was required to do so.[129] The strongest support for the Fed's action came from Barney Frank on the House Banking Committee. 'You [the Fed] didn't preempt us, we "disempted" ourselves....We didn't act for one reason: the people who were in a position of power didn't like the way the votes would have come out....Now that you have done it we'll probably pass a bill.'[130]

The motivations behind the Fed's action were spelled out on numerous occasions during the spring of 1989 by its board members. According to board member Walter Heller:

[O]ur existing legal framework presents a serious competitive handicap for them [commercial banks].... many of our foreign competitors do have broad-ranging rights to provide universal banking services. In some instances, they are even able to do so right here in the United States because their activities were grandfathered. What needs to be done? The Glass-Steagall barrier separating commercial and investment banking must fall. We are operating in a marketplace where this artificial distinction introduced half a century ago has outlived its usefulness.[131]

In justifying its actions, the Fed also emphasized the beneficial spillover effects of banking reform to the real sectors of the U.S. economy. In a speech entitled 'Improving America's Competitiveness', Heller stated that:

[O]ur American banking system is more fragmented and compartmentalized than that of any other country....contrast this situation with that prevailing in Canada, England, or Germany. There the hometown banker will also have branches and representative offices in key cities around the globe, and offer global financial services in support of the international trading efforts of his customer. When a factory owner or sales manager from a firm located in a small Swiss village or Dutch town steps off the plane in New York, he will be met by a representative from his own bank, ready to offer his services and advice as to how to conquer the American market. That is an advantage that the typical American small-town manufacturer will not have abroad.[132]

Encouraged by the Fed's rulings, money centre banks continued their campaign on Capitol Hill and in the public to press for a repeal of Glass-Steagall. 'Our appeals to the public good ring hollow as we engage in bitter disputes with...brokers, investment bankers, insurance agents, and...commercial bankers of different persuasions', complained Thomas Labreque, president of Chase Manhattan Bank.[133] Throughout the previous two years, money centre banks had realized that it was exactly this appeal to the public good — the threat of competition by foreigners both at home and abroad — that would eventually turn the tide in Congress.

Developments in U.S. and international financial markets continued to work in their favour as foreign penetration of the U.S. domestic financial market increased and the U.S. continued to lose its dominant role in the world financial markets. By 1989, not a single U.S. bank ranked among the top 25 in the world.[134]

Money centre banks now also argued that foreign banks were increasingly controlling important investment decisions and other activities in the U.S. economy. In late 1988, a bank consulting firm published a study finding that while U.S. companies had reduced the overall number of banks they use, they had been adding foreign banks, with Japanese banks leading the surge. Almost 40 per cent of American companies used a Japanese bank in 1988, up from 33 per cent in 1987.[135] According to the authors, the two primary reasons that foreign banks were gaining market share were: first, that many foreign banks were considered financially stronger than American institutions; and second, because foreign banks were more competitive, offering a wider variety of international services and innovative banking alternatives. U.S. banks had long claimed that in both cases, the Glass-Steagall Act was the major regulatory impediment preventing them from living up to these standards.

Other reports confirmed this trend. Between 1982 and 1988 the share of foreign banks in the domestic banking market had increased from 14 per cent to 21 per cent. Again, Japanese banks were leading. In California they now controlled 25 per cent of the banking market. Bankers warned that this was more than just a matter of national pride.[136] According to John Reed, Chairman of Citicorp, '[I]n a credit crunch [foreign] financial institutions would be faced with a choice: Which customers do you take care of? In such a situation, [foreign] banks would have a natural bias towards their hometown players.'[137] Other banks linked the spectre of another stock market crash to the need of the U.S. to maintain basic control over its financial system. They argued that in a financial crisis, control of credit often determines the outcome. When the stock market collapsed in October 1987, the Federal Reserve Bank of New York relied heavily on the big New York money centre banks to meet the cash needs of Wall Street firms. But would the banks have acted as quickly if the final decision had rested in Tokyo?

U.S. banks not only pointed to their declining market share at home but also abroad. By the spring of 1989, only 59 American banks and securities firms were represented in London. This was the lowest number of U.S. financial institutions in the city since 1977. The Japanese had increased their presence to 50 institutions. Banks warned that this decline would not only hurt the banks themselves, but American business would also be affected if they did not have the support of their hometown bank to promote their exports.[138]   The answer to these challenges, bankers argued, was to transform traditional commercial banks into institutions that could offer a wide variety of financial products, ranging from traditional loans to securities and insurance.   'I firmly believe that converging activities and international competition are sweeping us towards a new order, where universal banking will be the norm worldwide.'[139]

When Congress, having completed a substantial part of the S&L rescue package, returned to the issue of reforming the banking system in the summer of 1989, the Fed hoped to use this opportunity to appease those members of Congress that had revolted against the Fed's actions.   According to Greenspan, '...[T]here is no question that we are in effect being significantly suppressed by the Glass-Steagall restrictions....[I]f we repeal or significantly alter Glass-Steagall, that would in a major way improve our competitive abilities.'[140]   Similarly, Gerald Corrigan returned to Capitol Hill and reiterated his call for a prompt, progressive and comprehensive overhaul of the basic structure of the U.S. banking and financial system. However, in a sign that the tone of the debate had shifted away from deregulation to serve private sector interests and toward promoting the U.S. national interest, Corrigan's testimony was not part of a hearing on 'New Securities Powers for Commercial Banks.'[141]   Rather, the purpose of the hearing was 'to examine the condition and competitiveness of the U.S. industrial and financial bases and the implications for defense productivity and national security.'[142]   Corrigan reiterated his concern that the task of financial reform had become extremely urgent 'because it has important implications for the competitive position of U.S. firms and U.S. markets....'[143]   As intended, and as it did on earlier occasions, this line of reasoning struck a responsive cord.   According to Senator Dodd, '[I]t's unacceptable to most Americans that we should end up playing second fiddle to anybody in financial services.   I think a lot of differences we've seen [in Congress] in the past will evaporate.'[144]

Beginning in 1989, an additional factor raised the importance and influence of external pressures on the U.S. financial policy network.   For most of the 1980s, foreign institutions had little interest in the domestic political struggles among the various factions of the financial services industry.   This began to change as the market share of foreign banks in the U.S. grew.   For example, the Institute of International Bankers, which represents foreign banks in the United States, prepared a study for the Fed demonstrating how its member banks in foreign countries were operating safely and profitably as universal banks without any firewalls.[145]   British banks felt particularly strongly about Glass-Steagall.   They argued that since the Big Bang in London, competitive pressures in their home market had increased sharply.   'We didn't have a problem with liberalization in

London', said one banker.   'Now we'd just like to see some reciprocity.'[146]

By 1989, the issue of reciprocity between the U.S. and European financial markets had become the subject of considerable transatlantic controversy. As the European Community (EC) moved towards the goal of a single integrated financial market by 1992, there were indications that the EC was considering adopting a policy of reciprocity with respect to financial markets with non-EC members after 1992.[147]   Essentially, some EC member countries and banks argued that U.S. banks should only be permitted to engage in those activities in which Europeans were allowed to take part in the United States.[148] Congress had become increasingly concerned about the threat of retaliation by what had become known as 'Fortress Europe'.[149]

The EC dismissed U.S. fears as unfounded but at the same time said it would challenge the U.S. to open its own financial markets. According to Leon Brittan, commissioner of competition policies and financial institutions, '[W]here our partners have banking laws which are effectively nondiscriminatory but less liberal, these will be a matter for negotiation. And we are fully entitled to argue that our most liberal banking market is an example that the rest of the world will follow.'[150]   In addition, the Commission's official report on U.S. trade barriers and unfair trade practices specifically listed Glass-Steagall as part of a set of regulations that 'discriminate against non-US financial institutions.'[151]

U.S. money centre banks welcomed the additional external pressure. In fact, long before the issue of reciprocity became the subject of a major public policy debate in Washington, money centre banks had realized that '1992' could well spur financial market reform in the U.S., and consequently expressed strong support for the process of European economic integration. In a speech to European and American bankers in Zurich in the spring of 1988, Dennis Weatherstone, president of J.P. Morgan, predicted that '1992' would increase the pressure on the U.S. to reform its markets and that the EC's insistence on reciprocity could help overturn the Glass-Steagall Act.[152] Another banker commenting on the Commission's threat of reciprocity during the height of the debate sympathized with the EC's actions: 'I think it's important to note that we commercial banking organizations very much share the goals that the European Commission has expressed in terms of opening up the United States market. Specifically, we believe that the Glass-Steagall Act should be substantially liberalized.'[153] Opponents of a Glass-Steagall repeal quickly realized what '1992' would do to their efforts. 'Europe 1992 is going to make it tough.... This gives the banks a little more ammunition for the international competitiveness argument....They will try to make the argument that Europe is already cleaning our clock and this will make [European institutions] more competitive.'[154]

Regulators were also concerned about the developments in Europe. To its European partners, the Fed responded that the use of reciprocity would be a major step backwards and could provoke a protectionist backlash from the United States.[155] But at the domestic level, the Fed presented a rather different picture. According to Gerald Corrigan, the U.S. not only ran

> the very troubling risk of losing competitiveness — including jobs, income, and tax revenues in our major financial centers such as New York, Chicago, and San Francisco — but we also run the risk of fostering unnecessary and potentially dangerous political tensions concerning the right and privileges of institutions to operate freely in foreign markets. For example, while I am clearly encouraged by the recent steps taken in Brussels to respond constructively to expressed concerns about the reciprocity provisions in the European Community banking directive, I am certain that difficult problems lie ahead in this area so long as the basic structure of our system is so different from most others.[156]

Congress also reacted to the challenge from Europe. The Senate Banking Committee, including its leadership, saw its long held position that the U.S. had to respond to competitive pressures from foreign financial markets reaffirmed and reiterated that during numerous hearings. Indeed, it now considered 1992 its deadline for arriving at a comprehensive overhaul of the entire U.S. financial system — most importantly, a repeal of Glass-Steagall. According to Chairman Donald Riegle, '[L]et's get this done so that we get ahead of Europe 1992 — to get in front of events.'[157]

The impact on the House side was even greater. Gonzales, who had scheduled several hearings on the issue, acknowledged that, '[I]t's possible it [1992] could affect the outcome of the Glass-Steagall debate.'[158] During those hearings, the Administration and all federal bank regulatory agencies warned that the issue could have far-reaching consequences for relations among the countries involved.[159] Shortly after that, the House Banking Committee decided to form a 'Task Force on International Competitiveness of U.S. Financial Institutions'. According to its chair, John J. LaFalce, the purpose of the task force was to examine the issues surrounding the role of U.S. banks in the international economy. According to LaFalce, the banks 'face numerous obstacles in their efforts to match the foreign competition, some imposed by foreign competitors, some of our own making. If we do not remove those obstacles, the role of financial firms may diminish further.'[160] But more importantly, LaFalce flatly acknowledged that the committee could no longer be solely responsive to the concerns of small rural banks, which had been one of the two major impediments to a legislative compromise between the House and the Senate.

This issue should not only be of concern to those banks who hope to have an international presence. Our domestic market cannot be held sacrosanct for U.S. firms. Just as U.S. auto manufacturers have been forced to compete with Volkswagen and Toyota, U.S. regional and community banks will, in the not too distant future, find themselves competing against Deutsche Bank and Sumitomo.[161]

Another element that led to the dramatic change in the House's position on bank reform was the SIA's sudden withdrawal of its opposition to a repeal of Glass-Steagall. There had been some indications that the lobby was divided internally over the future course of its policy towards the banks, but few expected such a dramatic shift.[162] At the annual meeting in December 1989, the SIA's Board of Directors proposed a plan that would allow BHCs to engage in a broad range of securities and securities-related activities.[163] Importantly, the rationale that the SIA leadership gave for its change was that the proposal 'readies the nation, its banks and its securities firms for the global competition of the 1990s'.[164]

However, despite these dramatic policy shifts by those institutions that had long resisted bank reform, the repeal of Glass-Steagall was still anything but inevitable. Despite the passage of the thrift bailout bill, the Banking Committees' agendas remained crowded by hearings related to the collapse of the thrift industry. More importantly, the thrift bailout bill also called on the Treasury to undertake a major study of the U.S. financial services industry and develop a comprehensive reform proposal. The Treasury report was not due until early 1991 and Congress was unlikely to move on any important legislation before it had received the recommendations by the Treasury.[165] Still there was no doubt that the Administration, by means of the Treasury proposal, would pressure for a repeal of Glass-Steagall to improve the international competitiveness of U.S. banks.[166]

1990-1991

But the political momentum had shifted. It became increasingly difficult to portray the conflict in terms of banking reform. If anything, the S&L crises and the dwindling resources of the bank insurance fund as a result of the sharp increase in bank failures allowed those forces in the public and private sector opposed to the repeal to shift the debate away from the issue of international competitiveness and toward domestic safety and stability and the costs to the taxpayer resulting from congressional deregulation and careless supervision.[167]

The Administration and the regulators, who in 1989 had underestimated the extent of the S&L debacle and the required funds for the FDIC and had originally hoped to proceed with their effort to repeal Glass-Steagall once the crisis had been resolved, now responded by shifting their strategy.[168]

Even before the long-awaited proposal by the Bush Administration to overhaul the U.S. banking system was revealed, the Administration defended the suggested reforms as enhancing the safety and stability of the U.S. financial system.[169]   At the same time, the Administration knew that Congress had to pass bank legislation to replenish the bank insurance fund and tried to link it to other broad reforms.[170]   When the Brady Plan (named after Secretary of the Treasury Nicholas Brady) was released in February of 1991, it reflected a mixture of increased supervision and reform. In essence it consisted of five parts:

1. a reform of the deposit insurance system, including a limit on deposit insurance coverage
2. some early intervention measures and increased supervision for poorly capitalized banks
3. a consolidation of the regulatory structure
4. interstate branching
5. most importantly, new powers for commercial banks.[171]

The new powers for commercial banks were the most sweeping ever proposed. Not only were all provisions of the Glass-Steagall Act to be repealed for well-capitalized banks whose non-bank activities were confined to separately capitalized affiliates of holding companies, but commercial firms could own financial services holding companies. The global ranking and competitiveness of U.S. banks remained the principal argument for reform. According to Secretary Brady,

> What we are trying to do is...something about this situation here where the top bank in the United States is 27th in the world....[I]f there's one chart [referring to a table that in 1969 listed as the top three banks in the world U.S. institutions and in 1989 three Japanese] that's stuck in my mind since the very beginning of this study, that's it.[172]

Once again, the by now familiar process of mobilization and gridlock in the legislature resumed. In fact, it got worse. Given the broad-based nature of the bill, additional actors were mobilized and demanded to be heard in the deliberation of policy. For example, the IBAA, which not only expressed grave concern with the new powers that banks were to be granted but also with the establishment of interstate branching, was joined by state agriculture officials who argued that small banks would be pushed out of the market, leaving farmers without their principal source of credit.[173]   This in turn mobilized the House Agriculture Committee, which eventually opposed parts of the reform proposal.[174]   In addition, the high visibility of the S&L crisis had mobilized consumer groups into the debate over the U.S.

financial system. According to the Consumer Federation of America, the proposal would '...rupture our banking system, destroy the life savings of individual consumers and drive bank fees up.'[175]

In addition, some actors, while remaining in favour of a repeal of Glass-Steagall, strongly objected to other parts of the proposal. For example, the Treasury's attempt to consolidate the federal bank regulatory structure mobilized different regulators into an intense battle over regulatory turf. According to William Seidman, Chairman of the FDIC, the planned streamlining was '...an invitation to civil war.'[176] Resentment came also from the Fed, which objected to provisions included in the plan to remove some of the nation's largest banks from the central bank's supervision.[177] The Fed also objected to the Treasury's proposal to allow commercial firms to own BHCs.[178]

On Capitol Hill as well, the various factions regrouped for what was to become yet another fight based not just on different views of the future of the American banking system, but just as much on jurisdictional turf fights among various committees. In addition, the debate that followed the Administration's proposal made it clear that this time policymaking would be dominated by the experience of the S&L crisis and that Congress was likely to consider first the reform of deposit insurance before addressing the other aspects of the reform proposal.[179]

But the Administration pushed hard with respect to a repeal of Glass-Steagall and got the full support of the regulators and large banks.[180] In addition, as has been mentioned above, some of the strongest opposition from the securities industry had declined. Thus, when in early January the Fed permitted three more banks to underwrite stock, the SIA, rather than rejecting Glass-Steagall reform outright, called for legislative action to prevent the piecemeal dismantling of the act by the Fed. Pointing to the pressures of global competition, SIA President Edward O'Brien stated that 'the action cries out for Congress to deal with the issue if we want a globally competitive [financial services industry]....'[181] As a result, the securities industry did not strongly oppose the Treasury proposal, but instead called the Brady plan 'innovative', though in need of changes.[182]

On Capitol Hill, too, the proposal had its supporters. For example, Frank Annunzio (D-Il.), Chairman of the House Banking Subcommittee on Financial Institutions, strongly supported the Treasury proposal and introduced a bill which closely resembled the Administration's with respect to the bank powers issue.[183] To the surprise of many observers, the bill — though still in draft form — was approved by a vote of 36-0 in Annunzio's subcommittee. But while those supporting the overhaul of the banking system were elated, they also acknowledged that the real test would come when the bill moved to the full committee.[184] But again, by the middle of the year the bill passed the full committee with a surprising margin of 11 votes, even though the same committee had failed to act on a comparatively minor effort to repeal some restrictions on bank powers only three years previously.[185] It appeared that the Administration's strategy to exploit the need to deal with the depletion of the declining bank insurance fund had worked.

On the Senate side, the debate over bank powers was less sweeping. Chairman Riegle opposed the banking-commerce provisions contained in the Brady plan, but the committee was still expected to call for a broad-based repeal of Glass-Steagall.[186] Still, large banks were disappointed by the less sweeping nature of the bill when it passed the committee. In particular, they were opposed to the bill's requirement to offer new services to the poor, and some continued restrictions on banks' ability to enter the insurance business.[187]

The real source of opposition to an overhaul of the laws governing bank powers came once again from John Dingell. As soon as the Brady plan was made public, he expressed his opposition: '[A]llowing weak banks into the securities field or into insurance, which has solvency problems, will simply compound the problems of both.'[188] The fact that he had not been consulted by those advocating reform made him even less willing to consider such a move.[189] In response to a letter that Dingell wrote to House Speaker Tom Foley, his committee was given a broad mandate to draft its own bill. Moreover, to weaken the large banks' cause and in preparation for what was to develop into yet another battle between the House Banking and Energy Committees over market turf of their respective business constituents, as well as legislative turf of the committees themselves, Dingell publicly attacked Citicorp as technically insolvent.[190]

In what turned out to be a strategic mistake, the Administration threatened to veto any bill that deviated in any substantive way from the bank powers provisions contained in its proposal. Large banks, too, were unwilling to retreat from the proposal and continued to argue that a failure to reform the nation's banking laws in the face of globalization would hurt the entire U.S. economy. According to the president of the Chase Manhattan Corporation, this was no longer a matter of private but of public interest. '[B]ig banks are often seen as enemies, not as allies of the public good. This may have always been foolish, but with stiff competition in global markets, it becomes a fatal mistake.'[191]

The amendments to the Banking Committee bill that were pushed through by Dingell and his Democrat colleague Edward Markey, who chaired the Subcommittee on Telecommunications and Finance of the House Energy and Commerce Committee, represented a serious setback for large banks but were cheered by all other private sector actors that had a stake in the

debate.[192]   Among other things, the bill included a seven month
moratorium which would bar the Fed from authorizing new securities
powers for banks, thus closing the alternative policy avenue that had been
opened over the last few years.[193]   Given the urgent need to pass some
legislation in order to replenish the dwindling resources of the insurance
fund, the House Banking Committee had little choice but to accept some
form of compromise that could subsequently be reconciled with the Senate's
proposal. Large banks were strongly opposed to the bill that emerged from
the compromise and the Administration declared its outright opposition to
it, even though it became clear that its strategy had backfired.[194]   Those
favouring reform suddenly found themselves in the position of having to
defend the status quo with respect to Glass-Steagall and support a narrow
bill that would deal solely with the recapitalization of the bank insurance
fund.[195]

After ten months of debate, the legislature managed to agree on a bill that
granted the FDIC a $30 billion credit line with the Treasury to cover losses
in failed banks and that overhauled the deposit insurance system and gave
regulators new tools to close banks before they became insolvent. All other
aspects of the Brady plan disappeared from the legislative agenda.[196]
Given the direction the debate over new bank powers had taken in the fall
of 1991, large commercial banks were not too upset by the eventual
outcome, even though the promise of repealing the act in the early 1990s
was even more remote than before.[197]   As on earlier occasions, all
involved shared some responsibility for the renewed gridlock by showing no
willingness to move from their particular position.[198]

At the same time, those favouring a repeal had become accustomed to the
by now well-established alternative policymaking process that excluded most
of those opposing a repeal of the act and which was not closed by the bill
that finally passed Congress. Indeed, at the same time that the fully
mobilized policy network was moving toward gridlock, the alternative
policymaking process continued to undermine Glass-Steagall. The Fed,
which since late 1987 had essentially taken over policymaking with regard
to bank regulation, decided not to postpone its J.P. Morgan decision until
the Treasury issued its report. In April 1990, a federal court of appeals
rejected a challenge by the SIA which claimed that the Fed's rulings of
January 1989 had been illegal. At that time the Fed had also indicated that
the board would consider the possibility for the affiliates to underwrite and
deal in corporate stock within a year. On September 20, after a careful
examination of J.P. Morgan's capital position, the Fed approved its
application to underwrite corporate stocks. [199] Moreover, while the ruling
maintained the 10 per cent revenue limit, many analysts expected that the
limit would soon be raised to 40 per cent.[200]   In essence, this approval

amounted to a *de facto* repeal of Glass-Steagall. The House of Morgan had long ago been split into two unaffiliated firms (one was the commercial bank, and later bank holding company, J.P. Morgan & Co.; the other Morgan Guaranty Trust and Morgan Stanley, an investment firm) operating in two mutually exclusive financial markets by the Glass-Steagall Act of 1933; as of 1990, the institutional split remained but the two financial institutions had become the most formidable competitors in a single financial market offering both commercial as well as investment banking products — both of which Glass-Steagall sought to rule out.

In January of 1991, three more banks (Bankers Trust, the Royal Bank of Canada and the Canadian Bank of Commerce) were given permission to trade corporate stock. The applications of Citicorp and Chase Manhattan were still pending.[201] Shortly after that, the Fed granted applications of foreign banks to underwrite corporate debt and other securities directly, while U.S. banks that received permission still had to use affiliates for underwriting. The Fed was also looking into the possibility of allowing BHCs to combine investment advice and securities brokerage directly.[202] In February of 1991, around the same time that the Brady Plan was presented to Congress, a commercial bank (J.P. Morgan), based on the approval it had been granted by the Fed in the fall of 1990, was selected to underwrite a public stock offering for the first time since 1933.[203] In July, the Fed permitted a Pennsylvania-based bank to purchase a securities firm, which meant that for the first time a bank subsidiary could advertise bids and offers for securities on behalf of customers on electronic bulletin boards.[204] By November, around the same time that the bill had been defeated, Morgan had risen to seventh place as an underwriter of corporate debt in the U.S., and more than a dozen banks were allowed to underwrite debt issues (but not yet stock).[205]

Moreover, large banks also continued their pressure by exploiting either the differences in regulatory positions among federal regulators or the fact that the Glass-Steagall Act does not apply at the state level. For example, in February 1991, Citicorp asked a federal appeals court to reverse an order by the Fed that had barred a unit of Citibank in Delaware from selling insurance.[206] With respect to the regulatory structure, it was publicly demonstrated that commercial banks did not have to rely on the legislature to circumvent Glass-Steagall. All banks needed to do was convert to a state non-member bank and dissolve their parent holding company.[207]

In sum, the failure of the legislature to act did not mean that gridlock in policymaking would prevail. To the contrary, when the Administration's pointman on bank regulatory overhaul, Treasury Undersecretary Robert Glauber, reflected on the collapse of legislative progress at the end of 1991, he stated, '[I]t eventually will get to the situation where Congress will ratify what has already happened', indicating the degree to which some elements of the policy network had been demobilized and alternative mechanisms for policymaking had been found.[208]

NOTES

1. For both of those cases, see Hawley (1987).
2. *NYT*, 29 July 1980.
3. Bennett (1980); Butcher (1981).
4. *WP*, 7 June 1981; *NYT*, 25 August 1983; *WSJ*, 24 April 1984; *American Banker*, 28 November 1984; American Bankers Association (1986).
5. Walmsley (1986); *WSJ*, 24 April 1984.
6. *American Banker*, 7 August 1986.
7. *WP*, 20 November 1986; *American Banker*, 13 October and 21 November 1986.
8. *WP*, 11 August 1986; Brittan (1986).
9. Federal Reserve Bank of New York, 1986; see also Houpt (1988).
10. Corrigan (1986); see also *WP*, 21 November 1986.
11. For example, only moments after he was sworn in as a new Fed Governor, Robert Heller indicated that the future competitiveness of U.S. commercial banks in global finanical markets was one of his major concerns. See *American Banker*, 6 October 1986.
12. *WP*, 29 October 1986.
13. Address by Robert J. Clarke, 27 October 1986; see also *WP*, 28 October 1986; *Financial Times*, 28 October 1986.
14. Opening Statement of Chairman Garn, *The Internationalization Of Capital Markets*.
15. Statement of Dennis Weatherstone, Chairman, Executive Committee, J.P. Morgan & Co. Inc., and Morgan Guaranty Trust Co. of New York, *The Internationalization of Capital Markets*; see also Rose (1986).
16. Statement of Robert D. Hormats, Vice President, Goldman Sachs & Co., *The Internationalization of Capital Markets*.
17. *American Banker*, 5 December 1986.
18. Ibid.
19. *WP*, 21 January 1987; see also *American Banker*, 19 January 1987.
20. Ibid.; for some background on Gould, see *American Banker*, 17 July 1985; for similar comments by Secretary Baker, see *WP*, 13 January 1987.
21. *WSJ*, 11 March 1987; *CQ*, 14 March 1987.
22. *American Banker*, 20 February 1987.
23. *WP*, 22 February 1987; *American Banker*, 27 February 1987.
24. Statement of George D. Gould, Undersecretary For Finance, U.S. Department of the Treasury, *Strengthening the Safety and Soundness of the Financial Services Industry*.
25. Statement by Paul A. Volcker, Chairman, Board of Governors of the Federal Reserve System, *Strengthening the Safety and Soundness of the Financial Services Industry*.
26. Corrigan (1987); Statement by Gerald Corrigan, President, Federal Reserve Bank of New York, 'A Perspective on the Globalization of Financial Markets and Institutions', Senate Committee on the Budget, 6 May 1987; *The Economist*, 7 February 1987.
27. Corrigan, op.cit.; see also *WP*, 11 February 1987.
28. Statements by Seidman and Isaac in *Strengthening the Safety and Soundness of the Financial Services Industry*; see also Federal Deposit Insurance Corporation (1987).
29. *Status of the U.S. Financial System*; *Modernization of the Glass-Steagall Act*; *Financial Restructuring Proposal*; *New Securities Powers for Bank Holding Companies*.

30. Office of Technology Assessment (1987).
31. CRS Report No. 87-725 E.
32. For an approval of the globalization argument see the opening statements by Senator Garn, op.cit.; for a rejection, see the opening statement of Alfonse D'Amato in *Status of the U.S. Financial System.*
33. Interview with Kenneth McLean, 3 November 1988; see also *WP*, 23 September 1988; *WSJ*, 24 September 1987; *NYT*, 28 September 1987.
34. Opening statement of Chairman Proxmire, *Changes in Our Financial System: Globalization of Capital Markets and the Securitization of Credit.*
35. *WP*, 28 August 1987.
36. Statement of Roberto G. Mendoza, Jr., Executive Vice President, Morgan Guaranty Co., *Changes in Our Financial System: Globalization of Capital Markets and the Securitization of Credit.*
37. Statement of John Heimann, Vice Chairman, Merrill Lynch Capital Markets Group, *Changes in Our Financial System: Globalization of Capital Markets and the Securitization of Credit*; *WSJ*, 8 September 1987.
38. Testimony of Senator Hecht, in *Modernization of the Glass-Steagall Act.*
39. *Modernization of the Glass-Steagall Act.*
40. Statement of Senator Alfonse D'Amato, *Changes in Our Financial System: Globalization of Capital Markets and the Securitization of Credit.*
41. See SR1905, 'To Enhance the Competition of Financial Services Sector'. Staff members of other senators were stunned by D'Amato's move and they suggested that the Senator had put forward an even more radical proposal to undermine the legislative process. D'Amato angrily rejected these accusations and argued that piecemeal reform would not serve the real reason for the urgent need to legislate. According to D'Amato, '[T]he incremental approach seems inconsistent with a major objective of financial modernization since the "modernization" movement is aimed at enhancing the ability of our financial institutions to compete abroad.'
42. Statement of Paul A. Volcker, Chairman, Board of Governors of the Federal Reserve System, *Globalization of Financial Markets and Related International Banking and Supervisory Issues.*
43. Panel discussion, *Globalization of Financial Markets and Related International Banking and Supervisory Issues*; see also *American Banker*, 31 July 1987; for Barnard's views on bank reform, see *WSJ*, 26 February 1987.
44. Statement by Michael R. Darby, Assistant Secretary for Economic Policy, Department of the Treasury, *Globalization of Securities Markets.*
45. *Modernization of the Financial Services Industry*, 30 September 1987.
46. *Structure and Regulation of Financial Firms and Holding Companies.*
47. *Reform of the Nation's Banking and Financial Systems, Parts 1 & 2.*
48. Ibid.
49. Schumer (1987).
50. *NYT*, 28 June and 8 November 1987; *American Banker*, 3 November 1987; *WP*, 3 December 1987.
51. As discussed earlier, the SIA had filed suit against the ruling by the comptroller. *WP*, 15 January 1987.
52. *WSJ*, 8 April 1987; *ABA Bankers Weekly*, 14 April 1987.
53. *WSJ*, 23 June 1987.
54. *WSJ*, 30 April 1987; see also *United States Banker*, April 1987.
55. For a summary of the ruling and the dissenting statement by Volcker, see *American Banker*, 4 May 1987.
56. *American Banker*, 2 February 1987.
57. *American Banker*, 3 February 1987.
58. These relatively new securities are backed by consumer debt such as credit card or

automobile loans; see *NYT*, 16 July 1987.

59. As early as 1983, Greenspan, then heading his own consulting firm in New York, had advocated publicly what at the time was considered a radical deregulatory policy option for financial markets in the U.S.; see *WSJ*, 16 September 1983.

60. *WSJ*, 4 June 1987; *CQ*, 25 July 1987.

61. Guttmann (1987).

62. Statement by Alan Greenspan, Chairman, Board of Governors of the Federal Reserve System, *Role of Financial Institutions*.

63. Statement by Alan Greenspan, Chairman, Board of Governors of the Federal Reserve System, *Reform of the Nation's Banking And Financial Systems*.

64. Letter by Alan Greenspan to Fernand St. Germain, 5 February 1988.

65. *NYT*, 11 November 1987.

66. During the summer, the Administration stirred up a storm when George Gould stated in an interview that the Administration favoured the creation of five to ten universal banks that would rival the largest banks in Japan, West Germany, Britain and France. 'If we are going to be competitive in a globalized financial-services world we are going to have to change our views on the size of American institutions', said Gould in an interview with the New York Times. *NYT*, 7 June 1987; Gould (1987); *WSJ*, 4 November 1987.

67. *WP*, 13 November 1987; *CQ*, 28 November 1987.

68. Throughout the discussion the SEC had insisted that it could only agree on a bill if the agency were to get primary responsibility in regulating the securities activities of the subsidiaries; *WSJ*, 3 December 1987.

69. *Legislative Proposals to Restructure Our Financial System*.

70. Reinicke, paper presented at Heidelberg, 16-20 September 1992.

71. *WSJ*, 18 December 1987; on the changing tide in the House, see *NYT*, 4 January 1988.

72. Testimony by Alan Greenspan, Chairman, Board of Governors of the Federal Reserve System, *Legislative Proposals to Restructure Our Financial System*.

73. Statement by Alan Greenspan, Chairman of the Board of Governors of the Federal Reserve System, Subcommittee on Telecommunications and Finance of the House Committee on Energy and Commerce, 19 May 1988; *WSJ*, 29 October 1987; *WP*, 29 October 1987; *Financial Times*, 29 October 1987.

74. *NYT*, 8 January 1988.

75. The vote was 18-2. On the moratorium, see *NYT*, 29 February 1988. Proxmire and the committee had retreated to closed door sessions that would shield the senators from lobbyists; see *CQ*, 5 March 1988.

76. *CQ*, 27 February 1988; *National Journal*, 20 February 1988.

77. For an excellent overview of the bill, see Murphy (1988).

78. Verdier and Scarborough (1988); *Independent Banker*, April 1988.

79. United States General Accounting Office (1988).

80. One ad by Chemical Bank went as far as staging a fictitious conversation between a Chemical spokesman and former Congressman Henry Steagall. In the ad, Steagall initially resists a repeal of the act he himself wrote, but then quickly agrees to it after he is informed that 'when ranked by deposits, none of the world's 15 largest banks is a U.S. bank. All are Japanese and European.... [B]anking has become a truly global enterprise with the foreign banks gaining the lion's share.' See *NYT*, 26 January 1988; see also the ads in *WP*, 1 March, 15 June, and 12 July 1988.

81. *National Journal*, 5 March 1988.

82. *NYT*, 29 February 1988.

83. *WP*, 18 February 1988. The questionnaire was sent to 416 of the Fortune 500 and about half were sent back.

84. *NYT*, 24 March 1988; *CQ*, 19 March 1988.

85. Some advocated an amendment that would directly substitute the Senate bill, others offered

alternative legislation. *CQ*, 9 April 1988; *NYT*, 12 April 1988. John J. LaFalce and Stephen Neal proposed the amendment. In April, Doug Barnard introduced his own bill resembling closely the bill approved in the Senate, see *WP*, 14 April 1988.

86. *WSJ*, 13 May 1988.
87. The bill did not repeal Glass-Steagall but expanded bank powers while at the same time placing new and much more stringent limitations on the interrelationship between a bank and its securities subsidiary. In addition it kept most of the consumer provisions contained in the initial draft. *NYT*, 8 July 1988.
88. *CQ*, 30 July 1988; *WSJ*, 28 July 1988.
89. *CQ*, 9 July 1988.
90. *WP*, 24 April 1988.
91. *CQ*, 24 September 1988.
92. *WP*, 23 September 1988.
93. According to the vice president of the ABA, 'The Committee's action removes the only positive feature contained in the House bill — new securities authorities.' *American Banker*, 23 September 1988; for the IBAA's position, see the letter by its president J.R. Nunn to Jim Wright, Speaker of the House, dated 13 October 1988.
94. *CQ*, 24 September 1988.
95. *CQ*, 1 October 1988.
96. *CQ*, 8 October 1988.
97. *CQ*, 15 October 1988.
98. *Congressional Almanac--1988*; *National Journal*, 3 December 1988.
99. Ibid.
100. They included John J. LaFalce, Stephen Neal, and Barney Frank.
101. *WSJ*, 9 February 1988.
102. *NYT*, 14 June 1988.
103. *American Banker*, 4 November 1988; *Daily Report For Executives*, 4 November 1988.
104. *WSJ*, 11 November 1988.
105. Boyd and Graham (1988).
106. Ibid.; see also Brewer, Fortier, and Pavel (1988).
107. Speech by David S. Ruder, Chairman of the Securities Exchange Commission to the Annual Convention of the Securities Industry Association, 2 December 1988.
108. *American Banker*, 21 December 1988. This fear of losing influence was reaffirmed by an important ruling against the OCC in late December. A court in New York overturned a ruling by the Comptroller that permitted national banks to underwrite securities — in this case mortgage backed securities — backed by their own assets. The ruling was considered a major setback for national banks who wanted to engage in securities activities without converting to a bank holding company and implicitly gave the holding structure a competitive advantage; see *American Banker*, 19 December 1988; *American Banker*, 21 December 1988.
109. The bank holding companies were Citicorp, Chase, J.P. Morgan and Bankers Trust. Their applications differed somewhat as to the extent of underwriting permission requested; see *WSJ*, 26 October 1988.
110. *National Journal*, 11 November 1988.
111. *American Banker*, 14 November 1988; *WSJ*, 1 December 1988; *CQ*, 3 December 1988.
112. His close relationship with the S&L industry had led to allegations of impropriety and a series of investigations by the House Ethics Committee and the Justice Department. *WP*, 11 November 1988.
113. *American Banker*, 10 December 1988; *CQ*, 10 December 1988.
114. When the 101st Congress convened early in 1989, few members showed any interest in continuing the debate on bank powers. First, members of the banking committees were quickly overwhelmed by the S&L crisis. Second and more importantly, given that the problems of the thrift industry were closely attributed to the fact that S&Ls were allowed to

enter new businesses such as the real estate business during the early 1980s, no legislator in early 1989 wanted to hold extensive public hearings on a legislative package that essentially entailed similar provisions for commercial banks. *CQ*, 26 November 1988.

115. *American Banker*, 10 November 1988.
116. The degree of involvement of federal bank regulators did change, however, in the course of 1989 as the rescue of the S&L industry required the institutional participation of all three agencies, especially the FDIC.
117. The Fed was required to rule on applications by banks within 90 days.
118. *American Banker*, 19 January 1989.
119. As mentioned, corporate debt underwriting had to be conducted in a separate subsidiary and could generate not more than 5 per cent of the subsidiary's total gross revenue. In addition, the banks had to submit detailed proposals on how to capitalize the affiliate to ensure that the holding's capital would not be drained before the Fed would give its final approval. The Fed did however indicate that it was considering raising the limit to 10 per cent.
120. *WSJ*, 20 January 1989.
121. Edward O'Brien, President of the SIA, as quoted in *American Banker*, 19 January 1989.
122. *American Banker*, 20 June 1989.
123. *WSJ*, 27 July 1989.
124. The Fed had sought comment by other regulators and the private sector on the possibility of raising the limit. For a detailed account of the comments, see Federal Reserve, 21 September 1989; see also *NYT*, 14 September 1989; Federal Reserve Bank of Philadelphia, July-September 1989; for the SIA's reaction see *American Banker*, 5 July 1989.
125. *WP*, 19 January 1989.
126. *American Banker*, 25 January 1989.
127. As quoted in *NYT*, 19 January 1989; see also *CQ*, 21 January 1989. The investigation was to examine the board's functions, including monetary policymaking procedures, supervision of holding companies and services provided to banks, with the purpose of making the Fed more accountable to the public; see *Financial Times*, 26 June 1989.
128. The legislation would make the Treasury Secretary a member of the FOMC. It would also adjust the four-year term of the Fed chairman so that it would expire at the same time as the presidential term. Finally, the bill would require the FOMC to release its policy decision immediately. *WSJ*, 3 July 1989.
129. The fact that the Fed had postponed a final decision on equities for a year made the Fed's ruling more restrictive than the bill approved in the Senate in 1988 and gave Congress another year to act.
130. *American Banker*, 25 January 1989.
131. Heller (1988).
132. Speech by Robert H. Heller, Member, Board of Governors of the Federal Reserve System, Richmond Society of Financial Analysts, 23 March 1989; for similar statement by Fed members see W. Lee Hoskins, President, Federal Reserve Bank of Cleveland, Speech to the Community Bankers of Pennsylvania Annual Convention, 29 August 1989; *NYT*, 10 May 1989; *American Banker*, 3 May 1989.
133. *American Banker*, 21 August 1989.
134. Statement of Frank E. McKinney, Jr., Chairman, Association of Bank Holding Companies, Senate Committee on Banking, Housing and Urban Affairs, 9 March 1988.
135. *American Banker*, 27 December 1988.
136. *WSJ*, 12 October 1989; *WP*, 12 November 1989.
137. *WSJ*, 12 October 1989.
138. *American Banker*, 30 March 1989.
139. *American Banker*, 3 July 1989; *American Banker*, 22 June 1989.
140. Statement by Alan Greenspan, *Globalization of the Securities Markets and S.646, The International Securities Enforcement Cooperation Act of 1989*.

141. Title of a Senate hearing 6 August 1987.
142. *Oversight Hearings on the Condition of U.S. Financial and Industrial Base*. Other witnesses included several officials from DoD and CIA.
143. Statement by Gerald Corrigan, President, Federal Reserve Bank of New York, *Oversight Hearings on the Condition of U.S. Financial and Industrial Base*.
144. Panel discussion, *Globalization of the Securities Markets and S.646, The International Securities Enforcement Cooperation Act of 1989*.
145. *American Banker*, 14 February and 10 August 1989.
146. As quoted in *American Banker*, 19 March 1987.
147. See for example, Fitchew (1988); *WSJ*, 19 October 1988; *Financial Times*, 19 October 1989.
148. EC members were considerably divided over the issue of reciprocity. The division reflected the different degree of each country's financial system's involvement in the international financial markets: the deeper the involvement the greater the resistance to reciprocity.
149. *NYT*, 7 April 1989; *Europe 1992*, Joint Economic Committee, Congress of the United States, 18 November 1988; *Europe 1992: The Financial Services Industry*; Congressional Research Service (1989), Report 89-227; General Accounting Office (1990), GAO/NSIAD-90-99.
150. As quoted in *American Banker*, 25 July 1989; *Financial Times*, 16 July 1989.
151. Commission of the European Communities (1990); *Financial Times*, 21 September 1989.
152. *WSJ*, 21 June 1988.
153. Thomas F. Huertas, Vice President of Citibank, as quoted in *American Banker*, 17 April 1989.
154. Statement by a Washington lobbyist as quoted in *American Banker*, 25 July 1989.
155. *Financial Times*, 3 November 1988; see also the speech by Fed board member H. Robert Heller, World Economic Forum, 1 February 1989.
156. Statement by Gerald Corrigan, President, Federal Reserve Bank of New York, *Oversight Hearings on the Condition of U.S. Financial and Industrial Base*; see also testimony by Manuel H. Johnson, Vice Chairman, Board of Governors of the Federal Reserve System, *Oversight Hearings on European Community's 1992 Program*.
157. Statement by Senator Donald Riegle during testimony by William Seidman, Chairman, Federal Deposit Insurance Corporation, *Deposit Insurance and Financial Services Restructuring*.
158. As quoted in *American Banker*, 25 July 1989.
159. See the testimonies by David C. Mulford, Treasury Undersecretary for International Affairs, FDIC chairman William Seidman, and Comptroller of the Currency Robert Clark, in *Oversight Hearings on European Community's 1992 Program*; see also *CQ*, 30 September 1989.
160. Opening Statement by John J. LaFalce, Chairman, Task Force on the International Competitiveness of U.S. Financial Institutions, 8 May 1990.
161. Ibid.
162. *American Banker*, 2 December 1988.
163. The plan differed in some elements from the proposals made by the banks and its regulators and was thus likely to lead to some debate and an eventual compromise; Securities Industry Association (1990).
164. As quoted in *Washington Weekly Report*, 8 December 1990; see also *Financial Times*, 2 December 1989; Federal Reserve Bank of Dallas, Spring 1990. Some elements of the proposal, relating to tax and supervisory issues, were likely to generate opposition from the banks, but the SIA's decision had removed the most important impediment to a repeal of Glass-Steagall in Congress.
165. *CQ*, 2 December 1989; *Washington Report*, July 1990.
166. *CQ*, 27 May 1989; *Economic Report of the President* February 1990; Corrigan (1990).
167. For the three years of 1988-90 a total number of 574 insured banks assets and deposits totalling $80.6 billion and $63.5 billion respectively failed. Compare these figures to the

period 1980-82, where 62 insured banks, with total assets and deposits of $16.7 billion and $13.9 billion respectively, failed.

168. *CQ*, 27 May 1989.

169. *NYT*, 4 February 1991; *NYT*, 31 January 1991.

170. Indeed it was Congress that had required the Treasury to introduce deposit insurance reform under the 1989 law that salvaged the thrift industry.

171. U.S. Department of the Treasury (1991).

172. *CQ*, 9 February 1991.

173. *American Banker*, 6 March 1991.

174. Two other House committees — Judiciary and Ways and Means — were also given the opportunity to weigh in on the banking bill.

175. *CQ*, 9 February 1991; *Impact of Bank Reform Proposals on Consumers.*

176. Ibid.

177. *NYT*, 5 March 1991. For more on the proposal and the subsequent turf fights, see Reinicke (1991).

178. The Treasury's central thesis that banks need more capital was questioned by the Chairman of the New York Federal Reserve, Gerald Corrigan. *NYT*, 9 February 1991. Corrigan also underlined his stand against links between banks and commerce, saying that this would result in too much economic power in the hands of few. However, he argued favourably for the overhaul of other laws, such as the Glass-Steagall Act. *American Banker*, 12 April 1991; *American Banker*, 6 March 1991; Statement by Gerald Corrigan, President, Federal Reserve Bank of New York, *Financial Services Restructuring.*

179. *NYT*, 6 February 1991; *American Banker*, 11 February 1991; *CQ*, 9 February 1991.

180. On the Administration's approach, see *CQ*, 18 May 1991; on the large banks' lobbying efforts, see *American Banker*, 19 July 1991; Statement of Nicholas Brady, Secretary, Department of Treasury, *Strengthening the Supervision and Regulation of the Depository Institutions, Part 1*; Statement of Robert Glauber, Undersecretary, Finance, Department of the Treasury, *Financial Institutions Safety and Consumer Choice Act of 1991*; Statements by Alan Greenspan, Chairman, Federal Reserve Board; Robert Clarke, Comptroller of the Currency; William Seidman, Chairman, FDIC; Richard Breeden, Chairman, SEC, *Restructuring of the Banking Industry, Part 2.*

181. *WSJ*, 16 January 1991.

182. *CQ*, 9 February 1991.

183. Another strong supporter of the Administration's proposal was Rep. Doug Barnard, a member of the House Banking Committee.

184. In addition, Jim Leach (R-Ia.) had agreed at the Administration's request to withhold an amendment that would have deleted the section from the bill that permitted banks to affiliate with commercial firms. Statement by Peggy Miller, Legislative Representative, Consumer Federation, *Restructuring of the Banking Industry, Part 1*; Statements by Alan Greenspan, Chairman, Federal Reserve Board; Robert Clarke, Comptroller of the Currency; William Seidman, Chairman, FDIC; Richard Breeden; Chairman, SEC, *Restructuring of the Banking Industry, Part 2.*

185. The vote was 31-20; the favourable vote can be partly attributed to the dropping of both consumer provisions and the proposal to restructure federal bank regulation by the committee. *CQ*, 29 June 1991.

186. *American Banker*, 8 July 1991. Riegle initially had imposed several restrictions on the securities activities of commercial banks. However, as a result of strong lobbying efforts and at the insistence of Republican members, including ranking member Jake Garn, the Chairman dropped most of the restrictions. *American Banker*, 1 August 1991; *Financial Services Restructuring*; Statement by Nicholas Brady, Secretary, Department of the Treasury, *Strengthening the Supervision and Regulation of the Depository Institutions, Part 1*; *Strengthening the Supervision and Regulation of the Depository Institutions, Part 2.*

187. In fact, the relatively narrow margin (12-9) reflected the fact that even within the committee, divisions continued over the direction of banking reform. *American Banker*, 6 August 1991; *CQ*, 24 August 1991. Note that the bill that passed the House Committee had abandoned efforts to combat banks' refusal to lend in low-income or minority neighbourhoods.

188. *NYT*, 6 February 1991.

189. *American Banker*, 26 April 1991.

190. *American Banker*, 1 August 1991. According to some analysts, this could have helped large banks because it would show the urgent need for capital infusion into the banking system which could be achieved by allowing commercial banks to purchase banks. *American Banker*, 11 September 1991.

191. *American Banker*, 12 September and 16 October 1991.

192. In essence, the amendments would roll back many of the powers that banks had already been granted through administrative rulings. *American Banker*, 23 September 1991.

193. *American Banker*, 28 October and 8 November 1991.

194. *American Banker*, 25 October and 30 October 1991.

195. *CQ*, 2 November 1991.

196. *CQ*, 14 December 1991.

197. *American Banker*, 3 December 1991.

198. *American Banker*, 5 December and 24 December 1991.

199. *NYT*, 21 September and 25 December 1990; *WSJ*, 21 September 1990; *Financial Times*, 3 October 1990.

200. *WP*, 21 September 1990.

201. *WSJ*, 16 January 1991.

202. *CRS Issue Brief*, 21 February 1991.

203. *American Banker*, 15 February 1992.

204. *American Banker*, 10 July 1991.

205. *WSJ*, 13 November 1991.

206. *NYT*, 8 February 1991.

207. *American Banker*, 11 February 1991.

208. *CQ*, 4 January 1992.

7. The Domestic Politics of Capital Adequacy Regulation

MOBILIZING IN RESPONSE TO EXTERNAL PRESSURE

The process of international financial integration posed challenges not only to the economic interests of private sector actors — as demonstrated in the previous chapter — but also to the political capacity of the state and its actors and institutions. More specifically, the external shocks of the 1970s and the associated globalization of financial markets contributed to the erosion of banks' capital reserves. This generated growing fears among U.S. regulators that they could no longer guarantee the safety and stability of the U.S. financial system.

The global integration of financial markets contributed to the erosion of capital standards in several ways. As mentioned previously, the securitization associated with the external shocks and international financial integration, and the growing competitive strength of European and Japanese banks, sharply eroded U.S. commercial banks' competitive positions in both domestic and international financial markets.[1] In addition, high rates of inflation during the mid- and late 1970s, resulting from the external shocks, induced many banks to speculate that prices would chart a similar course in the future. At the domestic level, a large number of banks expanded their lending to energy and agricultural interests based on their assumption of rising commodity prices. On an international scale, money centre banks continued to broaden their portfolios to include more loans to non-OPEC industrializing countries, based on the expectation of continued inflation and low real interest rates.

Both developments put pressure on banks to engage in riskier behaviour and to make highly leveraged loans in order to regain market shares.[2] As a result, U.S. commercial banks began to experience declining capital ratios during the 1970s and early 1980s.[3] Among the large commercial banks, the proportion of bank capital to total assets declined from around 10 per cent in the early 1950s to 5 per cent by the mid-1970s.[4]

Meanwhile, the number of bank failures began to rise again after a long period of stability that had lasted since the 1930s. Several unprecedented failures of billion dollar banks during the 1970s raised the concerns of policymakers, as the size of banks that needed assistance from the Federal Reserve or the FDIC also grew. More than 20 banks with assets of over $50 million failed during the 1970s.[5]

By the late 1970s, the rising incidence of bank failures, the associated sharp increase in the FDIC's expenses, and the continued decline in capital asset ratios had generated increasing concern among U.S. regulatory authorities and the legislature.[6] These authorities perceived a threat to their capacity to ensure financial stability through regulatory supervision.[7] There was no doubt among policymakers that problem banks had ignored regulatory constraints because suggestions for change in bank behaviour were not always supported by all the agencies and could not be formulated in an enforceable manner.[8] Therefore, regulators and Congress agreed that some action on behalf of the policy network was necessary.[9]

The three federal bank regulatory agencies concurred that some type of regulatory reform to strengthen banks' capital adequacy standards was urgently needed.[10] The agencies agreed that part of the reason for the prior deterioration in capital ratios stemmed from the decentralized supervisory structure. Recognizing the inadequacies of their dispersed, subjective supervisory system, they decided to initiate a process of harmonization of their regulatory practices.

The federal regulators' decision in turn mobilized commercial banks to respond to the threat of new regulatory restraints on their activities. Within the commercial banking sector, two main groups of institutions were mobilized. The first group consisted of large money centre banks, which had become highly leveraged as a consequence of their exposure in industrializing countries. These banks feared that they would become the focus of regulatory efforts to tighten capital supervision because their deteriorating capital positions were responsible for most of the decline in the average capital ratio in the banking industry. The second group consisted of small banks, which were negatively affected by the existing system of capital regulation. Traditionally, authorities had required smaller banks to maintain higher capital standards than their larger counterparts.[11] This divergent regulatory treatment was based on the argument that large banks were safer because of their greater potential for portfolio diversification, and that small or 'community banks' might have a hard time raising capital in times of difficulty and therefore should be more highly capitalized than larger institutions. In light of the regulators' decision to re-examine the capital supervisory system in the early 1980s, the small banks mobilized because they saw an opportunity to redress perceived inequities in regulatory practices.[12]

THE FIRST STAGE OF CONFLICT: THE DOMESTIC POLITICS OF CAPITAL REGULATION

As was the case in the debate over Glass-Steagall, conflicts within the policy network over how to respond to external pressures were shaped by three factors. Two factors — the policy agenda and the range of participants in the policy debates — were inherited from the mobilization phase. Because regulatory agencies were the first actors to mobilize to the challenge of declining capital reserve ratios, they set the terms for the subsequent evolution of debate on regulatory reform and determined the policy proposals to which the other actors in the network were forced to respond. The regulatory agencies' calls for strengthening capital supervision not only set the terms of debate, they also determined the framework within which debate took place. By mobilizing a certain set of actors with a certain range of interests, the regulators' proposals defined the institutional and procedural context for conflict over policy responses.

These two factors dominated the process of conflict until 1982. Then in early 1983, a third factor, which involved a shift in the intensity of the external challenge, catalysed a series of changes in the domestic policy network and in the conflict over regulatory reform. The intensification of external pressure, in the form of the industrializing countries' debt crisis, shifted the terms of debate from a focus on the purely domestic aspects of regulatory reform to an increasing emphasis on the need for global regulatory coordination. In fact, the process of conflict can be divided into two stages: the politics of domestic capital adequacy regulation and the politics of international regulatory harmonization.

During the initial phase of the domestic political debate over capital supervision, there was relatively little disagreement among the public sector actors on the one hand and the private sector actors on the other. On the public sector side, for example, the three federal regulatory agencies concurred on the necessity of enforcing more stringent and uniform capital supervision.[13] They shared a strong interest in safeguarding the stability of the financial system and averting a systemic banking crisis. On the private sector side, both large and small commercial banks were united in opposing more stringent capital regulation.[14]

While both public and private sector actors articulated relatively united (though opposing) perspectives on the broad issues of capital regulation, there were differences within each group over policy details. For example, small commercial banks had a somewhat different set of policy concerns than large commercial banks: smaller banks wished to eliminate the regulatory disparity which forced them to maintain higher capital reserves, while large commercial banks were concerned solely with warding off an increase in general capital reserve requirements. Similarly, the public sector actors disagreed on exactly how to enforce more effective capital supervision, and they engaged in minor turf battles which reflected competing jurisdictional mandates and responsiveness to different private sector actors, as previously discussed.

The debate over the reform of capital adequacy regulation began after the regulatory agencies delegated the study of how to rationalize and strengthen their standards to a newly founded interagency body, the Federal Financial Institution Examination Council (FFIEC), in 1979.[15] At the same time, the OCC began to urge banks to shore up their capital positions, and in July of 1980 the agency proposed new and more stringent rules for the legal definition of capital.[16] Banks were united in opposing the new rules. The ABA urged the Comptroller to retain the present definition of capital while the trade association for bank commercial loan and credit officers opposed any implementation of new rules.[17] In general, banks responded with the familiar argument that 'the issues of bank capital and its adequacy are too important to be left to the regulatory authorities. Let's let the market make appropriate judgments and impose effective discipline with regard to bank capital.'[18]

But the Comptroller's Office was not alone in considering the tightening of capital standards. Throughout the summer and fall of 1980, Congress and other regulators also considered establishing mandatory capital-to-asset ratios.[19] For example, Fed Chairman Paul Volcker announced that many banks would soon have to improve their capital position voluntarily or else financial institution regulators might set specific minimum capital ratios.[20] Again the banks were quick to respond, arguing that an increase in capital reserve requirements would undermine their profitability and place them at a competitive disadvantage relative to those financial institutions which did not operate under similar regulatory constraints.[21] Banks also argued that they needed the flexibility to vary capital levels in response to changing economic conditions and market perceptions. For instance, a study by Citibank contended that, 'Unless banks are able to adjust their capital levels in ways that will minimize the impact of shifting economic winds, they risk being battered by them.'[22]

In addition to presenting this united front against any tightening of capital standards, small banks also used the renewed debate over capital adequacy to demand redress for the unfair treatment they had received with respect to this issue. For instance, in early 1981 the IBAA asked Congress to unilaterally lower their ratio requirements in order to bring them in line with the larger banks. In response to the pressure, Rep. David W. Evans, a Democrat from Indiana, which hosts many small community banks, introduced a resolution that called on regulators to reduce the gap.[23] Large banks quickly countered this move by putting pressure on regulators to maintain stricter requirements for smaller banks. A study by the ABA asked regulators to consider the fact that non-bank intermediaries did not have any capital requirements and that the ratios for thrifts were lower. They also challenged the small banks' drive for competitive equality, arguing that even 'in the absence of regulation, the market would require relatively more capital for small banks anyway.'[24] In sum, the private sector reaction to the regulatory agencies' intent to strengthen capital standards reflected a united opposition, even though there was some division among private sector actors.

In April 1981, the OCC announced that after having received hundreds of comments opposing its proposal to tighten the definition of capital, it had decided to leave the present definition in place. However, the OCC indicated that all three regulatory agencies were working to develop a *uniform* definition of capital for the determination of capital adequacy, which would be coordinated through the FFIEC.[25] Shortly afterwards the FFIEC issued a preliminary proposal containing a uniform definition of capital for bank supervision. The proposal specifically stated that 'the definition [of capital] being proposed by the examination council has as one of its purposes, promoting uniformity in supervisory policies among the Federal banking agencies....'[26]

The three regulatory agencies responded to the Council's recommendations within a month by agreeing upon at least a common set of capital supervisory guidelines. These guidelines, which reflected a major convergence among the regulatory agencies, had the following objectives:

1. to introduce greater uniformity, objectivity and consistency into the supervisory approach for assessing capital adequacy
2. to permit some reduction of the existing disparities in capital ratios between banking organizations of different sizes
3. to address the long-term decline in capital ratios.[27]

More specifically, the regulations established new definitions of bank capital and set guidelines for evaluating capital adequacy. In addition, the agencies set a minimum acceptable level for primary capital and established three zones for classifying institutions according to the adequacy of their total capital. However, the new guidelines did not completely harmonize capital standards across agencies, because the FDIC adopted somewhat different criteria than the OCC and the Fed. These divergences reflected modest differences in the goals of the regulatory agencies themselves, as well as differences in the interests of the private sector actors to whom they were responsive.[28]

In December 1981, the Federal Reserve and the Comptroller issued common guidelines based on the FFIEC's proposal for a dual-component concept of capital.[29] On the other hand, they rejected the FFIEC's recommendation to cease discriminating among banks based upon size. While they did lower somewhat the capital requirements for smaller banks, differences among banks remained. Both agencies continued to differentiate across size, grouping banks into three different categories: 'multinational', 'regional' and 'community' banks. The new standards applied to regional and community member banks and incorporated explicit numerical guidelines for the first time.[30] By contrast, no numerical standards were set for the 'multinational' group, despite the fact that the report by the FFIEC had shown that the decline in the average capital ratio in the banking industry in the late 1970s and early 1980s was almost entirely due to the deteriorating capital positions of large banks.[31] In addition, the regulators enlarged the multinational group from 11 to 17 banks.

Small banks strongly disagreed. They argued that the traditional position of the regulators, that large banks were less exposed to risk because of their greater potential for portfolio diversification, was no longer tenable. Small banks were able to point to the large international loans by multinational banks that were deemed highly risky, and argued that the social cost of failure would be greater in the case of large banks. Finally, since a considerable proportion of multinational banks' deposits were uninsured and since they had a similar portfolio structure, failure by a single large bank could easily lead to a system-wide crisis. [32] But the Federal Reserve and the Comptroller were not responsive to these arguments. While they lowered the standards for community banks somewhat and pledged to work towards an eventual harmonization of capital standards, differences continued after 1981.[33]

The multinational banks' exclusion from the new numerical capital reserve requirements reflected the responsiveness of the OCC and the Federal Reserve to the intense lobbying efforts of the money centre banks. Originally, the argument for the multinational banks' exclusion was that their business was so complex that it required individual subjective analysis. However, in subsequent years most MNBs boosted their ratios by issuing significant amounts of primary (equity) capital prior to their inclusion at the same minimum capital levels as the large regional banks. This suggests that their low levels of equity were the primary reason for their earlier exclusion.[34] In essence, the OCC and the Federal Reserve recognized that none of the money centre banks were capable of meeting the numerical reserve requirements without costly and possibly injurious consequences, at least in the short run.[35] They justified the regulatory exclusion on the basis of their special position in the banking system. Because the 17 multinational banks held almost half of all Fed member banks' assets, a sudden or sharp rise in capital requirements might have caused undue disturbance to the entire banking system. This underscored the Fed's concern about systemic disturbances in contrast to the FDIC's focus on the health of individual banks.

The agencies decided to apply strong informal pressure as an alternative to formal numerical targets in their efforts to raise the capital reserve ratios of the money centre banks. Regulators announced that their policies with respect to the MNBs would be amended '... to insure that appropriate steps are taken to improve over time the capital position of banking organizations in this group.'[36] As mentioned above, one of the objectives cited by the agencies for the new capital guidelines was 'to address the long-term decline in capital ratios, particularly those of the multinational group.'[37] In essence, large money centre banks were told that unless they substantially raised their capital base within the next few years, regulators would unilaterally impose strict numerical standards upon them.[38]

The FDIC differed in its new guidelines in several ways. While sticking to the FFIEC's principles of a fixed minimum capital ratio, the FDIC adopted a stricter definition of capital than the Federal Reserve and the Comptroller. The FDIC's more stringent capital definition, which included only equity capital, reflected the fact that as the main depository insurer it took a more conservative stand on bank safety than did the other regulatory agencies.[39] Secondary capital instruments, according to the FDIC, were not included in the evaluation procedure 'since they lack permanence, are not available to absorb losses...and impose mandatory servicing requirements.'[40] But although the FDIC did not develop a two tier system, all three of the regulatory agencies agreed that only equity capital could count as the prime factor in a definition of capital. As will be shown later, this agreement proved to be important when regulators from various countries were trying to arrive at a common definition of core capital.

In addition, the FDIC, in order 'to foster objectivity in the analytical process and provide a benchmark for evaluating capital adequacy', adopted common capital standards regardless of bank size.[41] The FDIC's common capital standards were a concession to the interests of the smaller banks which made up the majority of its regulatory constituency.[42] Thus, while not successful with the Fed and the OCC, small banks did manage to convince the FDIC that they should not be subjected to higher capital standards than large money centre banks.[43]

The new regulatory guidelines were thus not entirely uniform or objective. They continued to reflect divergent regulatory agency interests and ties to different private sector actors, obstructing a full consensus among the regulatory authorities. Yet these divergent agency interests and ties to private actors did not result in the formation of durable cross-cutting coalitions pitting different segments of the public and private sector against each other, as was the case in the debate over the repeal of the Glass-Steagall Act. The conflicts of interest among the regulatory agencies involved the specific details of capital standards rather than the general principle of capital adequacy regulation. As a result, any competing coalitions which arose among different public sector actors proved limited in scope and transitory in nature. These coalitions gave rise to minor variations in capital adequacy standards across regulatory agencies, but did not impede the formation of a more basic regulatory agency consensus on the need for stronger and more coordinated capital standards. And even the modest differences in approach taken by the various agencies disappeared after 1982, once the external pressures on the policy network intensified.

The policy announcements of 1981 reflected a major change: considerable institutional convergence among the regulatory agencies. First, by reacting to the declining ratios in such an assertive way, all three regulators were in agreement that the declining capital ratios presented a problem and that something had to be done. Second, all three agencies recognized the basic concept of capital adequacy as an important regulatory device in preserving the safety and soundness of individual banks and the banking system at large. Third, by announcing the new capital guidelines, all three agencies broke precedent by placing in the public domain their schedules of capital ratios, which would be used as benchmarks in judging the capital positions of sound and well-managed institutions. According to two officials from the OCC, the new standards represented a more objective and consistent supervisory approach to capital adequacy. Banks would benefit by being able to manage their capital positions with full knowledge of the likely supervisory posture and response. 'We consider the guidelines a superior approach to previous inconsistent methods, including formal and informal rules of thumb, reliance on peer group parameters, and published and unpublished standards.'[44]

Still, several institutional differences remained with respect to each of the stated goals at the time of promulgation. First, while the Federal Reserve and the Comptroller applied the same standards, the FDIC, as the insurer of commercial banks, applied more stringent standards. Secondly, two of the three regulatory agencies continued to differentiate among banks according to size. Finally and most importantly, not only were large banks allowed to maintain a lower capital ratio, but multinational banks were excluded from the new measurement entirely; the decision on their capital requirements was left to the individual attention of the appropriate supervisory agency, leading to charges that 'despite the labors of the FFIEC, the goal of unity among the regulators remains elusive.'[45]

Then in 1982-83, a significant change in the distribution of power and interests within the policy network occurred, and catalysed a decisive resolution of the capital adequacy issue at the domestic level. The most important catalyst to change was the sudden intensification of external economic pressures upon the policy network. More specifically, the emergence of the industrializing countries' debt crisis in 1982 exposed the low capital reserve levels of U.S. multinational banks to greater regulatory scrutiny than ever before, and raised urgent concerns that imprudent banking practices were undermining the safety and stability of the entire U.S. banking system. As in the case of Glass-Steagall, the intensification of external economic pressure gave rise to two critical shifts in the U.S. policy network. In the case of capital adequacy standards, it first mobilized Congress to enter the debate and empowered the legislature with strong leverage to force a policy resolution on the other major institutions in the policy network. Secondly, it supplanted the minor institutional conflicts of interest among the regulatory agencies with a complete consensus on the need for the immediate strengthening and complete harmonization of capital reserve regulations across agencies.

In early 1982, rumours surfaced that the resources of the International Monetary Fund may have been severely strained by the numerous financial problems of Latin American debtor nations. Then in August of 1982, Mexico announced that it could not meet the payments due on $81 billion in debt, $23 billion of which was owed to U.S. banks. On 18 November Argentina announced it was having financing difficulties and in early December Brazil notified its creditors it could not pay $100 million due on its external debt of $79 billion. Seen from the creditors' perspective, by the middle of 1982 the nine largest U.S. banks had lent over 140 per cent of their capital, which amounted to loans of $30 billion, to these three countries. Although at first resistant, in late 1982 the Administration agreed with most other creditor nations that an increase in the IMF's resources was urgently needed. Under a plan completed by the member nations of the IMF in early 1983, the Fund's resources were increased by 47 per cent, or about $32 billion.[46] The U.S. share of that increase was roughly $8.4 billion and had to be approved by Congress. The fact that this rescue required a congressionally mandated increase in the U.S. contribution to the IMF put Congress in a strong bargaining position vis-à-vis the regulatory agencies and the commercial banks.

Even before legislation authorizing the funds was sent to Capitol Hill by the Reagan Administration, there was strong opposition to the quota increase in Congress, given that the country was in one of the deepest recessions in its post-war history.[47]   During a hearing conducted by the House Banking Committee on 21 December 1982, Chairman St. Germain referred to the IMF and the demand for increased funding as a sophisticated bailout operation for large banks, and commented on the Administration's request to expand the IMF's resources: 'At a time when millions stand in unemployment lines and thousands of small businesses are filing bankruptcy petitions, the idea of an international bailout for adventurous U.S. bankers may not be the most popular item on the legislative agenda.'[48]   Similarly, at a Senate hearing conducted in early January of 1983, Senator Proxmire stated, 'It is going to be extremely difficult to get the Senate and the House to go along with this replenishment of the IMF. If you are going to lend $9 billion to anybody, why not provide it to home builders or automobile buyers?'[49]

The Administration, regulatory agencies, and private banks argued that an IMF quota increase was critical to forestalling a breakdown in the debt service capacity of the major industrializing countries, and to preventing a financial crisis for the heavily-exposed money centre banks, which would ultimately lead to chaos in the domestic and international financial system.[50]   In addition, as Federal Reserve Chairman Paul Volcker testified, the effects of refusing to approve the plan could be equally severe for the non-financial sector of the U.S. economy.   With their funds cut off, he argued, industrializing countries were likely to adopt strict adjustment programmes which would have drastic effects on U.S. exports to that region.[51]   Some members of Congress were well aware of that situation. As Senator Jim Sasser said, 'I think it is a Hobson's choice. We are damned if we do and damned if we don't.'[52]   Faced with this dilemma, Congress realized that it had little choice but to approve the plan.[53]   However, while the legislators knew that they could not forestall an eventual increase in the IMF quota for ever, they wanted to minimize any political backlash from their constituencies and were determined to attach amendments to the IMF quota increase that would ensure that a similar situation would not repeat itself.   In the Senate, Senators Heinz and Proxmire led the call to impose restrictions on the foreign activities of U.S. banks.[54]   On the House side, Henry Gonzales indicated in his opening remarks to the first hearing on the IMF increase that any further increase of the IMF's resources would not be allowed without extracting considerable commitments from both the regulatory agencies and the banks, and that a repeat of such a 'bailout' would not be possible.

During the course of a series of hearings on the quota increase, a congressional consensus developed that the regulators had been insufficiently alert to the unfolding international debt crisis, and had wrongly allowed large money centre banks to delay enforcement of the higher capital standards which would have protected the U.S. economy from the repercussions of the debt crisis. The sentiment in Congress towards regulators was probably best described by Senator Proxmire in a hearing on 16 February when he stated, 'Where were our bank regulators when all this foreign debt was piling up?... They did everything except regulate.'[55]

Initially, however, the regulators were not inclined to accept the blame. According to Volcker, the Fed had in 'process a re-evaluation of our current approach towards supervision. My own preliminary judgement is that the basic framework of the system introduced in 1979 is sound.' In addition, he warned Congress not to overreact with excessive regulations.[56] The FDIC, which is not responsible for the regulation of money centre banks and had been critical of their special treatment by the Fed, was more outspoken. In testimony before the Financial Institutions Subcommittee on 21 April 1983, FDIC Chairman William Isaac acknowledged the partial responsibility of the regulators for the severity of the debt crisis.

> As bank supervisors, we failed to effectively caution American banks to refrain from foreign lending growth. Although portfolio concentration was high, sufficiently firm steps were not taken to limit the concentration and leveraging of bank capital. Without question our supervisory efforts need buttressing.[57]

Clearly this statement was directed toward the Federal Reserve, which still had no firm guidelines set for the MNBs and continued to allow large banks to have lower capital ratios than smaller banks regulated by the FDIC.

Turning specifically to the issue of capital ratios, the Federal Reserve initially did not indicate it had any intention of committing itself to implementing specific regulations for the large MNBs. Volcker agreed that large banks had not done very well compared to small ones and that he 'would like to see them move generally higher'; he continued that 'there are a lot of pluses and minuses to any particular course of action' and that the Fed has 'some of these things under study.'[58] The Fed Chairman then reminded Congress that 'in the past decade there has been a view by some of the banking community that capital is irrelevant, and that one shouldn't worry much about capital ratios, and that capital ratios declining are not very important.'[59] In addition he told the legislature that 'banks undoubtedly have felt under very heavy pressure internationally, and carrying more capital is a cost.'[60] The Comptroller of the Currency took a similar position. While recognizing the need 'to strengthen lending procedures in order to reduce the future likelihood of accumulating large high risk exposures overseas', Conover did not endorse the introduction of specific lending limits based on bank capital in his proposals on how to strengthen the supervisory mechanisms.[61] And although the FDIC had earlier spoken of the need to strengthen regulation, no specific comments were made by its Chairman with regard to capital ratios.[62] Thus, while the regulatory agencies agreed in principle that capital regulation must be strengthened in order to preserve the safety and stability of the U.S. financial system, they resisted congressional calls for more stringent regulation on the grounds that capital supervision fell under the authority of the regulators.

On 7 April, in order to preempt any further action by Congress and to accelerate the IMF quota increase, the three regulatory agencies presented to Congress a five point programme to strengthen the supervision of international lending. The Fed in particular had become considerably more accommodating. The central bank now acknowledged that the regulatory system supervising the international activities of banks 'did not have sufficient force or impact on banker attitudes.'[63] However, the programme did not contain any specific policy proposal with regard to capital adequacy.[64] Rather, the agencies concluded that their existing statutory authorities were sufficient to implement their own reform programme and that legislation to implement regulatory reform was unnecessary.

The private sector was even more opposed to Congress imposing any regulatory restraints on its international activities in light of the debt crisis. According to the vice chairman of Chase Manhattan Bank, 'a tighter web of administrative controls around the foreign lending of banks, as some have suggested, would be unwise, unnecessary and counterproductive....[T]he fundamental situation [of the banks] is sound...if this is a temporary liquidity problem, and I am convinced it is....'; he also stated, '[F]rankly, I don't really feel that we need a whole lot of new regulation to solve this problem. This is really not the issue.'[65] Thus, bankers also opposed the five point reform proposal which the regulatory agencies had made to appease Congress and to get some control over the international activities of the money centre banks.[66]

The large money centre banks' opposition created a fierce backlash in Congress. In his response to the testimony by Ogden, Jim Leach reflected the feeling of the committee:

> that when Chase and other large banks appear before Congress, they are more concerned with this issue of fear and doubt [regarding the IMF quota authorization] than they are about telling the story. This couldn't be reflected more clearly than in the anomalies of your statement today, Mr. Ogden....Let's be honest with each other. You have screwed up....The dozen largest international banks had better increase their capital base and sell one whale of a lot of equity for Congress to be very sympathetic to their plight.[67]

There was widespread agreement among congressional committees that the money centre banks shared considerable responsibility for the debt crisis because of their imprudent and risky lending. In the eyes of the Senate, an enlargement of the IMF quota amounted to a bailout of the banks by the American taxpayer.[68] Thus, any increase in the U.S. contribution to the IMF had to be accompanied by a set of stronger capital adequacy regulations which would prevent the recurrence of bailouts in the future. In the words of Republican Senator Jake Garn, '[T]he price of an $8.4 billion increase in the IMF authorization in Congress is going to be legislation so that lawmakers can go home and report that "we did not bail out the banks".'[69] And while the Senate Banking Committee concurred with the agencies' five point programme it 'also concluded that specific legislative action is needed to mandate permanent improvements in the supervision and regulation of international lending....'[70]

The mood in the House concerning the attitude of the large banks and the proposal made by the three agencies was even more negative:

> [I]n 1977, such a recommendation [the five point plan by the agencies] would have been meaningful. In 1983, after six years of agencies' assurances, a reform proposal consisting of general comments and guidelines yet to be specified and addressing only the most short-term aspects of the international lending problem was insufficient. The long history of banker excess and regulatory neglect in the area of international lending made the agencies' proposal and legislative recommendations unacceptable.[71]

Throughout the spring of 1983, hearings continued to be held in the banking committees, both of which unequivocally endorsed harmonization and the strengthening of capital reserve requirements as integral elements for fostering prudent banking practices and preserving the safety and soundness of the U.S. banking system. For example, according to a bill introduced by the Senate Banking Committee, 'legislation also requires the bank regulatory agencies to establish uniform systems for requiring banks to maintain adequate levels of capital. The Committee believes this positive mandate is necessary to ensure that banking institutions, and especially larger banks, are adequately capitalized.'[72] The bill also emphasized that 'the Committee expects the standards developed under this Act will be uniform among the three bank regulatory agencies so that banks with the same characteristics are treated alike regardless of their regulatory status.'[73]

Although there initially appeared to be a standoff between regulators and Congress over the appropriate response to the debt crisis, a second development further altered the institutional power configuration and strengthened congressional leverage over the regulatory agencies. It was a legal challenge to the capital supervisory authority of the federal regulators by the banks. As discussed previously, banks lobbied against the new and stiffer requirements in 1981. However, no formal challenge was launched against the regulatory agencies. This changed in February 1983, when the

First National Bank of Bellaire challenged the Comptroller's authority to impose explicit capital requirements and issue a 'cease and desist' order if the bank did not comply with the order.[74] First National Bank of Bellaire obtained a ruling in its favour from the court of appeals, which set aside the portion of the Comptroller's cease and desist order requiring the capital levels of a particular national bank to be increased and maintained at a specified level.

Prior to this ruling, the bank regulators had assumed they would enjoy broad administrative discretion in enforcing their capital adequacy rules, pursuant to their powers to issue cease and desist orders under the statutory authority granted by the Federal Deposit Insurance Act. The court's decision in First National Bank of Bellaire vs. Comptroller of the Currency cast severe doubt upon the institutional capacity of the regulatory agencies and undermined their legitimacy to enforce the capital standards that were deemed necessary to maintain the safety and soundness of the banking system. The only way to reassert such institutional capacity was for Congress to step in and explicity legislate the ability and authority of the federal regulatory agencies to request and enforce the maintenance of capital standards that were deemed adequate. The agencies were left dependent upon Congress to reassert their threatened institutional authority.

The legislature indicated that it was willing to provide such authority if the agencies were willing to act on the other concerns it had raised. This was confirmed in a report by the Senate Banking Committee which stated,

> The Committee also believes clarification of existing authority is needed because the recent decision of the U.S. Court of Appeals...has clouded the authority of the bank regulatory agencies to exercise their independent discretion in establishing and requiring the maintenance of appropriate levels of capital.[75]

As one commentator suggested, '[C]ongressional pressure stiffened the backbone of the regulators in dealing with the big money center banks, who seemed to be calling the tune....'[76]

Given the legislature's determination to go beyond what the regulatory agencies had initially proposed; the regulators' dependence upon Congress to enact legislation that would restore their credibility in establishing adequate capital levels; and the urgency to get the IMF quota increase, the Fed, which had been most resistant to any specific ratios for MNBs, quickly acquiesced to Congress.[77] In a letter of 6 May to House Banking Committee Chairman St. Germain, Volcker defended the banks by pointing to the general increase in capital ratios of the biggest banks in the last year. However, he continued, 'we also believe it is now appropriate to implement specific minimum standards for all categories of banks.'[78]

On 13 June 1983, the Federal Reserve and the Comptroller issued a series of amendments to the 1981 guidelines in order to bring the MNBs, previously treated separately, under a uniform set of regulations. For the first time, the Federal Reserve and the Comptroller had set specific capital guidelines for U.S. multinational banks.[79] In addition, the agencies agreed to coordinate the capital adequacy requirements across agencies.

The new guidelines drew virtually no opposition from the large banks. First, money centre banks were dependent upon Congress for a major financial rescue operation and once it was apparent that both Congress and now the regulators as well were determined to implement tighter regulation, their initial resistance was quickly overcome by their overriding interest in ensuring the IMF quota increase. Both regulatory agencies and the banks were willing to accept any congressional conditions for capital adequacy in return for approval of the IMF quota increase. A second reason for the acquiescence of the large banks was that 12 of the 17 money centre banks had managed to raise their ratio above the required 5 per cent level by the time the regulation was implemented.[80] As one commentator put it, '...[T]he multinationals were deemed sufficiently rehabilitated to be brought into the fold.'[81] Accordingly, bankers agreed that they would have little trouble in meeting the new standards and did not mount any significant opposition.[82] This was confirmed by an internal memo from the Fed Board's Division of Banking Supervision and Regulation, in which the agency confirmed that the guidelines were not 'unduly burdensome.'[83]

The Senate responded quickly to the regulators' pledge to implement fixed minimum capital ratios for MNBs. On 8 June it approved a bill authorizing an $8.4 billion increase in the U.S. contribution to the IMF.[84] In the House, progress was much slower. As one lobbyist aptly described the situation in the House, '[N]obody, not one member of Congress, is going to win any votes back home on this unless [Citibank Chairman] Walter Wriston lives in their district.'[85] Despite these concerns, the bill was narrowly approved on 3 August.[86] The spectre of a sharp decline in world trade and a global financial collapse were the main reasons why those in favour of the bill were able to generate sufficient support.

In early November, after further negotiations, the bill was finally approved and Congress passed the International Lending Supervisory Act (ILSA). Section 908 of the Act directed 'each appropriate federal banking agency' to ensure that all 'banking institutions' would achieve and maintain adequate capital levels. The failure to maintain adequate levels was deemed to be 'unsafe and unsound.' To ensure the above mandate, ILSA provided the regulatory agencies with statutory authority for the enforcement of capital adequacy standards, thereby overturning the court decision in Bellaire vs. Comptroller.[87] As such, the Act conferred upon the regulatory institutions a new and additional enforcement device: the capital adequacy directive.[88]

In addition, ILSA addressed the anomaly of U.S. multinational and other major U.S. banking institutions engaging in substantial international lending without a statutorily-based comprehensive supervisory scheme.[89] Finally, Congress established the need for uniformity of capital standards through the enactment of ILSA, thus addressing the long standing dispute between small and large banks over the competitive inequality issue.

With the enactment of ILSA, the OCC, Federal Reserve and FDIC quickly undertook the congressionally-mandated task of strengthening and coordinating their approach to capital adequacy supervision. However, while the OCC joined the FDIC in issuing *regulations*, the Fed stuck to its policy of issuing *guidelines* for the 17 MNBs. According to the Fed, its rationale for doing so was that

> rigidly defining failure to meet certain capital levels in all cases as a per se violation of law could hamper the Board's efforts in working with banks and bank holding companies to strengthen their capital positions, and in evaluating capital adequacy in the context of a broader range of factors it must consider in acting upon applications.[90]

In addition, the agencies opened intra-institutional negotiations, with the aim of eliminating the remaining definitional and institutional differences in their regulatory standards and further strengthening the capital ratios.[91]

In July of 1984, the OCC and the FDIC announced a plan that would set new minimum standards for capital adequacy for *all* banks. When the two agencies announced their plan, it was unclear whether the Fed would agree to such a move, and some observers suspected that the Fed would be concerned that the proposal could be too tough on some large banks with heavy foreign loan exposure.[92] Within two weeks, however, the Fed responded to pressure from Congress and the other regulators, and announced a plan for the same increase in its minimum capital standards.[93] In line with its previous policy, however, the Fed continued to issue guidelines, as opposed to regulations, in order to retain some flexibility in handling individual cases.

By the end of the summer of 1984, the regulators had separately published their proposals for uniform and higher minimum capital standards for public comment.[94] The three proposals roughly approximated each other and from a technical perspective closely resembled the 1981 Comptroller and Federal Reserve guidelines. The regulators were now in full agreement that there should be uniformity of rules for banking institutions of all sizes, and that there should be effective enforcement procedures to ensure compliance with the rules. And while no formal agreement was announced during 1984, there was a clear indication that the agencies were already applying the higher capital standards to their client banks.[95] Larger banks were more severely affected by the new proposal. The Fed estimated that almost all large banks would be forced to raise new capital. The pressure on small banks was considerably less, since according to the FDIC only about 4 per cent of its members would have to raise their standards.

The intra-agency negotiations were concluded in early 1985, when all three regulatory agencies issued a set of common guidelines, with only a few minor differences remaining. The FDIC moved first in February, announcing its new rules (which were based on its proposal of July 1984) and stressing that the new regulations reflected an intra-agency compromise.[96] Shortly thereafter, the OCC followed suit with identical rules.[97] The Federal Reserve formally promulgated its own final revised guidelines in April of 1985.[98] As a Fed staff report noted, the new guidelines were coordinated with the regulations jointly adopted the prior month by the Comptroller and the FDIC. These guidelines led to the 'adoption of uniform minimum capital ratios for all federally supervised banking institutions...regardless of size, type of charter, membership in the Federal Reserve System, or the identity of their primary federal regulator....'[99] The regulations included uniform definitions for capital composition, a uniform minimum capital level of 5.5 per cent for all federally supervised banking institutions, and revamped enforcement procedures. Officials from the agencies stressed that an effort was made to achieve the greatest possible uniformity. Each of the regulators included comprehensive regulatory provisions regarding the issuance of capital directives and enforcement of capital adequacy standards.[100] Although the private sector was critical of the new regulations, there was relatively little opposition from the banks, as most of them had raised their ratios above the guidelines.[101]

In addition to specifying explicit regulatory procedures, the 1985 regulations and guidelines also incorporated, for the first time since the 1960s, the notion of risk assessment as an evaluation tool. In response to the higher reserve requirements contained in the 1981 guidelines, and especially after 1983, banks had shifted their portfolio structure from low-risk assets toward higher-risk, higher-return assets. This shift allowed the banks to partially compensate for the additional costs imposed by the new capital requirements of 1981. The 1985 agency statements also noted a dramatic increase in so-called off-balance sheet activities — activities which are not reflected on a banking institution's financial statement and are thus not included in the calculation of the capital-to-asset ratio.[102] Both developments suggested that banks were attempting to avoid the 1981 standards by increasing their proportion of both higher-risk-and-return assets and off-balance sheet activities, which in turn explains why there was relatively little opposition from the private sector. As one study suggested, if one incorporated stand-by letters of credit into the assets held by banks, the primary capital ratio for 12 money centre banks would have decreased from 6.3 per cent to 5.6 per cent during the first half of 1985.[103] From a regulatory perspective, it meant that 'the improvement we have seen in capital ratios in recent years overstates the real improvement in capital strength, measured against more realistic measures of risk.'[104]

Given their newly-acquired harmony and cooperative spirit on capital adequacy regulation, regulators were quick to react to attempts by the private sector to undermine their efforts, despite the fact that banks were strongly opposed to yet another round of new regulatory restraint. By the end of the summer, the Fed, in accordance with the OCC, announced that it would propose a risk-related capital requirement before the end of the year.[105] The new guidelines attempted to heighten the incentives to hold low-risk, highly liquid assets and lower the motivation to engage in off-balance sheet activities.[106] This time the regulators responded quickly, decisively, and, most importantly, in a uniform manner. In a joint press release by the three agencies in January of 1986, they officially announced their intention to develop risk-based capital adequacy standards.[107] The Fed soon proposed the new standards; the OCC and the FDIC were expected to follow with similar proposals.[108] By the middle of the year, regulators suggested that they could issue a uniform proposal for a system of risk-based capital requirements as early as October.[109]

Thus, in a relatively short period of four years, the U.S. regulatory system in the area of capital adequacy evolved from one of ad hoc and fragmented supervision to one of standardized and coordinated regulatory oversight. The relatively timely and coherent domestic response to the challenge of declining capital ratios reflected both the way in which the policy network had initially mobilized to confront the challenge, and the manner in which intensifying external pressures influenced the distribution of power and interests within the policy network.

The domestic coordination of capital standards demonstrates that policy gridlock is not inevitable in the decentralized U.S. financial policy network. Because of the way in which the policy network was initially mobilized to respond to the challenge of declining capital ratios, the 'structural possibility' of gridlock and fragmentation was never fully realized. The policy network was only partially mobilized, and the range of interests expressed by the major actors tended towards convergence rather than discord. The convergence of interests among the domestic public sector institutions and the relatively minor disagreements among private sector actors compensated for the structural fragmentation of the policy network, and allowed that network to formulate policy responses characteristic of a more centralized system. Then after 1982, the favourable preconditions inherited from the mobilization phase were reinforced by the intensification of external economic pressures upon the policy network. This allowed Congress to act as a powerful force to pressure regulators to completely harmonize capital ratios across the U.S. financial system.

However, increased domestic regulatory harmonization and institutional coordination in the area of capital adequacy were not only the result of the changing institutional power configuration in the domestic policy network. As early as 1981, U.S. regulators were well aware that any adequate solution to the capital adequacy question had to be of an international nature. As national financial markets became more and more integrated, regulatory tightening in U.S. banking would not necessarily protect the American financial system from a crisis in another country. Also, given the high degree of financial integration, unilateral strengthening of capital ratios would create competitive inequalities among banks from different countries competing in a single global market. As will be discussed in the next chapter, this international dimension of the capital adequacy issue had considerable influence in pushing U.S. regulators to arrive at a uniform, coherent U.S. position. Only a regulatory system that was uniform at the domestic level would allow U.S. regulators to work towards an international agreement on capital adequacy.

The intensification of external economic pressures not only fostered institutional cooperation and accelerated the coordination of reserve requirements at the domestic level; it also catalysed a process of unprecedented international cooperation among regulatory institutions and the international harmonization of capital adequacy regulation. At the same time Congress and the regulators reached agreement on the need for strengthening and coordinating domestic capital supervision, they also came to the realization that domestic supervision could only be effective in the context of a multinational agreement on capital adequacy standards. During the ILSA hearings, U.S. policymakers acknowledged that purely domestic regulatory action would be insufficient to safeguard the U.S. financial system from the repercussions of the industrializing countries' debt crisis. They felt the global integration of financial markets had progressed to the point at which higher capital standards in the U.S. alone could not insulate the American financial system from a crisis in another financial market. U.S. policymakers therefore felt compelled to carry their quest for financial stability to a supranational level, by seeking higher capital standards across all the major financial markets.

In addition, the global integration of financial markets meant that purely domestic regulatory action would not only fail to achieve the goal of protecting financial stability; it would also undermine the competitive position of U.S. banks in world markets. As Federal Reserve Chairman

Volcker testified before Congress during the ILSA hearings

[T]he globalization of financial markets has brought about a dramatic increase in international competition and an awareness that differences in rules among supervisory authorities around the world can create competitive distortions. The competitive disadvantages this could cause might make some supervisors reluctant to take otherwise necessary supervisory actions, knowing that the result of such actions could be the loss of competitiveness of their banking system.[110]

Large money centre banks were also acutely aware of the potential competitive asymmetries arising from the tightening of U.S. capital regulation. They argued against any such tightening on the grounds that it would place them at a competitive disadvantage vis-à-vis banks in less-regulated environments. Yet although U.S. policymakers acknowledged that a unilateral U.S. move to raise capital standards would place U.S. commercial banks at a disadvantage, they contended that a multilateral capital adequacy agreement would prevent such a competitive asymmetry from arising.

These concerns were clearly reflected in ILSA. ILSA demonstrated, for the first time, congressional concern for the convergence of international banks' capital standards by calling on federal bank regulators to consult with regulators from other nations. In fact, as will be discussed, it was ILSA that proved to be the key catalyst for the convergence not only of domestic capital adequacy standards, but also for the multilateral efforts of bank regulators to harmonize regulations. As such, ILSA's express intent of domestic and international convergence of capital standards evidenced the inseparability between the domestic and international dimension of bank regulation in an increasingly integrated global financial market.

NOTES

1.   Keeley (1988).
2.   Wall (1989).
3.   Marcus (1983).
4.   Orgler and Wolkowitz (1976); Federal Financial Institutions Examination Council (1980).
5.   Among them were four banks with assets of over $1 billion. The Bank of Commonwealth in Detroit, U.S. National Bank in San Diego, Franklin National Bank in New York and Security National Bank, Hempstead were either aided or merged to prevent failure (Commonwealth and Security National) or assumed by other banking institutions following foreclosure (U.S. National and Franklin National). The bailout of the First Pennsylvania Bank, with over $8.4 billion in assets, by the FDIC in April of 1980 raised the total assets of banks requiring assistance to over $20 billion. Maisel (1981); Spero (1980).
6.   Rose (1980); *WSJ*, 10 January and 31 July 1980; *American Banker*, 25 November 1980. The sharp rise in the FDIC's expenses heightened the attention and interest in increasing the stringency of bank capital regulation to limit the FDIC's exposure to losses and to blunt the

incentives for excessive risk-taking by federally insured banks.

7. This perception was conveyed to U.S. Bankers at the ABA's Annual Convention in October 1980 by all three regulators. *American Banker*, 15 October 1980.

8. Maisel (1981).

9. Wall (1989).

10. Ibid.; Maisel (1981); Spero (1980).

11. The Fed and the Comptroller strongly favoured higher ratios for small banks. *American Banker*, 15 October and 16 October 1980.

12. Small banks also found increasing support in the legislature; Congress pledged to look into the allegations by smaller banks that the regulators were discriminating against them. Rose (1980).

13. *American Banker*, 30 July 1980.

14. *American Banker*, 27 October 1980.

15. The FFIEC was established on 10 March 1979, pursuant to Title X of P.L. 95-630, the Financial Institutions Regulatory and Interest Control Act (FIRA). FFIEC (1987).

16. *WSJ*, 31 July 1980. The new definition excluded subordinated notes and debentures and loan loss reserves. *American Banker*, 24 July and 18 August 1980.

17. *American Banker*, 15 September, 26 September, 3 October and 17 October 1980.

18. *American Banker*, 12 September and 18 September 1980.

19. *American Banker*, 30 July 1980.

20. *American Banker*, 19 September 1980.

21. *American Banker*, 17 November 1980.

22. Howard and Hoffmann (1980); *American Banker*, 10 December 1980.

23. *American Banker*, 9 March 1981. The small banks achieved partial success when the OCC announced that it planned to lower its standards for small banks. *American Banker*, 26 March 1981.

24. American Bankers Association (1981); *American Banker*, 26 March 1980.

25. *American Banker*, 27 April and 12 June 1981.

26. FFIEC (1980); *ABA Banking Journal*, **74** (4), 1982; *American Banker*, 18 June and 22 June 1981. The FDIC did not agree with the Council's recommendation to include subordinated debt and limited life preferred stock in the definition of capital because these issues lacked permanence. They therefore considered them insufficient protection against losses and unforeseen events.

27. *Mid-Continent Banker*, February 1982; *Federal Reserve Bulletin*, January 1982.

28. Solomon (1982).

29. The new definition of bank capital included primary and secondary capital. Primary capital consisted of common stock, perpetual preferred stock, surplus undivided profits, mandatory convertible instruments (debt that must be convertible into stock or repaid with proceeds from equity), reserves for loan losses, and other capital reserves. These items were treated as permanent forms of capital because they were not subject to redemption or retirement. Secondary capital consisted of non-permanent forms of equity such as limited-life or redeemable preferred stock and bank subordinated debt. These items were deemed non-permanent since they were subject to redemption or retirement. Keeley (1988).

30. For community banks, which were defined as organizations with assets under $1 billion, the minimum primary capital-to-asset ratio was set at 6 per cent, while the minimum total capital-to-asset ratio was set at 6.5 per cent. For regional banks, which were defined as organizations with assets from $1-$15 billion, minimum primary capital was set at 5 per cent of assets, while minimum total capital requirements were set at 5.5 per cent. Historically, regulators relied on a peer group evaluation of capital adequacy that was deficient on at least two accounts: half the banks in a peer group were by definition always undercapitalized; and since the ratio was floating, there was never a clear signal what the adequate ratio was. Gehlen (1983).

31. FFIEC (1980).
32. Federal Deposit Insurance Corporation (1980); *Economic Review*, Federal Reserve Bank of Atlanta, 1982.
33. *Florida Banker*, April 1982.
34. Gehlen (1983).
35. *United States Banker*, January 1984; *National Journal*, 17 December 1983.
36. *Economic Review*, Federal Reserve Bank of Atlanta, 1982; *Florida Banker*, April 1982. According to John Ryan, Director of the Division of Bank Supervision at the Fed, 'Now this policy has changed in two ways: the Fed will be pushing harder on the very large banks to improve their capital positions, and the smaller banks will be permitted to reduce their ratios somewhat.' The OCC felt similarly that smaller banks had demonstrated resilience and strength. *United States Banker*, April 1982; *United States Banker*, December 1982.
37. Wall (1983).
38. For an early warning, see *American Banker*, 31 August 1981.
39. The FDIC refused to include other elements, such as subordinated debt and limited-life preferred stock. The reason for the FDIC's position was that both those components of capital lacked permanence and thus they were considered insufficient to protect against unforeseen events. Fed. Reg. 62963 (1981); *United States Banker*, April 1982; *American Banker*, 3 August 1981; *United States Banker*, January 1984.
40. *ABA Banking Journal*, 1982.
41. Statement of Policy on Capital Adequacy, 46 Fed. Reg. 62693 (1981). A threshold level of equity capital at 6 per cent of adjusted total assets and a minimum of 5 per cent was established for all banks. See for example *Federal Bar & News Journal*, 35/4, 1988; *American Banker*, 3 December 1981; *ABA Banking Journal*, April 1982.
42. *Bankers Magazine*, January/February 1982.
43. *Economic Review*, Federal Reserve Bank of Atlanta, 1982; *Florida Banker*, April 1982; *Bankers Magazine*, January/February 1982.
44. Noonan and Fetner (1983).
45. *United States Banker*, April 1982.
46. *American Banker*, 11 February 1983.
47. *CQ*, 15 January 1988.
48. *International Financial Markets and Related Matters*, 21 December 1983.
49. *Global Economic Outlook*, 10 January 1983.
50. *National Journal*, 19 March 1983.
51. *International Financial Markets and Related Problems*, 2 February 1983; *International Debt*, 17 February 1983.
52. As quoted in *CQ*, 19 February 1983.
53. *CQ*, 15 January 1983.
54. *National Journal*, 19 March 1983.
55. *International Debt*, 15 February 1983.
56. *International Financial Markets and Related Problems*, 2 February 1983; *American Banker*, 3 February and 11 February 1983.
57. *International Debt*, 14, 15, 17 February 1983; *International Financial Markets and Related Matters*.
58. *International Financial Markets and Related Problems*, 2 February 1983.
59. Ibid.; see also the statement by Volcker in *International Debt*, 17 February 1983.
60. Ibid.
61. Statement by C.T. Conover, Comptroller of the Currency, *International Debt*, 17 February 1983.
62. Ibid.
63. Hon. J. Charles Partee, Member, Board of Governors of the Federal Reserve System in *International Debt*, 14, 15, 17 February 1983; *International Financial Markets and Related*

Matters.

64. The five points were:
    1. Strengthening the existing programme of country risk examination and evaluation
    2. Increasing the disclosure of banks' country exposures
    3. Establishing a system of special reserves on problem foreign loans
    4. Promulgating regulations to account for rescheduling fees over the life of a foreign loan
    5. Strengthening the international cooperation with foreign bank lenders and through the IMF

65. *International Financial Markets and Related Problems*, 2 February 1983.

66. See for example the Statement by Peter C. Read, Executive Vice President, First National Bank of Boston, on behalf of the Bankers' Association for Foreign Trade, in *International Financial Markets and Related Matters.*

67. Ibid.

68. See SR No.122, 1983; HR No.175, 1983; *American Banker*, 9 February 1983.

69. *Financial Times*, 18 April 1983.

70. *Bretton Woods Agreements Act Amendments and International Lending Supervision*, 16 May 1983; Bench and Sable (1986), *North Carolina Journal of International Law and Commercial Regulation.*

71. *International Recovery and Financial Stability Act Report*, 16 May 1983.

72. *Bretton Woods Agreements Act Amendments and International Lending Supervision*, 16 May 1983.

73. Ibid.

74. 679 F.2d 674 (5th Cir. 1983).

75. *Bretton Woods Agreements, Act, Amendments, and International Lending Supervision*, 16 May 1983.

76. Statement of Karin Lissakers, *Review of the International Lending Supervision Act of 1983*, 25 June 1986.

77. *CQ*, 14 May 1983.

78. *Bretton Woods Agreements Act Amendments and International Lending Supervision*, 16 May 1983.

79. Joint press release of the Comptroller of the Currency and Federal Reserve Board. At a minimum these banks were expected to maintain a ratio of primary capital to total assets of at least 5 per cent, the same level that regional banks were required to hold since 1981. *Washington Financial Reports*, 20 June 1983; *American Banker*, 14 June 1983.

80. *Banking Expansion Reporter*, 4 July 1983.

81. *United States Banker*, January 1984.

82. The banks with ratios below the Fed's minimum guideline were: Citicorp (4.67 per cent), Bank America Corp. (4.79 per cent), Bankers Trust New York Corp (4.79 per cent), Irving Bank Corp. (4.83 per cent), and Chase Manhattan Corp. (4.98 per cent). *American Banker*, 27 June 1983.

83. Federal Reserve Board, Division of Banking Regulation and Supervision, 7 November 1983.

84. *CQ*, 7 May and 11 June 1983.

85. *CQ*, 23 July 1983.

86. The vote was 217-211. *CQ*, 6 August 1983.

87. Bench and Sable (1986); Liechtenstein (1985). As the Report that accompanied the Senate's version of the Act stated: 'The Committee also believes clarification of existing authority is needed because the recent decision of the U.S. Court of Appeals (Fifth Circuit) in First National Bank of Bellaire v. Comptroller of the Currency has clouded the authority of the bank regulatory agencies to exercise their independent discretion in establishing and regulating the maintenance of appropriate levels of capital.' SR No. 122, 16 May 1983.

88. In essence, the directive stated that if banking institutions fail to maintain capital at or above minimum required levels, the regulator may issue a directive requiring the institution to submit and then adhere to a plan describing the means and timing by which the bank will

achieve the required capital levels.

89. Bench and Sable (1986); Liechtenstein (1985).
90. Federal Reserve Board, *Press Release*, 6 July 1984.
91. With regard to definitional differences, the biggest among the regulators was the treatment of subordinated debt. The Fed's and OCC's interests are geared towards the protection of depositors and subordinated debt can be used to pay off depositors. However, loan losses can be charged against debt only if the bank is already in liquidation, so its usefulness is understandably limited from the FDIC's, the insurer's, point of view. See *United States Banker*, January 1984.
92. Under the proposal by the two agencies *all* banks they regulate would be required to meet a minimum acceptable ratio of total capital to total assets of 6 per cent. The minimum acceptable level of primary capital to assets would be 5.5 per cent. *American Banker*, 10 July 1984.
93. *American Banker*, 24 July 1983.
94. *Banking Expansion Reporter*, 6 August 1984; *Bank Executives Report*, 15 August 1984.
95. *American Banker*, 30 October and 19 November 1984; *Business Week*, 3 December 1984.
96. *Washington Financial Reports*, 18 February 1985; *NYT*, 11 February 1985.
97. *Washington Financial Reports*, 18 March 1985; *Banking Expansion Reporter*, 1 April 1985.
98. *NYT*, 2 March 1985; *Banking Expansion Reporter*, 18 March 1985. See also Gilbert, Stone and Trebing (1985); Wall (1989); *Economic Review*, Federal Reserve Bank of Atlanta, March/April 1989.
99. *WSJ*, 4 March 1985.
100. Gilbert, Stone and Trebing (1985).
101. *Fortune*, 7 January 1985; *Business Week*, 28 January 1985; *American Banker*, 25 January 1985; Mingo (1985).
102. Off-balance sheet activities had been the concern of bank regulators for quite some time. See *American Banker*, 29 March 1985; *United States Banker*, January 1984; *Bankers Monthly Magazine*, 15 December 1985; U.S. General Accounting Office (1988); Banca Nazionale del Lavoro, *Quarterly Review*; Khambata, (1989).
103. *Savings Institutions*, August 1985; Salomon Brothers Inc., 12 September 1985.
104. *Risk-Based Capital Requirements for Banks and Bank Holding Companies*, 30 April 1987.
105. *WSJ*, 19 July 1985; *American Banker*, 12 September 1985.
106. Wall (1989).
107. Federal Reserve Board Press Release, 24 January 1986.
108. *WSJ*, 16 January and 17 January 1986. For the reaction of the private sector, see *Business Week*, 3 February 1986.
109. *American Banker*, 11 July 1986 and 5 January 1987.
110. Testimony by Paul Volcker to the Subcommittee on General Oversight and Investigation, House Banking Committee, 30 April 1987.

8. Capital Adequacy and the Politics of Change

THE SECOND STAGE OF CONFLICT: THE POLITICS OF CHANGE

While the close link between aspects of domestic and international bank regulation had been appreciated publicly in Congress only since 1983, it had long been recognized by bank regulators in the United States and other major industrial countries.[1] By the time ILSA directed U.S. bank regulators to seek an international agreement on the harmonization of capital adequacy standards, an international institutional framework for such an agreement already existed and the issue of capital adequacy had already been raised on numerous occasions. The institutional framework that examined these questions was the Basle Committee on Bank Regulation and Supervisory Practices, also known as the Cooke Committee (for its second chairman, Peter W. Cooke).[2] This committee was established in 1974 by the central bank governors of the G-10 countries plus Switzerland and Luxembourg, under the administrative auspices of the Bank for International Settlements (BIS) in Basle, Switzerland.[3]

In the early 1970s, high inflation and increasingly volatile exchange rates, a downturn in the business cycles of the major industrialized countries, and the possibility that some countries might fail to honour their debts had undermined public confidence in financial markets — both domestic and international.[4] When confidence was further eroded by several well-publicized bank failures during 1974 which had international repercussions, bank regulators for the first time publicly recognized the need for international cooperation in the field of bank supervision.[5] Analogous to developments in U.S. domestic financial markets, regulators in the major industrialized countries attributed the bank failures to the fact that bank supervision had not kept pace with the increasing global integration of financial markets. In the words of Peter Cooke,

> There was in effect a supervisory vacuum in this new global market which needed to be filled. Neither the supervisors, nor indeed the banks themselves, had fully appreciated the degree to which the banking environment was changing in character and the new increased risks involved in international business.

Supervisors were still very much domestically oriented within the framework of different national banking systems.[6]

Turning briefly to the operational aspects of the Basle Committee, each nation has two representatives on the committee: one from its central bank, one from its bank supervisory authority.[7] The representatives meet approximately three to four times a year. The Secretariat of BIS serves as a staff for the Basle Committee. In essence, the committee acts as an advisory body whose recommendations require unanimous agreement of all its representatives. It has no power to require implementation of its agreements in the laws or regulations of its member nations. However, U.S. federal bank supervisory agencies, as well as bank supervisory agencies in other countries, have committed themselves to working to implement committee principles.[8]

The objectives of the Basle Committee are to provide a forum for bank supervisory officials from the major industrialized countries to exchange information about their respective regulatory structures, and to strengthen collaboration among national authorities in their supervision of international banking. In the committee's first decade of existence, representatives of its member countries supported the following principles for supervising banks' international operations, in the hopes of offering greater stability to the international banking system:

1. supervisory responsibility for banks' foreign offices should be allocated by agreement between parent and host-country supervisors
2. parent supervisory authorities should supervise their banks on a consolidated basis, thereby including all the business of a financial institution, whether at home or abroad
3. given the interdependence and shared responsibilities of parent and host supervisory authorities, each should identify the extent and adequacy of supervision practised by its counterpart authority
4. supervisors should identify the overall structure of a bank's organization to ensure that all its components are supervised
5. banks and supervisors should consider well-proven and committee-recommended practices when managing foreign exchange and country risks in international lending.

These principles are embedded in two agreements, referred to as the original and the revised Basle Concordat. The first concordat, adopted in December of 1975, represented an important step towards greater international supervisory cooperation.[9] However, it suffered from a number of deficiencies, which became apparent after 1978 and culminated in the conflict among regulatory authorities over culpability in the collapse of Banco Ambrosiano's Luxembourg subsidiary in 1983.[10] Regulators reacted quickly and adopted a revised concordat, with more precise guidelines for supervision, in June 1983.[11]

However, while the committee members recognized the need for international cooperation among regulators, especially in distributing supervisory responsibilities for the activities of international banks across national regulatory systems, they were still sceptical of the prospects of harmonizing regulatory standards across countries. In the words of George Blunden, governor of the Bank of England and the committee's first chairman:

> In spite of the trend towards integration of banking systems across international frontiers, there are still...great variations in national banking systems. Each country's supervisory system has had to be accommodated within each country's political and legal systems and an attempt to integrate it with the systems of other countries could often run into severe constitutional difficulties.... Even if these distinctive national characteristics did not exist, it would not be possible to move towards the integration of national banking supervisory systems into an internationally coherent system, without the creation of a new supra-national supervisory authority. The banking system of a country is central to the management and the efficiency of its economy; its supervision will inevitably be a jealously guarded national prerogative. Its subordination to an international authority is a highly unlikely development, which would require a degree of political commitment which neither exists nor is conceivable in the near future.[12]

Turning to the issue of capital adequacy, multilateral efforts to arrive at a convergence of capital adequacy standards among the leading industrial nations started during the late 1970s.[13] In fact, at the same time that U.S. regulators were beginning to reconsider the domestic structure of capital adequacy regulation, they were also starting to exchange information with bank regulators from other countries about different approaches to such regulation.[14] The reason for this was two-fold. First, other countries had experienced a similar decline in their banks' capital ratios and either had already taken preventive measures to halt any further erosion or were about to do so.[15] Second, U.S. regulators and banks were aware that any unilateral move to strengthen U.S. capital requirements would result in competitive inequalities for U.S. banks.[16]

In a communique issued by the BIS in 1980, the Governors of the G-10 central banks reaffirmed the cardinal importance which they attached to the maintenance of sound banking standards, particularly with respect to capital adequacy, liquidity and concentration of risks.[17] This consensus among the central bankers reflected the same concerns which were shared by U.S. policymakers: the fear of financial crisis arising from the worldwide erosion in capital ratios, and the desire to eliminate competitive asymmetries arising from divergent national capital standards. Member institutions of the committee were increasingly concerned with the continuing erosion of bank capital on a worldwide basis, and commenced the preparation of a report to the G-10 central bank governors regarding bank capital adequacy in relation to the international business of banks. The committee was of the view that further erosion of bank capital ratios was undesirable and that, in principle, it was desirable to achieve greater approximation in the levels of capital employed by major international banks.

While realizing that it would be unrealistic to attempt any formal legal harmonization of capital adequacy internationally, the committee did see its role as trying to achieve a 'greater convergence among its members with regard to national definitions of bank capital for supervisory purposes...' due to 'the undesirability of any further erosion of banks' capital ratios.'[18] The main thrust behind this conclusion was prudential concern for the safety and soundness of major international banks and the international banking system.

In addition to its immediate concerns, the Basle Committee also set an agenda for further work in the capital adequacy area. The committee pointed to the 'desirability, in principle, of greater homogeneity in the levels of capital employed by major banks operating internationally,' and agreed to undertake further work with a view toward achieving greater convergence among its members with regard to national definitions of bank capital for supervisory purposes.[19]

In June of 1982, the year in which the extent of the debt crisis would be fully appreciated by policymakers, the Basle Committee presented a study to the G-10 central bank governors, who endorsed the committee's main conclusion: 'that in the current and prospective environment, further erosion of capital ratios should be resisted, and that in the absence of common standards of capital adequacy, supervisors should not allow the capital resources of their major banks to deteriorate from the present levels, whatever those levels may be.'[20] In addition, while the regulators recognized that capital requirements differed across nations, both in terms of techniques of measurement and definitions of capital used, they pledged to continue to address some of the more technical aspects of capital adequacy. One aim was 'to work towards a common view among member countries of the main constituent elements of capital....'[21] Another important element was the analysis of different kinds of ratios (risk-asset vs. gearing vs. large loan-exposure ratios), with the goal of assessing their usefulness and 'mak[ing] recommendations for the application of such ratios within the supervisory arrangements of member countries.'[22]

Thus, as early as 1980, there was widespread consensus among the G-10 regulators that capital adequacy was one of the central elements in guaranteeing the stability and safety of individual banks as well as the domestic and international banking systems.[23] In addition, most regulators were acutely aware of the fact that divergent capital requirements across different countries would have adverse prudential effects, as the weaker standards of one nation drove other nations to lower their standards in an effort to protect the competitive standing of their banks. As one supervisor stated, 'In such a situation both the ability to maintain capital adequacy and the wish to do so could be reduced.'[24]

However, despite the fact that the committee members agreed on the general need to address the issue on an international scale, each country differed in its approach to the issue of capital adequacy in three critical respects:

1. how to define and value capital
2. how to develop a formula that measures capital's adequacy
3. the minimum level of capital considered 'adequate'.[25]

The fact that all three issues had to be resolved among the 12 countries before they could achieve their goal of a common standard that provided a level playing field for banks competing in the global financial market made it an almost insurmountable task. Given the long historical tradition of each country's financial structure and the legal and fiscal differences among them, it was clear to the committee that individual nations were not about to give up their national supervisory systems.

Just as in the case of domestic regulation of capital adequacy, ILSA also proved to be a major stimulus with regard to the international efforts at capital adequacy regulation and their harmonization across the major industrialized countries. During the ILSA hearings in 1983, a clear congressional and agency consensus developed on the fact that the viability of the U.S. banking system could no longer be ensured solely through domestic regulation, and that the fundamental objectives of regulatory supervision in the area of capital adequacy could only be achieved through global regulatory cooperation. First, to ensure that banking crises in other countries would not spill over into the U.S., ILSA directed the Chairman of the Board of Governors of the Federal Reserve System and the Secretary of the Treasury to 'encourage governments, central banks, and regulatory authorities of other major banking countries to work toward maintaining, and where appropriate strengthening, the capital bases of banking institutions involved in international lending.'[26] Second, in response to pressure by the private sector and statements by the regulatory agencies during the hearings, Congress had become increasingly sensitized to the competitive inequalities that might arise from divergent bank regulations in an increasingly integrated global banking market. Representatives from the private sector complained that any unilateral imposition of higher capital ratios would prove to be a major hindrance for American banks trying to compete in international markets. Fed Chairman Paul Volcker stated,

> There are intense competitive pressures in these markets, and this is an area where it is important, to the degree possible, to have a common international approach....I would also note that — not as any kind of excuse, but as a fact — banks undoubtedly have felt under very heavy pressure internationally, and carrying more capital is a cost. From the viewpoint of an individual institution, if it feels its competitors, particularly in this business which is literally worldwide, have a competitive advantage, this is not an atmosphere in which it is easy to get capital increases....It is an area that has international as well as domestic dimensions.[27]

In response to these pressures, Congress asked regulators not only to ensure that other countries would raise their capital standards to avoid a collapse of the international banking system, but also to seek an international agreement on capital adequacy standards within the framework of the Basle Committee, and to report back to Congress within a year on the progress towards such an agreement.

The pressure that ILSA exerted upon U.S. regulators was thus not only reflected at the domestic level, culminating in the harmonization of capital adequacy rules for all U.S. banks. U.S. regulators were also increasingly pressing the other members of the Basle Committee to continue to search for ways to arrive at an international agreement to resolve the same issues at the global level. During 1983, such efforts were reflected in the committee's agreement to develop a 'general framework' for measuring capital. As members were quick to point out, this framework would not replace individual national standards. Rather, the framework would be used to compare and analyse capital positions of international banks by means of the different approaches used in the committee's member countries. For example, the framework included several alternative definitions of capital, such as strict vs. loose, reflecting the variety of definitions among members.[28] In calculating the capital positions of the major banks in each member country, the committee also assigned various weighting schemes to different classes of assets.

The study was conducted with two aims in mind. The first was to determine the usefulness of international comparisons of bank capital. Second, while the members were aware that this particular effort could not result in any narrowing of national capital adequacy standards, they did not lose sight of this long-term goal. By engaging in this comparative effort the members were hoping that they would be able to identify the specific differences among the G-10 countries, revealing the exact degree and nature of the modifications necessary to arrive at an eventual narrowing of different capital adequacy standards.[29]

Referring specifically to the mandate given to the Fed and the Treasury by Congress, the G-10 central bank governors subsequently approved further work by the committee toward a framework of 'functional equivalence' of capital measurement.[30] The different mechanisms by which supervisors in different countries measured capital was considered one major obstacle to an internationally coordinated and consistent increase in capital standards. Thus, it was hoped that the work of the committee would in part overcome national differences and make possible the development of a common definition of capital and common capital adequacy measurement methods. In September of that year, the committee presented the G-10 governors with a framework for measuring capital adequacy that had the broad support of all committee members. It was subsequently approved by the governors. However, as the report stressed, 'this framework is still at an early stage of development.'[31]

By 1985, the issue of capital adequacy had become the top priority of the Basle Committee, and concerns about an increasingly integrated global financial market without any complementary regulatory framework in this particular area were now voiced publicly by the committee and individual central banks.[32] Work among regulators toward a generally accepted concept of capital, its adequacy, and its measurement continued throughout 1985.[33] But while members could agree that there were indeed various mechanisms for measuring capital, this only highlighted the diversity of the national systems and the difficulties in devising meaningful and acceptable common standards.[34]

Two additional factors further complicated the work of the committee. First, as it became increasingly clear that regulators were determined to come to some form of agreement to further strengthen, and at the same time harmonize, national capital adequacy regulation, the respective domestic regulatory authorities came under increasing pressure from their banking constituencies not to adopt any kind of regulation that would adversely affect the competitive position of *their* banking system in global financial markets.[35] A second factor was the recognition that no matter what the final agreement on capital adequacy might look like, it could not avoid the increasing importance of off-balance sheet activities. The risk-weighing approach to capital adequacy had been long established in most European member countries. When the U.S. authorities, in early 1986, announced that they were ready to introduce a risk-weighing measure of capital adequacy into their own system, it proved to be an important step towards a common standard.[36] In fact, the U.S. domestic proposal specifically notes that '[I]n addition, adoption of this proposal would begin to move capital adequacy policies in the United States more closely in line with those of other major industrial countries.'[37] But while this promoted further convergence on the more general and broader aspects of the capital adequacy issue, since all G-10 countries by now either had introduced or were seriously considering risk-weighing approaches, it also posed a new and 'urgent challenge to existing supervisory methods and procedures.'[38] By 1984, the committee had already commenced a survey to determine the extent to which off-balance sheet risks were being captured in the G-10 countries' supervisory mechanisms and the degree to which they were subject to capital requirements. It soon became clear that there were significant differences in the national treatment of many of the more traditional off-balance sheet activities, and that formal systems for measuring capital adequacy did not extend to the new forms of off-balance sheet activities. These findings would further complicate the formation of an internationally acceptable measure of capital and its adequacy, as perceptions of different assets' riskiness were likely to differ across countries. A preliminary report was released in March of 1986, and though no specific capital requirements for various risk categories were prescribed, the central bankers emphasized that they had arrived at a series of common definitions for the plethora of off-balance sheet instruments and the degree of risk they entailed.[39]

By the end of 1986, it was generally accepted by policymakers that global regulatory harmonization was required to stem the increasing tendency of private actors to engage in regulatory arbitrage. At the same time, regulators were well aware of the pressures on national policymakers to engage in competitive deregulation in a global financial market characterized by different national regulatory regimes.[40] A widely publicized report by the BIS that explored the emerging global financial market confirmed these concerns: 'as markets become more integrated, there's a good case for supervision of these activities and for closer cooperation and approach to the supervision of these markets.'[41] It was this pressure that led to progress toward developing a consensus in member countries on the technique for measuring capital adequacy.

There existed a broad agreement in the Basle Committee on the necessity to strengthen as well as harmonize capital ratios across the G-10 countries. In fact, through its efforts the committee had, by the end of 1986, succeeded in the formulation of a complex definition of capital that all countries agreed on. The definition contained a variety of characteristics that were used in some, though not all, countries' regulatory systems, reflecting the increasing willingness of members to contemplate changes in their own system in the interest of greater convergence among the countries represented on the committee.

When banking supervisors from around the world met for their fourth international conference in October 1986, capital adequacy was the major theme. Stressing the importance of convergence towards higher standards of capital adequacy of major banks, H.J. Müller, Chairman of the Basle Committee and Executive Director of the Netherlands central bank, presented the current status of the Basle Committee's work on the issue of capital adequacy.[42] In general, there was broad agreement among the regulators on 'the importance of a high degree of supervisory co-operation in an increasingly global marketplace.'[43] Stressing the central importance of capital adequacy, the statement continued that 'there was a broad measure of agreement on what should constitute the constituents of capital...[and] that the risk ratio approach was the preferred approach.'[44]

However, while a model for convergence was beginning to take shape, there was no clear sense of how to transform the technical agreements achieved in the committee into practical applications in the respective banking systems. At a meeting in Basle in early 1986, central bankers commented that it seemed unlikely that standard capital requirements would be introduced. The development of actual regulations would have to remain at the discretion of the national authorities. Given the committee's lack of political authority and inability to enforce new rules on the maintenance of capital, the political initiative had to come from individual members. However, national regulators, for the most part, faced considerable opposition from strongly entrenched interests in their respective banking industries, since any change in the regulatory structure, and especially a tightening of regulations, would result in new costs to the industry.[45] The only members of the Basle Committee that would likely take the necessary political initiative were those who either would face little domestic opposition to a change in capital adequacy standards or actually had an interest in an international agreement.

The U.S. was such a member, and had throughout the exercise been a strong supporter of the Basle Committee's efforts. More specifically, at the domestic level the U.S. had little to lose in proposing new and more stringent capital levels that would force the private sector to adapt; at the international level, the U.S. regulators actually had a great interest in promoting an international agreement. With respect to the former, and as discussed above, U.S. regulators themselves were in the midst of reconsidering their own measurement techniques and had put forward their own risk-based proposal to the banking community for comment in 1986. In fact, when the U.S. developed its original proposal, the regulators deliberately considered the work done in Basle and incorporated some elements into their own framework in order to minimize the differences. Similarly, since the middle of 1985, the Federal Reserve and the FDIC had been publicly discussing the idea of implementing even more stringent capital regulations in the U.S. that would raise the ratio for total capital-to-assets to 9 per cent.[46]

As to the international level, broadening the debate to include the international dimension of bank regulation represented little, if any, political cost. In fact, since the domestic conflict was already fully underway, U.S. regulators had a great interest in promoting an international agreement. One of the arguments banks made in resisting a renewed round of capital adequacy regulation was that it would deepen the competitive inequality among banks' operations internationally. By seeking such an agreement, regulators would be able to counter these charges by banks. Congress, too, with the implementation of ILSA, had given the regulators a mandate and had urged regulators to seek an international agreement. Moreover, regulators were required to report back periodically on the progress toward such an agreement.[47] During these hearings, regulators came under increasing pressure from both the private sector and Congress to ensure that an international and domestic agreement on capital adequacy would be reached in congruence. The private sector and the legislature insisted that U.S. regulatory policy could not be conducted in isolation from other national banking systems. As one banker put it, '[W]hile capital is important it should be emphasized that American banks must compete with banks around the world. Some of these banks have no or low capital requirements. It is essential that the U.S. banking system is competitive in the world marketplace in order to finance U.S. exports and U.S. industry in general.'[48]

Given the domestic pressure exerted upon the agencies, U.S. regulators, and especially the Federal Reserve, which had been very active in Basle, became increasingly impatient with the slow progress of the Basle Committee. By the latter half of 1986, the issue of competitive inequality had become so important at the domestic level that it was difficult to conceive of a policy solution that would separate the domestic regulation of U.S. capital standards from the international efforts to not only raise the levels, but to harmonize them as well.[49] To further its interest in the Basle Committee, the U.S. needed an ally that would support its call for urgent action.

Throughout the international negotiations, the Bank of England had also been a strong proponent of an agreement among the G-10 countries. London, together with New York, still represented a major centre of activity for multinational banks, and a severe crisis in global financial markets would have especially strong negative repercussions for the city. In addition, just as in the U.S., British regulators were in the midst of revising their own system to incorporate a wider range of off-balance sheet activities, and were eager both to move forward with the implementation of a revised rule and to address the issue of competitive inequality.[50] In the fall of 1986, regulators in the U.S. and the U.K. agreed to postpone further work on their own national proposals and to consider — parallel to the ongoing discussions in Basle — the development of a common approach to the issue of capital adequacy. Given the importance of New York and London as international banking centres, regulators felt that an agreement on a uniform risk-based capital framework implemented in both countries would represent a major step forward in international convergence.[51]

A series of confidential, bilateral negotiations was concluded as early as January 1987, when the U.S. authorities and the Bank of England agreed on a definition of primary capital and capital adequacy assessment.[52] Officials from the regulatory authorities in both countries hailed the agreement as a 'landmark in international supervisory cooperation' and a step toward international consistency, which would minimize the distortion in international competition.[53] One reason for this rapid convergence of supervisory perspectives was that the Fed had considered, and thus was familiar with, the risk-based capital approach the Bank of England had adopted when it revised its own risk-weighing scheme in early 1986.[54] However, observers also admitted that no one had expected the conclusion of an agreement within such a short time period. They concurred that it reflected the concern and the increasing urgency felt by regulatory authorities in the two countries over the soundness of global financial markets, as well as pressure from the private sectors in the two countries to deal with the competitive inequalities arising from regulatory inequities in a single global financial market.[55]

There were four central elements in the U.S.-U.K. accord where commonality was established: the definition of the primary capital base of banking institutions; the deductions to be made from primary capital in computing a bank's capital base; the weighing scheme for risky assets and off-balance sheet activities; and a ratio of primary capital to weigh its risk asset. Although a precise figure for the capital-to-asset ratio was not made public at the time, the regulators indicated that they would arrive at a common minimum ratio and make it public in the near future.

The conclusion of the agreement called for 'the convergence of supervisory policy and capital adequacy assessments among countries with major banking centers' and invited other countries to join them on an individual basis.[56] At the same time, the U.S.-U.K. accord also specified that if the Basle Committee did not reach a prompt agreement among the major industrial countries, the U.S. and the U.K. would proceed alone with their bilateral harmonization plan.[57] The agreement was to take effect in May 1987, after a period of comment in each country.

Not all member countries of the Basle Committee, let alone the committee

itself, were enthusiastic about the bilateral accord between the U.S. and the
U.K.. According to Peter Cooke, the agreement at first sight appeared to be
counterproductive to the multilateral objectives of the Basle Committee.[58]
In fact, Markus Lusser, the Vice Chairman of the governing board of the
Swiss National Bank, saw it as

> ...political pressure by the economic superpowers....[A]t least in the representative of
> a small country the agreement between the United Kingdom and the United States
> arouses somewhat mixed feelings. In light of the urgency of the problem, the
> reassurance originating from the agreement between the two countries to come to an
> accord in the concrete case of regulations of capital adequacy is acceptable. However,
> should the example set a precedent and the strategy of the two powers be extended
> to other fields of harmonizing banking supervision — as a substitute, so to speak, for
> internationally negotiated compromises — then the willingness to co-operate
> internationally could suffer damage in the long run. In view of the problems that
> need to be solved, this would be a harmful development.[59]

The U.S. and the U.K., however, not only stuck to their accord but they
increased the pressure on other countries to join the agreement. Both
countries indicated that they might take action against foreign banks that did
not comply with the agreement. For example, in a statement to Congress,
Paul Volcker noted that the U.S. had

> ...not applied extraterritorially U.S. bank capital standards on a consolidated basis to
> foreign banking organizations seeking to expand in the United States. However, the
> U.S.-U.K. risk-based capital proposal represents a step forward toward a more
> consistent and equitable international norm for assessing capital adequacy. For this
> reason, we believe such a framework can, under appropriate circumstances, assist in
> evaluating the capital positions of foreign banks trying to acquire U.S. institutions.[60]

Asked specifically about the possibility of applying 'mandated reciprocity',
Volcker suggested that U.S. regulators 'could move in that direction.'[61]

Pressure was specifically directed at the Japanese, whose inclusion in the
agreement was considered essential in order to get a level playing field in
global financial markets. 'If I were a Japanese banker or bank supervisor
I would be a little worried about being thought to be lagging behind',
commented the head of banking supervision at the Bank of England, and
added 'I would be very disappointed if this initiative were to founder on a
negative reaction from the Japanese.'[62]

Congressional and private sector reaction was mixed in the U.S.
Regulators admitted that while the majority of the 14,000 banks in the U.S.
would not be affected by the plan, some of the 50 largest banks might be
adversely affected as they would have to raise more capital to meet the
standard, which could depress those banks' stock prices and increase
investor uncertainty. Thus, some banks rejected the new proposal as they

had done with previous ones, arguing that 'the banking industry is already sufficiently capitalized.'[63] Other banks were more cautious. '[I]t is a good start, a necessary start', said one banker, but noting that the agreement was bilateral and not multilateral, he stated, 'until it goes further there will continue to be inequities.'[64]   The private sector's critique did not go unnoticed in Congress, especially among representatives from the states of New York and California. In his introductory statement at a hearing on the agreement before the Subcommittee on General Oversight and Investigations, Chairman Carroll Hubbard noted that 'sectors of the banking industry have expressed serious reservations about the proposal....'[65]

But regulators were determined to go ahead with the implementation of the proposal at the domestic level, despite potential anticompetitive effects. During the same hearing, Volcker reiterated the Fed's

> ...interest in the competitiveness of U.S. banks. Only a strong, competitive and profitable banking system can remain healthy in the long run and fulfill the strategic role banks play in our economic and financial system. In considering the issue of competitiveness, it is possible that banks that are permitted to operate with lower capital levels may have a competitive advantage...[b]ut from the standpoint of appropriate public policy those considerations have to be balanced against the long-range safety and soundness of the banking system.[66]

RESOLUTION: THE BASLE AGREEMENT AND THE GLOBAL REGULATION OF CAPITAL STANDARDS

The Anglo-American determination to go ahead with a set of common capital rules intensified their diplomatic efforts to persuade other members of the Basle Committee to join the agreement. At the same time that the two countries publicly declared that if necessary they would implement the new regulatory scheme on a bilateral basis and retaliate against foreign banks that did not adhere to their standards, the U.S. and the U.K. intensified their informal contacts with other members of the Basle Committee to examine the possibility of a broader agreement. In order to achieve such an agreement it was clear to the American and British regulators that some compromise was necessary. Thus, they indicated to the other countries, both in private and in public, that they were willing to make some adjustments to accommodate other regulatory regimes. For example, Gerald Corrigan, President of the Federal Reserve Bank of New York, which had been instrumental in achieving the accord, stated only a few weeks after the agreement that 'it is an approach which can be easily adapted to future developments as they occur.'[67]

The existence of the bilateral agreement between the U.S. and the U.K., and the possibility of retaliatory action by the two countries, allowed other members of the Basle Committee to take the political initiative both at home and abroad. At the domestic level, a debate over restructuring capital adequacy regulation was justifiable given the negative repercussions it might have on the private sector. At the international level, the Basle Committee and its member countries saw their reputation and central role in the field of global bank cooperation and regulation challenged, if not undermined, and consequently intensified their activity. Failure to reach an agreement would cast doubt on both the institutional capacity of the committee to function effectively on future issues, and on previous agreements, such as the two concordats.

The committee responded — as the U.S. and the U.K. had hoped it would — and accelerated its own negotiations on capital adequacy in order to regain the initiative it had lost. It immediately set to work on integrating the U.S-U.K. proposals into the framework which had been developed in Basle, with a self-imposed deadline of the end of 1987.[68]

At its first meeting in 1987, the committee decided to use the U.S.-U.K. agreement as a basis and expand the agreement to encompass the other member countries. In addition, the committee laid out a timetable, which was endorsed by the governors, that would produce a multilateral agreement by the end of the year. This was a tremendous challenge, given the complexity of designing an internationally acceptable definition of capital. As mentioned previously, each country had its own definition of regulatory capital. Each of these concepts reflected a different set of country-specific accounting practices, banking activities, and supervisory philosophies. Moreover, the slightest change in the definition of capital would greatly affect measured capital ratios within the banking system and thus alter the market's perception of the financial strength of the banking organization in that system.

Despite these difficulties, as a result of a meeting which took place in early April in Basle, U.S. regulators were cautiously optimistic that 'some countries are likely to adopt a scheme that is quite similar to this relatively soon.'[69] Canadian banks had already given a positive response and U.S. regulators also cited substantial progress with individual European nations and the European Community. The greatest challenge for the Basle Committee was to get an agreement with the Japanese. On the one hand, committee members realized that they needed to convince Japan, which by 1987 had become a formidable force in international financial markets, to be part of the agreement or risk a major backlash from the private sector in their own countries, complaining about competitive inequality, that would lead ultimately to a breakdown of the agreement.[70] On the other hand, there existed substantial differences, especially with regard to the definition of bank capital, between the Japanese and the other members of the committee. Japanese banks maintain sizeable unrealized gains on their equity positions. These unrealized gains have traditionally been realized when necessary to offset losses. In fact, Japanese regulators had recently introduced new capital guidelines to bring their capital standards more in line with those of the other major industrialized countries. The new guidelines also explicitly recognized these gains (also referred to as hidden reserves) as a form of capital and allowed banks to include 70 per cent of unrealized gains as capital.[71] Other countries on the committee did not recognize hidden reserves at all, which created a major obstacle to an early conclusion of an agreement.[72]   Still, U.S. regulators were cautiously optimistic that an agreement could be reached.

> I think they [the Japanese] understand it. The capital position of their banks is quite different, which is a complication, but I think it is really imperative that we reach greater international coordination...and Japan has to be a part of that....Whether they will adopt a full-blown system of this sort, in what time period, I would not hazard a guess. I think that will partly depend on whether some other countries will come along. I don't think that the Japanese in the end can be the odd man out.[73]

In the short term, however, tensions increased between the U.S. and Japan. Japanese authorities were under great pressure by their banks not to subscribe wholesale to the U.S.-U.K. agreement, which was considered unfair from the competitive perspective of the Japanese banking industry. In fact, Japanese banks went so far as to directly appeal to U.S. authorities. While recognizing the need for greater harmony in national bank regulations, the chairman of the Japanese Federation of Bankers Association argued that sufficient consideration must be given to conditions in every nation in working out regulations governing primary capital ratios. In a letter to the Fed on behalf of Japanese banks, he called for part of the value of banks' holdings of stocks and other securities to be included as capital.[74] At the same time, the Fed increased the pressure on the Japanese. Under a recent agreement between the U.S. and Japanese regulatory authorities on financial disclosure required for applications to set up subsidiaries in their respective countries, the Fed demanded that five Japanese banks supply such information. More importantly, the Fed asked the banks to furnish data on their capital structures in line with the capital adequacy rules and definitions of primary capital agreed upon by U.S. and U.K. bank regulators.[75] Faced with increasing U.S. pressure, Japan took the first, and major, step toward breaking the impasse when Toyoo Gyohten, vice minister for international finance, announced publicly that his country, in principle, had agreed to go along with the U.S.-U.K. accord.[76]

Several more meetings were held during the spring and summer of 1987, amidst ever-increasing concern by regulators over the rapid pace of structural change in global financial markets and their increasing inability to supervise the international activities of banks.[77]   According to the Annual Report of the BIS, the liberalization of national financial markets that had occurred since the early 1980s had not always had beneficial effects, and 'capital market liberalization may even have had harmful effects on the real economy.'[78]   Indicating the determination of the regulators to act in concert, the report concluded that these developments made it even more pressing that countries make only those regulatory responses which were achieved in a cooperative effort among the authorities.

At a meeting in June 1987, a new formula was proposed. Given the diversity of capital definition among the countries, the formula recognized shareholders' equity as the only and primary element in the definition of capital (termed core capital). At the same time, it allowed all other elements of capital admitted in the various national supervisory schemes to be recognized as supplementary or secondary capital. The amount of secondary capital was limited to 50 per cent of total capital.[79]   One element that was central to the success of this particular formula was its ability to account for the continued definitional differences among member countries. Basically, countries were not required to include within their own national definition all the elements that the formula contained. More specifically, in order to comply with the secondary capital requirement, countries were free to use as many or as few of the non-core elements as they wished. If they preferred, they could even use additional core capital to fulfill the requirement. In essence, the formula combined the regulatory consensus on the notion of core capital with the differences reflecting long-established national traditions of individual banking systems, and forged an acceptable compromise among the G-10 countries.

Given the substantial progress that was made throughout the spring and summer of 1987, the U.S. and British authorities decided to delay the implementation of their proposal to allow for a broader agreement by the Basle Committee members in the near future. As Paul Volcker said, during his last appearance as Chairman of the Federal Reserve before Congress,

> I would like to report we have a comprehensive international agreement. I cannot report that this morning. We were on the verge of an international agreement with the British. We have not pulled that off, for what I think is a constructive reason. We have a chance of getting a much broader agreement, and I would hope that by the end of the year, while a few difficult problems remain, my successor and the other banking agencies will come back to report that indeed we have a basic agreement on capital among virtually all major developed countries.[80]

Commenting specifically on Japan's attitude, Volcker agreed with the statement by Representative Schumer from New York that the Japanese have a 'real desire to accelerate things and be included in the system and not to take some temporary advantage on being outside the system.' And Volcker continued, 'I think it is going to be done. I am sorry I am not going to be here in this particular position, but I think it is going to be done. I think it is that close.'[81]

After further negotiation in the fall of 1987, compromises were also found on a number of other issues where national differences remained significant: a weighting scheme, an exact minimum ratio of capital, and a time frame for the implementation of the agreement. Policymakers also indicated that Japan was close to reaching an agreement with the other members of the Basle Committee.[82] The most controversial issue remained that of hidden reserves. In the meetings, the Japanese originally suggested that in accordance with national regulations, 70 per cent of their average unrealized gains over the past five years should be counted towards their capital for the purpose of the ratios, while other countries argued for less than 30 per cent.[83]

In December of 1987, the central bank governors announced that they had agreed on a common approach to the issue of capital adequacy and its measurement.[84] A consultative paper was issued for banking associations from the member countries, supervisory authorities outside the G-10 countries, and other interested parties.[85] With regard to the most controversial issue, the agreement allowed commercial banks to include up to 45 per cent of unrealized capital gains on equity holdings as part of the secondary component of total capital.[86] The committee also agreed that banks' capital should be raised to at least 8 per cent of assets by 1992, of which 4 per cent of total capital must consist of primary or core capital.[87] Countries also agreed to the risk weights assigned both to assets and off-balance sheet exposure.[88]

However, according to some member countries, certain issues remained unresolved and, in their view, raised doubts about if and when an agreement could be reached.[89] For example, the concessions made for the Japanese provoked resentment in some European authorities who argued that such concessions could weaken their own national capital requirements. West Germany, in particular, argued that the idea of including secondary capital would weaken rather than strengthen its capital requirements.[90] In addition, French authorities argued that loan-loss reserves should count as capital, something the proposal did not allow. Throughout the 1980s, French banks had built up large loan-loss provisions that equalled about 40 per cent of their exposure to major debtors among the industrializing countries. They now argued that this explained why they compared so poorly with other members of the committee, and insisted that they were not prepared to change this policy.

The committee itself, however, was much more optimistic, and described these disagreements within the committee as 'minority views', indicating that they would not prove to be an obstacle to an eventual agreement.[91] Similarly, some members of the committee, most notably the authorities from the U.S. and the U.K., were very optimistic. 'It is a major accomplishment to have got to this point', Brian Quinn, one of the British chief negotiators stated.[92] Peter Cooke dismissed reports that some countries disagreed with the final proposals and described the agreement as 'a document that everybody is prepared to subscribe to.'[93] Cooke also stated that the accord was both credible and realistic; it was credible in that it incorporated the right concepts and realistic in that it took into account the current requirements of national banking systems. Only nine months before, when the U.S. and U.K. regulatory authorities published their joint proposal on capital adequacy, it seemed unthinkable that the rest of the world's major countries could be marshalled into line so quickly.

The immediate reaction from the international banking community was mixed. British, Swiss and West German banks appeared to be least affected by the accord. On the other hand, French, Belgian and Japanese banks were expected to face pressure to raise their capital base.[94] In the U.S., the bank analysts suggested that only 26 banks would need to raise funds to meet the requirements in the long run. These banks included most of the money centre banks in New York, California and Chicago, and a number of financially troubled banks in the Southwest. Given the fact that the October stock market crash had depressed interest in new stock offerings in financial markets, most of the initial capital would have to be raised through retained earnings. Only J.P. Morgan and Bankers Trust were thought to be able to meet the new requirements now.[95] Thus, opposition to the proposal came almost exclusively from money centre banks that considered the proposal 'detrimental' and argued that foreign banks still had a built-in competitive advantage over U.S. banks.[96]

A full-fledged domestic debate in the various countries over the international proposal had to wait until national regulators published their specific proposals. Given that the original proposal allowed national bank regulators considerable discretion as to exact interpretation and implementation of the Basle proposal, there was some hope in the private sector that regulators would not be too stringent in their interpretation.

The U.K. regulators were the first to publish the proposed guidelines for their banks, and the hopes of the British bankers were quashed.[97] The three U.S. regulatory agencies coordinated their proposal and followed shortly after.[98] The Fed's announcement indicated that it would follow the lead of the Bank of England and choose a conservative interpretation of the international agreement. Most importantly, in a departure from the proposal accepted in Basle, the Fed proposed that the standards would apply to *all* U.S. banks, not just multinational institutions. The intention here obviously was not to recreate domestic competitive inequalities while creating a level playing field at the global level.[99]

The ensuing conflict between the banks and the regulators not only focused on the proposal's competitive implications at the international level, but also at the domestic level. In the domestic financial markets, money centre banks found their domineering position in the credit markets increasingly challenged by a small number of strong regional banks, sometimes also referred to as superregionals, that were benefiting from relaxation in the interstate banking laws and expanding across borders into neighbouring states. Given the restraints the new capital rules would put on asset growth, the money centre banks would have to sell some of their assets and retain most of their profits. Superregionals, on the other hand, were not affected by the Basle decision. As of 30 July, the average core capital ratio of the ten largest regional banks was 5.5 per cent. Thus, the money centre banks' drive to expand through acquisitions and mergers to counter the superregionals in the U.S. domestic markets would be slowed down considerably if the Basle agreement were to be implemented in its present form.[100]

Criticism came not only from the private sector but also from Congress. The same committee that in 1983 requested regulators to 'cause banking institutions to achieve and maintain adequate capital by establishing minimum capital levels' and that asked the three regulatory agencies to 'encourage governments, central banks, and regulatory authorities of other major banking countries to work toward maintaining and where appropriate strengthening the capital bases of banking institutions'[101] was now conducting hearings on the competitive implications of the Basle agreement. The majority of the House Banking Committee members, while approving the fact that an agreement had been struck, were critical of many aspects of the agreement. Particular pressure to change some aspects of the accord came from representatives of states that hosted large money centre banks. Charles E. Schumer (D-Ny.) and Norman D. Schumway (R-Ca.) circulated a document among members of the Banking Committee identifying several 'flaws' in the Basle agreement that 'place American banks at a competitive disadvantage to their foreign counterparts.'[102]

The regulators responded quickly and displayed a remarkable degree of harmony and cooperation in defending the agreement reached in Basle.[103] The agencies also indicated that they were prepared to defend the institutional authority that ILSA had attributed to them. As William Taylor, staff director of the Fed's Bank Regulatory and Supervisory Division, pointed out to Congress, the agencies were not only doing their work as bank regulators but they had taken 'an important step in carrying out the congressional mandate' given to them by ILSA five years ago.[104]

While regulators were prepared to consider some of the criticisms that were made, they were not willing to introduce any major changes and thus attempt to renegotiate the agreement at the international level. While admitting that a small number of banks would have to raise additional capital, an official from the Federal Reserve rejected the notion that the new standards would leave U.S. banks at a disadvantage, arguing that the agreement was consistent with the more recent U.S. domestic capital adequacy standards. This was confirmed in a letter from a New York investment firm specializing in banks to Rep. Schumer, who had asked the company to comment on a document he had circulated among committee members to gather support for the cause of the money centre banks. Ironically, the investment firm did not agree with the charge by Rep. Schumer that the implementation of the agreement would cause a reduction in U.S. banks' participation in the U.S. economy. Rather, the company argued that financial intermediation would shift away from money centre banks to regional and superregional banks. They agreed 'that a threat to money center bank competitiveness...is real. However, that threat may come more from domestic regional banks than from foreign institutions.'[105] This supported the position of the regulators, who at this point were less concerned with the political consequences of domestic intra-industry conflicts over market shares than with the long-term health of the banks.[106] The letter by the investment company also confirmed what U.S. regulators were much more concerned about during the negotiations — namely, that the new rules and capital levels would not put an unrealizable burden on the banks. '[W]e are not greatly concerned about the money center banks' ability to reach the 4 per cent tangible, 4 per cent common equity requirement by 1992. Even the weakest of the money center banks (Bank of America and Manufacturers Hanover) have indicated that they can reach this target....'[107]

Apart from the fact that a positive response by the regulatory agencies to the particularistic interests of money centre banks would have been met with strong criticisms from the regional and small banks across the country that regulators (and especially the Fed) were once again giving in to the interests of the large and powerful banks in New York, Chicago and California, it would have created gridlock at the international level. Having gone through the delicate negotiations and compromises necessary to achieve an agreement among the ten most powerful economies in the world, during which everybody had to make some concessions, it was clear to U.S. regulators that domestic competitive concerns of a relatively small, though important, number of banks would not be taken seriously by the other regulators represented on the Basle Committee. Any such unilateral manoeuvre would lead not only to criticisms from the other regulators on the committee, but would be met with strong opposition from the private sectors in the other countries, jeopardizing the entire agreement.

The importance of the international dimension of the agreement, and the degree to which domestic policy manoeuvrability had become limited in order to maintain the agreement, became evident during the hearings on the Basle Accord. For example, several congressmen, including Schumer, also challenged the notion that the Basle definition of core capital should exclude perpetual preferred stock. Perpetual stock, according to the committee, had always been included in the U.S. definition on the basis that from a liquidity perspective it is essentially the same. Regulators agreed with Congress that indeed preferred stock serves very much the same purpose as common equity, but explained that 'the reason it was excluded is that the whole international agreement represented a lot of compromise and to include the preferred stock would have been to open up the question of including other high-grade instruments that other countries feel should get equal standing.'[108]

Regulators went even further in defending the agreement by publicly applauding the Japanese, against whom most of the private sector criticisms were directed. Referring to the difficult negotiations over the issue of unrealized gains in equity values, Taylor of the Federal Reserve described the Japanese as 'extremely cooperative' and stated, 'The Japanese...have been forthcoming in this proposal to try and meet the concerns of the rest of the world, and I think they have done a pretty good job of it.'[109] And as to the distribution of the burden of adjustment by the various domestic banks, Taylor continued, 'I think the greater burden probably does fall on the Japanese.'[110]

Pressure on the Fed by both the private banks, who accused the agency of 'betraying' U.S. banks, and Congress continued to mount, and they urged the Fed to propose several changes to the Basle Committee at their next meeting in July. At the initiative of Schumer, who now described the proposed standards as having a 'devastating impact on the international competitiveness of the largest American banks',[111] 30 out of 50 members of the House Banking Committee sent a letter to Alan Greenspan charging that if implemented the proposed capital standards would impose serious and, at least in the case of perpetual preferred stock, clearly unwarranted constraints on the competitiveness of U.S. banks during a particularly crucial period. But the regulators remained firm in their determination not to jeopardize the larger objective of the entire enterprise — an international agreement that had been so carefully worked out. Only one day after

Schumer had sent the letter to the Fed, one commentator aptly described the regulators' position:

> It is not the technicalities that are important here, but the recognition that the world's finance is no longer carried on by separate national banking systems dealing with each other at arms' length. It is dominated by multinational institutions that will soon have grown entirely beyond the reach of country-by-country regulation, unless the world's regulators can get together to enforce these kinds of rules.[112]

When the Basle Committee announced its final version of the report in July of 1988, the central features of the committee's report were reaffirmed.[113] The protests by U.S. banks and Congress had little effect and only a few minor changes were made. The committee did not modify the basic definition of capital.[114] It also confirmed that the minimum ratio of 8 per cent had to be achieved by 1992, with an interim step to be taken by the end of 1990. Officials at the Fed estimated that the major American banks at the time of announcement had tier one capital equal to about 3.2 per cent of their assets and that five of the nation's largest banks would have to raise as much as $12 billion to $15 billion combined in the next four and a half years. But they were also quick to point out that Japanese banks would have to raise $20 to $35 billion combined during the same time period to meet the new standard.[115]

But the domestic debate over the specific application of the international agreement was far from over. In the spring of 1988, the Fed, which regulates bank holding companies and thus all money centre banks, had announced that the new capital rules not only applied to the bank subsidiary but to the entire holding company as well. This did not come as a great surprise. Since the early 1980s, the Fed had always insisted that the guidelines should be applied to the entire holding company. Banks had always opposed this, but saw little chance of convincing the Fed to apply the guidelines to the bank alone. The debate over the exact interpretation of the Basle agreement at the domestic level provided an opening for bankers and some in Congress to raise this particular issue again.[116]

Their chances were all the more promising since this was one of the few areas where regulators disagreed over the application of the rules.[117] Such a disagreement, if it turned out to be unresolvable, could have detrimental effects on the entire effort, since the international accord could be undermined by domestic differences. This disagreement among the regulators surfaced as early as April of 1988, during congressional hearings on the Basle agreement. The Fed rejected suggestions by some members of the House Banking Committee to apply the standards only to the bank affiliate of the holding company, arguing that this would lead to a situation where the consolidated organization could be materially more leveraged than the banking part of it. The Comptroller's office agreed with the Fed's position that the standards should be applicable to the holding company as well. The FDIC, however, disagreed. The director of bank supervision explained the agency's position by arguing that 'substantial firewalls are developed between the holding company and the individual banks.'[118]

The debate intensified during the summer. In an interview in late June, William Seidman, Chairman of the FDIC, said he had tried to exempt bank holding companies from the requirement because it would be unfair to apply the new standards both to themselves and their banking subsidiaries.[119] In addition to the $15 billion in capital that needed to be raised by banks and banking subsidiaries, the FDIC estimated that the 150 bank holding companies operating in the U.S. would have to raise an additional $14.1 billion in capital so that they themselves could meet the requirements. In commenting on his staff's findings, Seidman stated that

> [T]he Fed is about to place United States banks at a competitive disadvantage, since they will have to raise a lot more money.... If you properly keep the bank separate so that its capital cannot be drained by the holding company the bank should stay sound no matter what happens to its parent.[120]

The Comptroller too, who on earlier occasions had supported the Fed, now argued that it was important to regulate bank holding companies' capital requirements differently from the banks.

The Fed, on the other hand, defended its position.[121] Stressing its role as the primary regulator of BHCs, the Fed stuck to its long-held doctrine that in times of stress the resources and strength of a bank holding company are to be used to help a troubled bank. In addition to the domestic argument for maintaining the status quo, the Fed — as it had done on earlier occasions — claimed the international agreement was a constraint on its ability to unilaterally alter some aspects of the agreement. Regulators argued that the extension of prudential supervision, including the application of capital standards and reporting requirements, to banks on a consolidated basis had long been encouraged by international supervisory authorities as a way to strengthen an increasingly interdependent international financial system.[122] In accordance with these principles, the Basle accord expressed concern that bank ownership structures or affiliations with other firms not be allowed to weaken the capital position of the bank or expose the bank to undue risks. In addition, as the primary regulator of bank holding companies, the Fed could ignore, for the most part, criticisms from the other agencies. With some minor exceptions, it stuck to its plan to require bank holding companies to maintain similar capital levels.[123]

Despite the efforts by money centre banks to influence the final outcome of the Fed guidelines, bankers and banking analysts in general agreed that they 'can live with it'[124] and expected banks to have few problems obtaining the additional capital because of the long transitional period.[125] The next step was to coordinate the agencies' rules and come up with a final ruling that all three regulators could agree on, to ensure harmony across the agencies. The Fed adopted the final version of its risk-based capital guidelines on 16 December 1988, and the other agencies followed shortly after that.[126]

Analyses of the U.S. domestic policy network usually assume that the network is too structurally fragmented, and too ad hoc and reactive in its mode of operation, to formulate coherent and aggressive policy responses to external pressures — much less take the initiative in formulating an internationally coordinated response to such pressure. Yet as the formation of the Basle Agreement reveals, the U.S. policy network took relatively coordinated and decisive steps to resolve the challenge posed by the worldwide decline in banks' capital ratios. Moreover, as it became clear that a solely domestic response to the external pressure would not be sufficient, the U.S. led the G-10 group of countries in a coordinated effort to respond to the external challenge.

NOTES

1. Heimann (1979).
2. For the history of the Basle Committee, see *BIS Press Review*, No. 121.
3. For more on the BIS, see *Banker*, 1979; Klein (1978); Lemke (1977); *WSJ*, 10 October 1980. The membership of the committee is comprised of the representatives of the central banks and other authorities with formal responsibilities for the prudential supervision of banking institutions from these 12 leading industrial countries.
4. Blunden (1977).
5. The bank failures were those of the Herstatt Bank in West Germany and the Franklin National Bank in the U.S.
6. Cooke (1981); Blunden (1977).
7. Given its dispersed regulatory structure, the United States represents something of an anomaly. At the committee meetings the U.S. is currently represented by four bank regulatory officials — two from the Fed, and one from the OCC and the FDIC respectively.
8. U.S. General Accounting Office (1986).
9. The precise text of the concordat is reproduced in International Monetary Fund (1981); see also U.S. General Accounting Office (1986); Cooke (1984).
10. Dale (1983).
11. For a reprint of the second concordat see *International Legal Materials*, July 1983; see also *Washington Financial Reports*, 18 July 1983; Cooke (1984).
12. Blunden (1977). For another sceptical view of the future of international regulatory cooperation see Dale (1982).
13. Norton (1989).
14. Basle Committee on Bank Supervision (1989); Pierre Jaans in *International Conference of Bank Supervisors*, 5 and 6 July 1979; *Institutional Investor*, January 1985.
15. *American Banker*, 28 November 1980, 24 December and 28 December 1981; *The Banker*,

June 1983; Ossola (1980).

16. *American Banker*, 30 July and 7 November 1980; *NYT*, 2 June 1980.
17. Cooke (1984).
18. Committee on Banking Regulations and Supervisory Practices (1982).
19. Ibid.
20. Committee on Banking Regulations and Supervisory Practices (1983).
21. Ibid.
22. Ibid.
23. For a more detailed discussion of the importance of this consensus, see Kapstein (1989).
24. As quoted in U.S. General Accounting Office (1986).
25. Bank capital as defined by most countries includes stockholders' equity and accumulated earnings. Some countries, however, permitted capital to be adjusted by reassessing fixed assets to reflect market values. Others carried these assets at cost minus depreciation. Another difference in the valuation of capital that proved to be an important issue was that securities owned by banks were included at cost in some countries and at market value in others. This resulted in substantial differences in capital. Finally, some countries consider subordinated debt and reserves set aside for loan losses (whether disclosed or not) as capital; others do not. All of the above amounted to substantial differences, even if the countries could concur on how to measure capital adequacy. Here too, countries differed: some use a capital-liability ratio while others use a capital-to-asset ratio. Moreover, different countries attach different weights to asset categories when assessing the riskiness of a bank portfolio. Finally, even countries that could agree on a common definition and form of measurement would still need to agree on an appropriate minimum level.
26. Public Law 98-101, Sec. 908, (b)(3)(C), 97 Stat. 1281.
27. *International Financial Markets and Related Problems*.
28. Strict definitions comprise only stockholders' equity. More lenient definitions include such assets as reserves for loan losses and subordinated debt.
29. Committee on Banking Regulations and Supervisory Practices (1984).
30. The notion of functional equivalence was put forward by Volcker to encourage convergence towards a generally accepted quantitative guideline for banks' capital adequacy by measuring and comparing standards of capital adequacy on a common basis.
31. Committee on Banking Regulations and Supervisory Practices (1984).
32. *Financial Times*, 29 August and 26 November 1985.
33. 50 Fed. Reg. 16,063, 24 April 1985.
34. Norton (1989).
35. Bardos (1987-88); Committee on Banking Regulations and Supervisory Practices (1984).
36. *Financial Times*, 22 January 1989.
37. 51 Fed. Reg. 3976 cont. (31 January 1986); see also Statement by Paul Volcker, *Risk-Based Capital Requirements for Banks and Bank Holding Companies*. The Canadians and Japanese were also issuing their own risk-weighing measures, albeit based on each country's domestic banking environment.
38. Committee on Banking Regulations and Supervisory Practices (1986); *Financial Times*, 19 September and 29 October 1985.
39. *Financial Times*, 11 March and 17 March 1986.
40. 'The battle to keep tabs in the face of rapid change', *Financial Times*, 23 February and 23 May 1986.
41. Statement by the Chairman of the report as quoted in *Euromoney*, June 1986. Bank For International Settlements (1986); see also *Financial Times*, 21 April and 9 May 1986.
42. Müller (1986).
43. Press Release, *4th International Conference of Banking Supervisors*; *Financial Times*, 22 October 1986.
44. Ibid.

45. *Financial Times*, 11 March and 30 October 1986.
46. *NYT*, 13 September 1985; *Financial Times*, 18 September 1985. For a dissenting view from the Comptroller, see *WSJ*, 23 October 1985.
47. *Review Of The International Lending Supervision Act of 1983*, 25 June 1986.
48. Statement of Carleton R. Haswell, Senior Vice President, Chemical Bank, *Review Of The International Lending Supervision Act of 1983*, 25 June 1986.
49. Holland (1986).
50. *Financial Times*, 2 January 1986.
51. Bardos (1987-88). The Bank of England had developed its approach in 1980 and had been using it as an integral part of its prudential supervision procedures. Bank of England, September 1980.
52. For a copy of the agreement, see Bank of England, *Quarterly Bulletin*, February 1987; for an in-depth discussion of the proposal see *Staff Report* by the Federal Reserve Board, reprinted in *American Banker*, 14, 15, 20 January 1987.
53. *WSJ*, 9 January 1987.
54. The Bank of England had included risk-weighing in its own measurement technique since 1980. See *Federal Register*, 31 January 1986.
55. *Financial Times*, 9 January 1987.
56. *American Banker*, 9 January 1987.
57. For further discussion of the accord, see Murray-Jones and Spencer (1987); *Harvard Law Review*, 1987.
58. Cooke (1990).
59. Markus Lusser, in speech delivered in Boppard am Rhein, 13 March 1987.
60. *Risk-Based Capital Requirements for Banks and Bank Holding Companies*, 30 April 1987.
61. Ibid. The committee was aware of the fact that the U.S. and the U.K. were trying to come to an agreement with Japan and there was some fear that once a trilateral agreement had been reached other countries' banks could be barred from the three most important financial centres which would be a major blow to their ability to remain competitive. They therefore pressured their government to cooperate internationally; see also Markus Lusser, speech delivered in Boppard am Rhein, 13 March 1987.
62. Brian Quinn, quoted in *American Banker*, 20 January 1987.
63. Donald Ogilvie, Executive Vice President of the ABA, in *American Banker*, 9 January 1987.
64. Statement by the senior vice president and general manager of the London bureau of Morgan Guaranty Trust Co. in *American Banker*, 20 January 1987; but in the U.S. the competitive concerns were not only directed at the international financial market. Since the new guidelines also included capital market activities, where commercial banks are in direct competition with securities firms, bankers also complained about inequities with regard to the investment banks. For a discussion of the different regulations, see *Quarterly Review*, Federal Reserve Bank of New York, Autumn 1987; for a more detailed examination of the various criticisms made during the comment period, see *American Banker*, 27 May 1987 and 9 July; *NYT*, 9 January 1987.
65. *Risk-Based Capital Requirements for Banks and Bank Holding Companies*, 30 April 1987.
66. Ibid.; see also *American Banker*, 20 January 1987.
67. Gerald Corrigan, Remarks before the Overseas Bankers Club Annual Banquet, 2 February 1987.
68. Committee on Banking Regulations and Supervisory Practices (1987).
69. *Risk-Based Capital Requirements for Banks and Bank Holding Companies*, 30 April 1987.
70. U.S. regulators had already approached the Japanese on a bilateral basis in late 1986.
71. Under the guidelines issued in May 1986, Japanese banks were required to raise their capital-to-asset ratios to 4 per cent by 1992. Banks with overseas branches were required to raise their capital-to-asset ratios to 6 per cent by April 1987. United States General Accounting Office (1988).

72. Bardos (1987-88).
73. Statement by Paul Volcker, *Risk-Based Capital Requirements for Banks and Bank Holding Companies*, 30 April 1987.
74. *Financial Times*, 13 May 1987.
75. *Financial Times*, 21 May 1987.
76. *Financial Times*, 12 June 1987.
77. Cooke (1990).
78. Bank for International Settlements (1987).
79. Initially Germany was opposed to any widening of the definition of capital beyond pure shareholders' equity. They argued that to accept supplementary (from their perspective, less reliable) forms of capital would lower standards and undermine the main prudential objective of the exercise: to improve the overall level and quality of capital in international banks.
80. Statement by Paul Volcker, *Globalization of Financial Markets and Related International Banking and Supervision Issues*, 30 July 1987; see also *NYT*, 31 July 1987.
81. Ibid.
82. *Financial Times*, 25 September 1987.
83. *WSJ*, 23 October 1987.
84. *American Banker*, 10 December 1987; *Financial Times*, 9 December 1987.
85. Committee on Banking Regulations and Supervisory Practices (1987).
86. U.S. regulators believed that including more than 45 per cent in the computation would have been unwarranted given the price volatility of Japanese banks' securities holdings and the relatively thin markets for those securities.
87. Two aspects characterize the transitional phase: banks have to attain a minimum of 7.25 per cent by the end of 1990; at the same time, the components of capital are not as strictly defined as in the final rules.
88. The committee established five weights, 0, 10, 20, 50, 100 per cent. Compared to the initial U.S.-U.K. accord, the Basle Committee's proposal thus not only had some substantive differences but also went further in specifying what constitutes capital and what minimum standards banks were expected to achieve.
89. *Financial Times*, 11 December 1987; *Banker*, February 1988.
90. Gossling (1988).
91. One such minority view continued to be the F.R.G.'s (not named in the report) that 'in the context of the Committee's work to improve the quality of banks' capital, an international definition of capital should effectively be confined to core capital elements', see Committee on Banking Regulations and Supervisory Practices (1987). In the end, German insistence on a narrow definition of capital was undermined by the EC's proposal to establish a two tier system, with an 8 per cent ratio to be established by 1992. Minor differences also existed with respect to the weighting scheme, and two member countries — believed to be Germany and France — were 'reserved on the appropriateness' of the 7.25 per cent interim minimum standard to be achieved by the end of 1990.
92. *Financial Times*, 11 December 1987.
93. *American Banker*, 11 December 1987.
94. *Financial Times*, 14 December and 15 December 1987.
95. The core capital of J.P. Morgan and Bankers Trust was 5.95 per cent and 4.12 per cent, respectively, as of 30 June 1987. The average ratio of the eight largest banks excluding these two was 2.5 per cent as of 30 June 1987.
96. *WP*, 8 February 1988; *WSJ*, 11 December 1987.
97. *American Banker*, 19 January 1988.
98. *Federal Register*, 15 March 1988; see also *American Banker*, 28 January 1988.
99. One surprise was the Fed's decision to put home mortgage lending in the 100 per cent category, i.e. among the riskiest types of loans. Not only are mortgages commonly believed to be less risky than other loans, but more importantly the international agreement had placed

mortgages in the 50 per cent category. Consequently, the Fed's decision would give foreign banks a competitive edge in this particular field.
100. *NYT*, 1 February 1988; *American Banker*, 29 November 1988.
101. Public Law, 98-181, 30 November 1983, Section 908, (3)(C).
102. Statement of Charles E. Schumer, *Risk-Based Capital Requirements for Banks and Bank Holding Companies*, 21 April 1988. See also a letter to Alan Greenspan dated April 1988 from the House of Representatives, asking the Chairman of the Federal Reserve Board to revise several aspects of the accord, reprinted in the above hearing.
103. The FDIC took some exception to the applicability of the agreement to small rural banks; see ibid.
104. Statement by William Taylor, *Risk-Based Capital Requirements for Banks and Bank Holding Companies*, 21 April 1988.
105. Letter from James McDermott, Jr., Director of Research, Keefe, Bruyette & Woods, Inc. to Congressman Schumer, Re: Comments on Schumer/Schumway 'Dear Colleague' letter in reference to risk-based capital guidelines, 19 April 1988; see also Salomon Brothers, Research Department (1988).
106. Statement by Paul G. Fritts, Director, Division of Bank Supervision, FDIC, *Risk-Based Capital Requirements for Banks and Bank Holding Companies*, 21 April 1988.
107. McDermott, Jr. (1988).
108. William Taylor, in *Risk-Based Capital Requirements for Banks and Bank Holding Companies*, 21 April 1988.
109. *WSJ*, 30 December 1987.
110. Taylor, op. cit.
111. *WSJ*, 7 April 1988.
112. *WP*, 8 May 1988.
113. *Banking Report*, 25 July 1988; *Banking Report*, 8 August 1988.
114. German authorities maintained their view that they would prefer the definition of capital to be confined to core capital alone. The Bundesbank served notice that it would continue to try to exclude any other capital for purposes of the standard. However, these reservations did not prevent them from accepting the final document. See *WP*, 13 July 1988.
115. *NYT*, 12 July 1988.
116. *Issues in Bank Regulation*, Summer 1988.
117. Another issue that regulators disagreed on was the Fed's desire to see the new standards applied uniformly across the entire U.S. banking industry. The FDIC, representing the small banks, argued that the agreement only applied to multinational banks. Since small banks had no trouble in meeting the standards, however, the agency did not insist on that. In fact as it turned out small banks were much better off under the new regulations. See *American Banker*, 30 November 1988.
118. Paul G. Fritts, Director, Division of Bank Supervision, FDIC, *Risk-Based Capital Requirements for Banks and Bank Holding Companies*, 21 April 1988.
119. *NYT*, 13 July 1988.
120. *NYT*, 15 July 1988.
121. For an extended discussion of the Fed's position, see 'Fed Staff Summary and Recommendations on Risk-Based Capital Plan', reprinted in *BNA's Banking Reporter,* Bureau of National Affairs, 8 August 1988.
122. These principles are contained in the two Concordats of the Basle Committee.
123. *NYT*, 4 August 1988; *WP*, 4 August 1988.
124. Peter J. Tobin, Executive Vice President and chief financial officer of Manufacturers Hanover Corp., as quoted in *WP*, 13 July 1988.
125. *WSJ*, 5 August 1988.
126. *American Banker*, 16 December 1988; *WSJ*, 19 December 1988.

9. Conclusion

DEFENDING THE NATIONAL INTEREST: U.S. COMPARATIVE RESPONSES TO EXTERNAL ECONOMIC SHOCKS

As shown in the previous chapters, the external economic shocks of the 1970s and the subsequent integration of financial markets across the major industrial countries confronted both U.S. commercial banks and their regulators with powerful challenges to their economic and political interests. In the case of Glass-Steagall, large commercial banks argued that the restrictions placed upon their activities in the national financial system increasingly eroded their competitiveness in domestic and international financial markets, ultimately threatening the strength and viability of the American financial system and the economy at large. In the case of capital adequacy, international financial integration and competition among banks led to an erosion of banks' capital reserves worldwide. This confronted U.S. policymakers with the possibility of global financial collapse arising from risky, over-leveraged lending practices by commercial banks.

As the previous chapters have shown, the U.S. policy network responded to the two regulatory challenges posed by global financial integration in two very different ways. This divergence in the response pattern of the U.S. financial policy network can be explained through cross-case comparisons of the three phase adjustment model — mobilization, conflict and resolution. The mobilization phase is defined as the stage in which the external shock penetrates the domestic policy network, creating several challenges to the national policy network. Each challenge activates a specific response pattern by domestic institutional actors. The cause of divergence in the response pattern and the subsequent policymaking process is explained by a comparative analysis of the two challenges along the following three dimensions: which actors' interests were initially threatened by the external challenge; what kind of compensatory policy changes those actors sought; and which other actors were mobilized in the debate over how to respond to the challenge.

The two challenges posed by the external pressures initially mobilized *different* sets of actors with *different* policy goals. In the case of Glass-Steagall, large U.S. commercial banks mobilized against a steadily declining market share, defending their economic interests and demanding a repeal of Glass-Steagall. The challenge of declining capital ratios, on the other hand, mobilized the regulators to defend their political capacities, initiating a coordinated effort to harmonize and enhance the capital standards of U.S. commercial banks. Thus, contrary to the case of Glass-Steagall, where one private sector segment of the financial services industry mobilized to press for financial market *deregulation*, the case of capital adequacy resulted in a concerted effort by all federal bank regulators toward financial market *reregulation*.

The efforts of large commercial banks and regulatory authorities to meet their respective challenges and realize their objectives in turn mobilized the U.S. policy network to differing extents, and involved the participation of different public and private sector institutions. The money centre banks' effort to overturn Glass-Steagall mobilized a wide array of public and private sector institutions. Initially, large banks built alliances with public sector institutions that had expressed some concern for their interests, and were thus perceived to be essential allies in an effort to repeal the act. These were primarily the three federal bank regulators, with the Comptroller and the FDIC most sympathetic to the cause of the money centre banks. Another strong ally was the newly elected Republican Administration. In the legislature, support was not as broad and banks were only able to form a small and rather fragile alliance with the Republican leadership in the Senate Banking Committee. At a later stage, once conflict had already erupted, the large banks formed coalitions with state legislatures and regulators that were supportive of their cause.

At the same time that money centre banks were building coalitions with public sector institutions to strengthen their efforts, other institutions whose position in the policy network would be adversely affected by a repeal of Glass-Steagall mobilized against those banks. On the private sector side, the securities industry strongly opposed any change in the regulatory structure that had protected its own market from the competition of commercial banks for almost fifty years. Investment banks quickly established the necessary ties in the legislature to build a strong coalition that could block any change in the act. Both House committees with jurisdiction over banking and securities matters were receptive to the investment banks' concern. Similarly, small banks, fearing that a change in the Glass-Steagall Act would lead to increased competition from the large banks and erode their market share, forged alliances with public sector institutions. Small banks found most of their support in the House Banking Committee, where there was a long populist tradition of fighting financial concentration in large banks. The committee had always supported regulations that would preserve small rural banks. In addition, during the first half of the 1980s, small banks received some support from the Fed, which favoured only a very limited entry of commercial banks into the securities business.

Finally, some institutions did not build specific coalitions with either the private or public sector, but mobilized because a change in the Glass-Steagall Act would have repercussions on their role in the policy network. For example, the SEC took a position that was solely geared towards the defence of its own regulatory turf in case the Glass-Steagall Act were repealed.

In sum, the efforts to revise or repeal Glass-Steagall mobilized numerous federal regulatory agencies, several congressional committees in both the House and Senate, state legislatures and regulators, and multiple lobbying organizations, including those representing large money centre banks, small commercial banks, and securities firms, thus fully activating all institutions in the dispersed and decentralized policy network.

Contrary to the case of Glass-Steagall, the efforts by regulators to raise the capital standards of commercial banks mobilized a more restricted range of private and public sector actors in the policy network. In addition, the primary conflict did not revolve around an inter-industry struggle over market shares. The regulators were in basic agreement on the policy goals and did not need, nor did they feel compelled, to build any coalitions with the private sector institutions. Still, just as in the Glass-Steagall case, those adversely affected by a possible change in the regulations that governed the policy network responded by mobilizing to prevent change. However, since only commercial banks would be affected by higher capital standards, other private sector institutions, such as the securities industry, which played an integral role in the conflict over Glass-Steagall, remained completely demobilized on the issue of capital adequacy regulation. In addition, while the banks themselves were deeply divided over Glass-Steagall, they were united in their opposition to increased capital levels and did not exert conflicting pressures on the regulators and Congress.

On the public sector side as well, few other institutions felt compelled to respond to the agencies' regulatory efforts. The SEC lacked interest and jurisdictional power over banking issues, as did the House Energy and Commerce Committee. Similarly, state legislatures and regulators had no authority in bank capital regulation. Moreover, those committees in the legislature that were eventually mobilized in the debate over capital adequacy were supportive of the regulators' efforts. In sum, the attempt by regulators to raise the capital levels of commercial banks mobilized a much more limited range of institutions, both private and public, than did Glass-Steagall. In addition, given the interests of the institutions involved, there was little or no room for the formation of the close public-private sector coalitions characteristic of the mobilization in Glass-Steagall. Rather, the coalitions that did form were for the most part either among private or among public sector institutions, and were not as stable as in the case of Glass-Steagall.

But a mere listing of the institutions mobilized and the coalitions formed reveals little about the policymaking process itself, i.e. how the policy network responded to the challenge. In order to explore these dynamics, it is necessary to examine in greater detail the evolving goals and institutional interests, as well as the patterns of conflict which those interests generated. In each case, the process of conflict over policy responses was divided into two phases: an initial phase, which was largely shaped by the factors inherited from the mobilization phase; and a second phase which reflected the intensification of external pressures upon that policy network and the way they impinged upon that network.

Turning first to Glass-Steagall and its initial phase, one central element inherited from the mobilization period involved the identity and interests of the institutions which first reacted to the challenge. In the case of Glass-Steagall, large commercial banks set the policy agenda and essentially determined *what* was debated. Money centre banks and their coalition partners in the public sector appealed to Congress to permit them to enter the securities business. In doing so, the banks set the parameters of subsequent conflict within the policy network, predisposing the network to consider a specific set of demands — the deregulation of banking.

The response pattern and the identity of the institutions responding to the money centre banks determined *how* the repeal of Glass-Steagall was debated. The institutions that responded in support of or against the large commercial banks espoused a wide disparity in interests and policy goals, within both the public and private sectors of the policy network. As a result, the main lines of conflict were not between a unified public sector and a unified private sector; instead, there were multiple lines of conflict both within and between the public and private sectors. The resultant public-private sector coalitions generated the maximum potential for conflict and policy gridlock.

Within the public sector portion of the policy network, the various legislative and administrative bodies with jurisdiction over product regulation initially espoused widely divergent regulatory philosophies and positions on Glass-Steagall. The OCC and the FDIC strongly supported the repeal of Glass-Steagall. This goal reflected their market-oriented regulatory philosophy, which held that the efficiency of the U.S. financial system would be optimized through promoting competition and removing restrictions on banks' activities. By contrast, the Federal Reserve opposed a complete repeal of Glass-Steagall, because it put greater emphasis on ensuring the stability of the financial system than it did on promoting competition. In addition, the Fed's resistance to a repeal of Glass-Steagall reflected its fears that deregulation would undermine its control over the banking system and thus its capacity to conduct monetary policy. Congressional committees with jurisdiction over the separation between commercial and investment banking were equally divided. The conflicts within Congress reflected both divergent interpretations of the goals of regulation and differences in the private sector interests to which particular committees were responsive. Generally speaking, the Senate Banking Committee was more inclined to revise Glass-Steagall, because it was more attuned to the regulatory goal of promoting competition and somewhat more responsive to the interests of large commercial banks. By contrast, the House committees were more concerned with safeguarding financial stability, more inclined to indulge in anti-bank populist rhetoric, and more responsive to the political lobbying efforts of the securities industry and the small banks. These divergent interests and philosophies impeded the formulation of a coherent congressional position on the repeal of Glass-Steagall, and created the possibility for cross-cutting coalitions with opposing private sector interests.

In addition to the divisions in the public sector, the private sector was divided by both inter-industry and intra-industry conflicts. The inter-industry conflict revolved around the diametrically opposed goals of commercial and investment banks, as commercial banks attempted to invade the long-protected and jealously-guarded markets of the investment banking industry and as non-bank banks were making inroads into the traditional consumer loan market of commercial banks. Meanwhile, the intra-industry conflict revolved around the divergence in interests between large and small commercial banks. Large banks pressed for a repeal of Glass-Steagall to retain their customer base while smaller institutions resisted out of fear that deregulation would lead to further financial concentration and erosion of their own market shares.

The mobilization of competing private sector interests into a policy network already characterized by considerable conflicts among public sector actors maximized the potential for cross-cutting public/private coalitions. Each group of private sector actors sought public sector allies who were strategically well-placed in the policy network to facilitate or obstruct policy outcomes. But congressional committees were not only at odds over the appropriate regulatory structure of the U.S. financial system; their responses to the commercial banks' demands also reflected their own institutional interests, which would be affected by a change in the Glass-Steagall Act. This was most obvious in the case of the House Energy and Commerce Committee, which in the late 1980s formulated its policy position on the basis of its ability to expand the committee's jurisdictional turf rather than on its long-held tradition of denying commercial banks access to the securities business. In the Senate, too, institutional self-esteem prevented the legislature from arriving at a compromise, when Chairman Garn refused to step away from the Senate's 89-5 vote on a deregulation bill that was unacceptable to the House.

The conflict among the various committees went so far as to impede legislative progress in other fields of financial regulation unrelated to the issue of Glass-Steagall, particularly when the committees attached Glass-Steagall legislation to other banking bills and refused to act unless they would be considered jointly. To sum up, both the actual policy differences over the future regulatory structure of the U.S. financial system in a rapidly changing domestic environment, and the implications of what this restructuring of financial regulation would entail for the political and economic power of institutions in the network, led to a complete impasse in the legislative segment of the policy network throughout the 1980s.

However, the inability of Congress to achieve even minimal compromise did not entirely forestall policy progress. Throughout the first half of the 1980s, large commercial banks skilfully exploited the decentralized structure of financial regulation and were able to extract some concessions in their bid to enter the securities business. Large banks applied pressure at various levels in the policy network. First, banks turned to individual state legislatures and pressed for a more liberal set of bank regulations. The effect of such an action was two-fold. By allowing state chartered banks to engage in some securities activities that were not permitted at the federal level, the banks were able to argue that the regulatory system had created competitive inequalities which had to be eliminated by adjusting federal bank regulation to the more liberal standards of the states. In addition, given the more liberal environment at the state level, banks could threaten to change their charter and seek supervision at the state level, challenging and eventually undermining the power and reach of the federal bank regulators. Both tactics by the banks added pressure on the regulators to become more responsive to the demands of the large banks. A second strategy of the banks was to exploit the philosophical and institutional differences among regulators at the federal level. Banks pressured those regulators that were more inclined to allow them to enter the securities field to issue more liberal rulings within the existing set of legal statutes. In some cases, it was even the regulators themselves that issued such rulings to increase political pressure on the legislature to act. For example, throughout the period under consideration, both the Comptroller and the FDIC issued more liberal rulings for banks chartered under their jurisdiction than did the Federal Reserve. Such rulings by the FDIC that allowed state-chartered non-member banks to engage in a variety of securities activities, including the underwriting of corporate debt, and the Comptroller's rulings that opened the financial services industry to non-financial companies through the non-bank loophole (both of which were strongly opposed by the Fed) are the most prominent examples. Both rulings weakened the competitive position of those banks that were regulated by the Fed and increased pressure on the Fed to act in the same fashion.

Another example is that of the regulators' position on discount brokerage. In late 1982, when the Fed was considering permitting BHCs to enter discount brokerage, both the OCC and the FDIC had already given permission to the banks that they regulated to engage in those activities. A ruling by the Fed against discount brokerage would have led to an outcry by the BHCs that the Fed was creating competitive inequality among the commercial banks and would have led some holding companies to give up their charter. As discussed, the Fed ruled in favour of discount brokerage in early 1983.

But the rulings alone were not sufficient to ensure the banks limited entry into the securities business. Each ruling by the regulators was challenged by the securities industry in court. Moreover, whatever the judicial ruling, it was always appealed to the next highest level of the judiciary by that industry that the court had ruled against. Thus, by the middle of the 1980s, numerous court cases at various levels were pending in the judicial system, only to be resolved by the Supreme Court after years of litigation. In the initial stages of the conflict, the courts were not willing to relieve Congress of its responsibility to execute bank regulatory policy and to delegate it to the administrative segment of the policy network. As the judge who wrote an early decision in the commercial paper case stated, '[T]he realignment of our nation's financial industries is for the elected representatives of our nation to bring to fruition by comprehensive legislation', and should not be the result of 'fiat by judicial decree or by administrative policymaking.'[1]

Thus, while the dispersed and decentralized regulatory structure produced some policy outcomes in the administrative realm, leading to some minor adjustments of bank regulatory policy (as in the case of discount brokerage), the policymaking process was piecemeal and ad hoc. Policy outcomes were the result of conflicting pressures among regulatory agencies rather than policy consensus among the institutions responsible for bank legislation. In addition, all policy decisions were temporary in nature, as only a Supreme Court decision would finalize the jurisdictional dispute among the litigating factions within the policy network. Even a ruling by the Supreme Court could eventually be overturned by Congress, as both House committees with jurisdiction over bank regulation had threatened on several occasions. As a result, throughout the first half of the 1980s, the U.S. financial policy network displayed a remarkable degree of confusion, incoherence and inconsistency, leaving many participants in, as well as observers of, the policymaking process to question whether it was in fact capable of generating any coherent policy response to the changing conditions in the financial markets.

The case of capital adequacy regulation provided a strong contrast. The institutions that mobilized in response to the initial challenge created by declining capital levels were not from the private but from the public sector. In addition, their primary interest was not to deregulate the U.S. financial markets but to reregulate them. Also, contrary to the case of Glass-Steagall, where those initially mobilized represented a small segment of the private sector, all three federal bank regulators mobilized jointly and initially delegated the development of a response to the challenge to the Federal Financial Institution Examination Council, an institution specifically created to promote greater cooperation among the bank regulators. This willingness to delegate some of the decision making to another institution reflected the broad convergence of interests and goals among the regulators initially mobilized.

Once regulators announced their intent to raise capital levels, the pattern of those institutions who responded was also different than in the case of Glass-Steagall. Congress concurred with the regulators that the maintenance of an adequate capital base was critical to the stability and soundness of the banking system, and that the erosion in banks' capital reserves had to be reversed through stronger, more coordinated regulatory controls. As a result, the mobilization of additional public sector institutions in the debate did not weaken the public sector stance, as in Glass-Steagall, but strengthened it.

The private sector, on the other hand, did mobilize against higher capital levels. But the regulatory agencies and Congress were not confronted with the multiple and conflicting pressures that emanated from the private sector in the Glass-Steagall case. In fact, commercial banks were largely united in their opposition to higher capital standards. Yet this unity did not translate into any significant capacity to influence the decision making process, as it had with Glass-Steagall. While commercial banks *had* to rely on public sector institutions to change Glass-Steagall, regulatory agencies did not need the complete consent of the banks to raise capital standards. This reduced the ability of the private sector to exert pressure on the regulators and minimized the role of private/public sector coalitions in the policymaking process. Moreover, given that banks faced a public sector that was unified in its goal to raise capital levels, they could not exploit the decentralized structure of the regulatory system in the same fashion as they had in Glass-Steagall. Thus, within two years of announcing their intention to establish numerical capital standards for all commercial banks and to narrow the differences among them, regulators had made considerable progress in achieving their original policy goal.

This is not to say that the challenge of declining capital ratios did not generate any conflict. As shown, multinational banks were primarily concerned with resisting strict numerical capital adequacy standards, while the smaller banks focused on eliminating the competitive asymmetries arising from the higher capital standards which they were required to maintain. These differences were projected into the public domain, with the FDIC and the Fed forming loose coalitions with their respective client banks and defending their interests in the policymaking process. As a result, by late 1982, a policy gridlock seemed to emerge over the final steps toward the original policy objective, as the Fed continued to resist implementing specific ratios for its client institutions: the big multinational banks. Similarly, differences also continued to exist in the ratios the FDIC applied to its banks and the ratios required by the OCC. Just as in the case of Glass-Steagall, some change in the policy network had to occur to overcome this impasse.

In sum, the comparative analysis of the Glass-Steagall and capital adequacy cases during the mobilization and early conflict phases has revealed striking differences in the political process of formulating responses to external challenges by the same policy network. These differences can be explained by the nature of the challenge, the institutions that mobilized initially to the challenge in order to adjust the regulatory system to the changing conditions in the financial markets, and those institutions that responded to preserve the status quo. As argued in Chapter 2, this implies that one cannot predict the policymaking process by simply examining the structural possibility of dissension and fragmentation. The U.S. financial policy network has often been characterized as fragmented and prone to conflict because it encompasses a multiplicity of public and private institutions linked together through decentralized channels of authority and decisionmaking. However, as has been demonstrated, it would be misleading to predict policy responses based on the structure of the entire domestic financial policy network without considering the specific circumstances to which the policy network responds. More specifically, any external pressure will create different challenges and different challenges will activate different segments of the same policy network. Only if the challenge activates a wide array of public and private sector institutions, and only if both the public authorities and private institutions in the network are divided by internal conflicts of interest, will the structural possibility of dissension and fragmentation be fully realized. If, on the other hand, the challenge mobilizes only a small segment of the decentralized U.S. financial policy network, and if powerful institutions in that segment express broad agreement over how to resolve the challenge, that network will respond in a manner typical of a more centralized system.

The preceding discussion has compared how different institutions in the U.S. financial policy network initially responded to the external pressures of the late 1970s. However, as the two cases have shown, a comparison of the mobilization and initial stages of conflict is insufficient to fully understand the evolving conflicts and to predict the eventual policy outcomes in each case. In fact, the patterns of conflict and coalition-building within the policy network did not remain constant over time. In both cases, the accelerating process of international financial integration, and the associated intensification of external pressure, caused shifts in the interests of some of the major institutions in the policy network, and subsequently in the coalitions that had shaped the policymaking process. These shifts in turn caused important changes in the way in which the policy network responded to the challenges which they confronted, and ultimately facilitated and conditioned the way the conflict was resolved.

Turning first to the case of Glass-Steagall, the progressing globalization of financial markets contributed to two major sets of changes in the financial policy network. First, it allowed those institutions that had long advocated a repeal of Glass-Steagall to alter the nature of their argument. Rather than calling for deregulation, proponents of a Glass-Steagall repeal now called for banking reform — the failure of which would cause an irreversible erosion in the competitiveness of the American financial services industry, and subsequently the industrial strength of the entire U.S. economy. What had long been portrayed as the pursuit of individual interests for private profit had become a matter of national interest in the pursuit of the public good.[2]

This new and different perspective led several important institutions to change their position toward a repeal of Glass-Steagall in a critical way. Probably the most important shift took place at the Federal Reserve during 1986-1987. Beginning in 1986, the Fed became increasingly concerned about the declining profitability, and ultimately the stability, of the American banking system. Members of the Fed Board and staff pointed out that the decline of the American banking system was in part the result of their inability to effectively compete with less-regulated foreign financial institutions in the U.S., as well as in international financial markets. Since foreign banks were not about to adopt U.S. regulations, U.S. banks had little choice but to adjust to foreign and international regulatory standards. Board members also pointed to the inconsistency in financial regulation — U.S. commercial banks were allowed to undertake many securities activities abroad not permitted in their own domestic market. The change in the Fed's position was strengthened by the fact that between 1985 and 1986, President Reagan had appointed several new governors to the Fed Board.

The new appointees indicated that they were acutely aware of the international pressure on domestic financial markets and were strong advocates of bank deregulation, including a repeal of the Glass-Steagall Act. It was these changes that led the Fed to consider the applications of Citicorp, Bankers Trust, and J.P. Morgan to underwrite commercial paper, mortgage-backed securities, and municipal revenue bonds through separate affiliates. When the Board, in the spring of 1987, voted to permit the activities, the narrow 3-2 vote reflected the internal division that had erupted within the institution as a result of the changing external circumstances. Since Chairman Volcker remained opposed to such a blatant breach of Glass-Steagall, the decision would not have its intended effect of promoting policy progress either in Congress (by passing a bill) or in the judiciary (by upholding permissive rulings by the regulators).

This would change with the departure of Paul Volcker and the appointment of Alan Greenspan as the new chairman of the Board of Governors in the summer of 1987. Greenspan's appointment led the Board to unanimously endorse the repeal of the Glass-Steagall Act and united federal regulators in their position on this particular aspect of bank reform. But the mere fact that all three regulators now had a single unified position towards bank reform did automatically translate into actual policy change. Primary policymaking authority in the network still rested with Congress. Any adjustment in the rules that governed commercial banks still had to be implemented through legislative action by Congress. But the legislature remained locked in a gridlock that by the late 1980s had deteriorated into jurisdictional turf battles among two House committees, and left no hope for any legislative resolution of the conflict.

With the inability of Congress to act, the entire burden of regulatory adjustment had been shifted to the agencies, and especially the Fed, since its client banks were the most vocal advocates of a repeal of Glass-Steagall. In fact, in their applications to be granted the power to underwrite a whole series of securities in the spring of 1987, the money centre banks provided the Fed with the legal loophole that would enable the central bank to reinterpret existing legislation and open the securities business to commercial banks. This time, the Board did not hesitate, and granted the banks sweeping new powers that would enable them to better compete at home and abroad.

As on previous occasions, the mere reinterpretation of existing statutes, however, was not sufficient to overcome the vigorous resistance of the securities industry. Given that every ruling by the Fed that would lower the barrier between commercial and investment banking was contested by the SIA in court, the Fed's ability to implement regulatory change depended on the judiciary's willingness to allow such permissive interpretations of the statutes within the existing framework of banking law. On earlier occasions, the courts had resisted relocating policymaking authority from Congress to the agencies, and on several occasions rejected the sweeping reinterpretations of the banking statutes by the Fed and other regulators. However, in the spring of 1987, when the SIA asked the Supreme Court to hear an appeal against a lower court ruling regarding the banks' ability to sell commercial paper, the high court refused to hear the appeal, arguing that due to the Fed's expertise in these matters the regulator must be given greatest deference in interpreting the statutes of the banking law. In other words, though the rulings of the Fed proved to be in vain on earlier occasions because the courts were unwilling to participate in the policymaking process and referred the regulators back to Congress, the judiciary now had become a vital link in the policymaking process by legitimizing the Fed's rulings. More specifically, by giving the Fed far greater latitude in interpreting the banking statutes on a whole range of issues, the courts, by the late 1980s, had effectively relocated the policymaking process away from the legislature to the regulatory agencies.

But the Fed still had to weigh its newly gained freedom from the legislature in the field of bank regulation against a possible curbing of its autonomy in the conduct of monetary policy. Some members of Congress vigorously opposed the Fed's role as a policymaker and threatened to drastically reduce the agency's power if the Fed began to repeal Glass-Steagall through administrative rulings. However, with the rising threat of foreign competition, even the legislature began to reconsider its position, and those opposing change were challenged by a new bipartisan faction in Congress that fully endorsed the need for banking reform in light of the globalization of financial markets. In the Senate, this group included the Democratic and Republican leadership in the Banking Committee. This bipartisan coalition emerged after Chairman Proxmire, a longtime supporter of the Glass-Steagall Act, reversed his position in light of the increasing competitive pressures on U.S. commercial banks. After 1986, several members in both the Senate and the House began to publicly challenge St. Germain's position on Glass-Steagall, eventually forcing him to introduce a bill that proposed moderate securities powers for commercial banks.

There were two principal reasons why even those members that had long resisted the deregulation of banking now agreed to introduce some reform of the system. First, once the SIA had decided to abandon its long-held resistance to a repeal of Glass-Steagall — because in the long run it might be more effective to restructure the domestic system and face competition at home in order to be able to compete better internationally — the most formidable public-private sector coalition opposed to change for the previous two decades ceased to exist. Secondly, a House member who was against deregulation, and defended his position by appealing to such broad notions as the country's traditions and value system, could continue to do so by arguing for reform. During the first half of the 1980s, many Congressmen rejected the deregulation of banking on the grounds that it would lead to undue concentration in the financial services industry and eliminate many of the smaller rural banks, a central characteristic of the U.S. economy. The same members now advocated the reform — not deregulation — of the banking system as a matter of national interest to preserve the independence and strength of the U.S. financial services industry, but also to preserve jobs, provide cheap capital, and improve the rising trade deficit. The persuasive power of the threat of foreign competition and its populist undertone had such an impact that by 1989, numerous congressmen in the House and Senate publicly encouraged the Fed to approve the pending applications by the money centre banks. In doing so, they relinquished their policymaking power to the Fed and the courts, undermining the credibility and legitimacy of their own institution, the primary policymaking body in the network. Given this strong support and encouragement, the Fed decided to ignore the threats from those opposing its role as a policymaker and approved many of the applications, which led to a *de facto* repeal of Glass-Steagall.

Thus, despite the fact that the fragmented policy network remained fully mobilized, a policy resolution was eventually achieved. Two interrelated factors explain this unusual outcome. The shifting policy positions led to a much greater degree of consensus in the fragmented policy network. By the middle of 1989, only one congressional committee was opposing some reform of the Glass-Steagall Act. Still, the structural position of the committee allowed it to block any policy progress in the legislature. But this newly established consensus also convinced those institutions in favour of a repeal of Glass-Steagall to take charge of the policymaking process by excluding the political forces that were capable of blocking a resolution. By forging a strategic alliance, the Fed and the judiciary demobilized the legislature by excluding it from the policymaking process, reducing the structural possibility of gridlock. Within a relatively short time, the network generated a policy resolution.

In sum, the progressive internationalization of financial markets and the intensification of foreign competition generated important shifts in the interests of some powerful public and private sector institutions in the U.S. policy network. These shifts eliminated many of the conflicts and competing coalitions which had previously contributed to the policy gridlock in the network. However, these shifts were not sufficient to break the legislative gridlock over Glass-Steagall. In a decentralized policy network characterized by dispersed regulatory authority, shifts in the positions of some major actors could not produce a legislative repeal of Glass-Steagall as long as any one congressional institution remained opposed to change. Yet the absence of legislative action did not imply continued gridlock. Based on the new policy consensus, the agencies, with the support of the courts, issued a series of rulings that have resulted in a *de facto* repeal of most of the restrictions embodied in the Glass-Steagall Act.

Turning to the issue of capital adequacy, the intensification of the external economic pressures upon the U.S. policy network also generated significant shifts within the policy network. Despite the initial success of moving toward a common domestic standard, a policy impasse had developed by late 1982. It soon became clear that resolution of the challenge posed by declining capital ratios was not an automatic process. Just as in the case of Glass-Steagall, regulatory adjustment required changes in the positions of some important actors, in this particular case the Fed and the large multinational banks. The industrializing countries' debt crisis in 1982-83 would prove to be the external catalyst, leading to several important changes in the policy network that allowed a policy resolution to emerge.

Most importantly, the debt crisis mobilized Congress to participate in the debate over capital adequacy and shifted the distribution of political power in the policy network towards the legislature. It mobilized Congress, because the debt crisis presented a threat to the safety and stability of the U.S. banking system and to the entire U.S. economy. As a result, Congress felt compelled to act in order to prevent a recurrence of such a crisis. It shifted the distribution of power in the policy network because in order to avert a default by several Latin American countries, the banks, the regulators, and the Administration all desired an increase in the U.S.'s contribution to the IMF, which required congressional approval.

Congress had long favoured specific capital standards for multinational banks, but also advocated higher and more uniform standards for *all* banks. Yet throughout the first years of the debate over capital standards, the regulators (especially the Fed and the OCC) were successful in defending their administrative turf against any incursion by the legislature. But once the extent of the debt crisis unfolded, Congress was in a position to blame the regulators for their negligence in allowing capital ratios to deteriorate and for failing to supervise the international activities of U.S. banks, thus challenging the agencies' institutional capacity in this particular area of bank regulation. The fact that any IMF quota increase needed congressional approval empowered the legislature to make its consent to such a quota increase conditional upon the regulators' agreement to implement higher and equal capital standards across *all* banks, including the multinationals.

A second reason why Congress found itself in a more powerful position to influence policymaking was the fact that the Bellaire case had effectively undermined the regulatory capacity of the agencies and left them dependent upon legislation that would reestablish their regulatory power. Finally, multinational banks, while still resisting a capital increase, had lost much of their political leverage as a pressure group. First, the debt crisis revealed in a dramatic way the dangers inherent in the low capital reserves held by the large money centre banks. This discredited the long-held argument by multinational banks that bank size is a proxy for safety and thus justifies lower capital reserves. Secondly, since their own imprudent lending practices had left the money centre banks vulnerable to the industrializing countries' debt default, they were dependent upon congressional approval of an IMF quota increase for their continued financial viability, and thus were hardly in a position to challenge Congress's demands for higher capital standards.

Thus, just as in the case of Glass-Steagall, external pressures generated changes that enabled the policy network to resolve the initial challenge. The shift in the distribution of political power in the policy network allowed Congress to force a policy resolution upon the other major actors, as the regulatory agencies and the banks were willing to accept congressional conditions on capital adequacy in return for the approval of the IMF quota increase. Clearly, given the original consensus and the considerable progress that had already been made towards a resolution of the problem by the time external pressure increased, policy progress was much easier in the case of capital adequacy than in the case of Glass-Steagall. More specifically, the network did not have to resort to a strategy of exclusion to arrive at the necessary consensus. To the contrary, it was the additional involvement of Congress in the decisionmaking process that led to a policy resolution.

But the external pressure had an even more profound impact in the case of capital adequacy than in the case of Glass-Steagall. In both cases, increasing external pressure caused a policy resolution. But while the original policy objective and the process by which that objective was achieved remained the same in the case of Glass-Steagall, the increasing external pressure altered the process by which the policy objective was achieved in the case of capital adequacy. During the congressional hearings that led to the passage of ILSA, a broad consensus among the public sector actors in the policy network developed; that is, the original policy objective could no longer be achieved solely through domestic regulation. Policymakers realized that globalization of financial markets had advanced to such a degree that higher capital standards in the U.S. alone could not insulate the American financial system from a crisis in another financial market. In addition, banks and policymakers concurred that a unilateral U.S. move to raise capital standards would place U.S. banks at a disadvantage in an integrated global market by forcing them to conform to stricter regulations than their competitors. Moreover, money centre banks had indicated that they would be more inclined to acquiesce to higher capital standards if such a move were to include other countries as well. Thus, by the time ILSA was passed, the objective to raise and harmonize capital standards in U.S. domestic financial markets had been expanded to the long-term goal of achieving an international agreement to strengthen and harmonize capital standards across the major financial markets. As a result, it was not only the actual policymaking *process* that differed across the two cases. Globalization of financial markets also generated divergent policy *outcomes*. In the case of Glass-Steagall, the challenge to the U.S. financial policy network was resolved by *domestic adjustment and deregulation*. The only way to resolve the challenge of declining capital ratios, on the other hand, was through *international cooperation and reregulation*.

Finally, both case studies demonstrate the central role of institutions in structuring the political and economic conflicts in the policy network and ultimately determining their outcome. In both cases, it was primarily institutional interests that defined the nature of the conflict in the policy network. Probably the most striking example is the jurisdictional turf battle among the two House committees, which was not even related to the actual issues over which the conflict originally erupted, but led to complete gridlock in the policy network and ultimately to the exclusion of Congress from the policymaking process. Another important example is the institutional competition that evolved among the regulators over the depth and pace of deregulation. Many of the rulings issued by individual agencies can be explained by the institution's desire to expand or defend its regulatory turf and institutional standing with its client banks. The case of discount brokerage or the FDIC's ruling with regard to state chartered non-member banks comes to mind. Finally, the Fed's hesitance even after the Board had unanimously endorsed the repeal of Glass-Steagall can only be explained by the threat to its institutional interest in preserving its independence in the conduct of monetary policy.

But while institutions were central in explaining the larger processes of mobilization, conflict and resolution, they were not always capable of explaining some of the most critical junctures in the conflict — the incidence of change. Clearly, in the case of capital adequacy, it was Congress's entry into the conflict phase that provided the required impetus to change and policy resolution. But in the case of Glass-Steagall, it was the individual actors who emerged as the most important sources of change and conflict resolution. First, Alan Greenspan's appointment to the Fed and his influence as chairman over the Board of Governors turned the Fed into an ardent advocate of the Glass-Steagall repeal, uniting all three regulators in pressuring Congress to change the law. Secondly, and even more importantly, the final impetus to a *de facto* repeal of Glass-Steagall did not come about because the Fed had changed its position. Rather, it was the encouragement of several congressmen that led the Fed to move on the applications. But those congressmen were not acting to promote their institutional interest in preserving congressional authority over banking legislation; rather, they made their decisions as individual actors who were resigned to the institution's inability to execute bank regulatory policy. The importance of individual actors in inducing institutional change in the case of Glass-Steagall supports the contention that theories of institutional change do not provide clear guidance on the thresholds necessary to induce change.[3]

Turning to the process of institutional change itself, the analysis of Glass-Steagall has demonstrated that institutional breakdown is not as sudden and abrupt as the wording might imply and as others have portrayed it. For example, when Congress, as an institution, was finally excluded from the policymaking process, it was the culmination of a decade-long conflict, during which the legislature gradually drifted to the point of complete paralysis while the external pressure steadily increased. *The politics of institutional change and breakdown* involved a long struggle among numerous public and private sector institutions and actors over market shares in the financial services industry, as well as regulatory jurisdiction and influence among government institutions. In addition, institutional breakdown in Congress did not occur in isolation from the rest of the policy network. Rather, by the time Congress had been demobilized and excluded from the policymaking process, the Fed and the judiciary had filled the political and policy vacuum that the legislature would have left behind. Thus, the network continued to function, albeit with newly distributed powers, and the policymaking process did not collapse. Other institutions and individual actors mediated the process of change. Focusing on the incidence of institutional breakdown alone would neglect much of the political dynamics characteristic of the financial policy network.

Lastly, institutional breakdown is not always necessary to enact change. To the contrary, in the case of capital adequacy the institutions in the policy network adjusted to avoid breakdown. The adjustment transformed the policy network from a purely domestic set of institutions into an international institutional framework that could effectively regulate the emerging global financial market. As early as 1987, Paul Volcker addressed the political consequences of the globalization of financial markets for domestic regulatory policy: 'There is a sense in which all of us, perhaps in this area more dramatically than in other areas, lose sovereignty in developing regulations and supervision that is just directed toward our domestic markets.'[4] Indeed as shown in Chapter 8, in order to keep the policy network operational and to arrive at the international agreement, the interests of foreign regulators and banks were more important in determining the policy outcome than those of domestic — public and private — institutions, reflecting the extent to which the politics of capital adequacy regulation had become an international issue rather than a domestic one.

NOTES

1. As quoted in *WSJ*, April 29, 1981.
2. Reinicke (1992), ECPR Inaugural Pan-European Conference, Heidelberg, 16-20 September.
3. See also Ikenberry et al. (1988).
4. Statement by Paul Volcker, *Globalization of Financial Markets and Related International Banking and Supervision Issues*, 30 July 1987.

References

A great variety of sources were employed in the writing of this study. For the purposes of organization, the author lists them below under eight separate categories.

Books, book chapters, and working papers

Angermüller, Hans A. (1988), 'The Evolution of Banking Strategies and Services: The Dilemma Facing Today's Bankers', in Mikdashi, Zuhayr (ed.), *International Banking*, New York: St. Martin's Press.

Benston, G. (1990), *The Separation of Commercial and Investment Banking: the Glass-Steagall Act Revisited and Reconsidered*, New York: Oxford University Press.

Bhala, Raj (1989), *Perspectives on Risk-Based Capital*, Bank Administration Institute.

Born, K.E. (1983), *International Banking in the 19th and 20th Centuries*, Leamington Spa: Berg Publishers.

Bröcker, G. (1990), *Competition in Banking*, Paris: OECD.

Cargill, T. and Garcia, G. (1983), *Financial Deregulation and Monetary Control: Historical Perspectives and the Impact of the 1980 Act*, Stanford: Hoover Institution Press.

Carosso, V. (1970), *Investment Banking in America: A History*, Cambridge: Harvard University Press.

Carron, A. (1983), *The Political Economy of Regulation*, Washington, D.C.: The Brookings Institution.

Cohen, B. (1987), *In Whose Interest?*, New Haven: Yale University Press.

Cooke, Peter (1990), 'International Convergence of Capital Adequacy Standards' in Gardener, Edward (ed.), *The Future of Financial Systems and Services, Essays in Honor of Jack Revell*, New York: St. Martin's Press.

Cooper, K. and Fraser, D. (1986), *Banking Deregulation and the New Competition in Financial Services*, Cambridge: Ballinger Publishing Co..

Cox, Andrew, ed. (1986), *State, Finance, and Industry: A Comparative Analysis of Post-War Trends in Six Advanced Industrial Economies*, New York: St. Martin's Press.

Dale, R. (1986), *The Regulation of International Banking*, Eaglewood Cliffs, N.J.: Prentice Hall.

Edwards, Franklin and Scott, J.H. (1979), 'Regulating the Solvency of Depository Institutions: A Perspective for Deregulation' in Edwards, F.R. (ed.), *Issues in Financial Regulation*, New York: McGraw-Hill.

Einzig, P. (1967), *The Euro-Dollar System*, New York: Macmillan.

Eisenbeis, R. (1983), 'Bank Holding Companies and Public Policy' in Benston, George (ed.), *Financial Services: The Changing Institutions and Government Policy*, Englewood Cliffs, N.J.: Prentice Hall.

Evans, P., Rueschemeyer, D. and Skocpol, T., eds. (1985) *Bringing the State Back In*, Cambridge: Cambridge University Press.

Feis, H. (1965), *Europe, the World's Banker, 1870-1914*, New York: Norton.

Flannery, Mark (1985), 'Economic Evaluation of Bank Securities Activities', in Walter, Ingo (ed.), *Deregulating Wall Street: Commercial Bank Penetration of the Corporate Securities Market*, New York: Wiley and Sons.

Frankel, J. (1984), *The Yen/Dollar Agreement: Liberalizing Japanese Capital Markets*, Washington, D.C.: Institute for International Economics.

Frankel, Jeffrey (1989), 'Quantifying International Capital Mobility in the 1980s', *NBER Working Paper*, No. 2856, National Bureau of Economic Research, February.

Freeman, Harry L. (1987), 'Implications of Global Financial Intermediation' in Mikdashi, Zuhayr (ed.), *International Banking*, New York: St. Martin's Press.

Friedman, Benjamin (1987), 'Postwar Changes in the American Financial Markets' in Feldstein, Martin (ed.), *The American Economy in Transition*, Chicago: University of Chicago Press.

Gerston, L., Farleigh, C. and Schwab, R. (1988), *The Deregulated Society*, Pacific Grove, CA: Brooks/Cole.

Giddy, Ian H. (1985), 'Domestic Regulation versus International Competition in Banking' in Krümmel, Hans-Jacob (ed.), *Internationales Bankgeschäft, Beiheft zu Kredit und Kapital*, No. 8, Berlin: Duncker & Humblot.

Goddin, Steward and Weiss, Steven (1981), 'U.S. Banks' Loss of Global Standing' in Staff of the Office of the Comptroller of the Currency, *Foreign Acquisitions of U.S. Banks*, Richmond: Robert F. Dame.

Goldberg, Lawrence and White, L., eds. (1979), *The Deregulation of Banking and Securities Industries*, Lexington, MA: Lexington Books.

Goldsmith, R. (1958), *Financial Intermediaries in the American Economy Since 1900*, Princeton, N.J.: Princeton University Press.

Goodhardt, C. (1988), *The Evolution of Central Banks*, Cambridge, MA: MIT Press.

Hall, P. (1986), *Governing the Economy: The Politics of State Intervention in Britain and France*, New York: Oxford University Press.

Hammond, B. (1957), *Banks and Politics in America*, Princeton, N.J.: Princeton University Press.

Hawley, J.P. (1987), *Dollars and Borders: U.S. Government Attempts to Restrict Capital Flows, 1960-80*, New York: M.E. Sharp.

Horvitz, Paul (1987) in *Thrift Financial Performance and Capital Adequacy*, Federal Home Loan Bank Board.

Houpt, James (1988), 'International Trends for U.S. Banks and Banking Markets' in *Staff Study 156*, Washington, D.C.: Board of Governors of the Federal Reserve System, May.

Howard, D. and Hoffmann, G. (1980), *Evolving Concepts of Bank Capital Management*, New York: Citicorp.

Huertas, Thomas (1983), 'The Regulation of Financial Institutions: A Historical Perspective on Current Issues' in Benston, George (ed.), *Financial Services: The Changing Institutions and Government Policy*, Englewood Cliffs, N.J.: Prentice Hall.

Ikenberry, John, et al. eds. (1988), *The State in American Foreign Economic Policy*, Ithaca: Cornell University Press.

Jesse, M. and Selig, S. (1977), *Bank Holding Companies and the Public Interest*, Lexington, M.A.: Heath.

Kane, Edward J. (1987), 'Competitive Financial Reregulation: An International Perspective' in Portes, Richard, and Swoboda, Alexander (eds.), *Threats to*

International Financial Stability, New York: Cambridge University Press.

Katzenstein, Peter, ed. (1978), *Between Power and Plenty: Foreign Economic Policies of Advanced Industrial States*, Ithaca: Cornell University Press.

Katzenstein, P. (1984), *Corporatism and Change*, Ithaca: Cornell University Press.

Katzenstein, Peter, ed. (1989), *Industry and Politics in West Germany: Towards the Third Republic*, Ithaca: Cornell University Press.

Kaufman, H. (1971), *The Limits of Organizations*, University of Alabama Press.

Keeley, Michael (1988), 'Deposit Insurance, Risk and Market Power in Banking', *Working Paper 88-07*, Federal Reserve Bank of San Francisco, September.

Kelly, E. (1985), 'Legislative History of the Glass-Steagall Act' in Walter, Ingo (ed.), *Deregulating Wall Street: Commercial Bank Penetration of the Corporate Securities Market*, New York: John Wiley and Sons.

Kelly, J. (1977), *Bankers and Borders: The Case of American Banks in Britain*, Cambridge, MA: Ballinger Publishing Company.

Kennedy, S. (1973), *The Banking Crisis of 1933*, University of Kentucky Press.

Kindleberger, C. (1974), *The Formation of Financial Centers: A Study in Comparative Economic History*, Princeton Studies in International Finance, No. 3: Princeton University.

Kindleberger, C. (1984), *A Financial History of Western Europe*, London: George Allen & Unwin.

Klebaner, B. (1974), *Commercial Banking in the United States: A History*, Hinsdale, IL: The Dryden Press.

Klein (1978), *Wesen und Funktion der BIZ*.

Krasner, S. (1978) *Defending the National Interest*, Princeton: Princeton University Press.

Krooss, H. and Blyn, M. (1971), *A History of Financial Intermediaries*, New York: Random House Publishers.

Lemke (1977), *Die BIZ*, HdWW.

Litan, R. (1987), *What Should Banks Do?*, Washington, D.C.: The Brookings Institution.

Maisel, Sherman, ed. (1981), *Risk and Capital Adequacy in Commercial Banks*, Chicago: University of Chicago Press.

March, J. and Olsen, J. (1989), *Rediscovering Institutions: The Organizational Basis of Politics*, New York: The Free Press.

Meerschwam, David (1989), 'International Capital Imbalances: The Demise of Local Financial Boundaries', in O'Brien, Richard and Datta, Tapan (eds.), *International Economics and Financial Markets*, Oxford: Oxford University Press.

Obstfeld, Maurice (1986), 'Capital Mobility in the World Economy: Theory and Measurement' in Brunner, Karl and Meltzer, Allan (eds.), *The National Bureau Method, International Capital Mobility, and Other Essays*, Amsterdam: North-Holland Publishing Company.

Ogata, S., Cooper, R., Schulmann, H. (1989), *International Financial Integration: The Policy Challenges*, Triangle Papers No. 37, The Trilateral Commission.

Orgler, Y. and Wolkowitz, B. (1976), *Bank Capital*, New York: Van Nostrand Reinhold Company.

Pauly, L. (1988), *Opening Financial Markets: Banking Politics on the Pacific Rim*, Ithaca, N.Y.: Cornell University Press.

Pavel, Christine and Rosenblum, Harvey (1984), 'Financial Services in Transition: The Effects of Nonbank Competitors', *Staff Memoranda*, SM84-1, Federal Reserve Bank of Chicago.

Pecchioli, R.M. (1983), *The Internationalization of Banking: The Policy Issues*, Paris: OECD.

Pecchioli, R.M. (1987), *Prudential Supervision in Banking*, Paris: OECD.

Polakoff, M. (1970), 'The Evolution of the U.S. Money and Capital Markets and Financial Intermediaries', *Financial Institutions and Markets*, Boston: Houghton Mifflin and Co..

Redlich, F. (1946-51), *The Molding of American Banking, Vol. I & II*, New York: Hafner Publishing Company.

Revell, J. (1983), *Banking and Electronic Fund Transfer System*, Paris: OECD.

Revell, J. (1986), 'Implications of Information Technology for Financial Institutions' in Fair, Donald (ed.), *Shifting Frontiers in Financial Markets*, Boston: Martinus Nijhoff Publishers.

Roll, Richard (1988), 'The International Crash of October 1987' in Kamphuis, R., Kormendi, R. and Watson, J.W.H. (eds.), *Black Monday and the Future of Financial Markets*, Mid-American Institute, October.

Rosenbluth, F. McCall (1989), *Financial Politics in Contemporary Japan*, Ithaca, N.Y.: Cornell University Press.

Rosenthal, J. and Ocampo, J. (1988), *Securitization of Credit: Inside the New Technology of Finance*, New York: Wiley.

Sametz, A., ed. (1981), *Securities Activities of Commercial Banks*, Lexington, MA: Lexington Books.

Saunders, Anthony and White, L., eds. (1986), *Technology and the Regulation of Financial Markets*, Lexington, MA: Lexington Books.

Savage, Donald (1978), 'A History of the Bank Holding Company Movement, 1900-1978', in Board of Governors of the Federal Reserve System, *The Bank Holding Company Movement to 1978: A Compendium*, Washington, D.C.: Federal Reserve Board.

Skowronek, S. (1982), *Building a New American State: The Expansion of National Administrative Capacities*, New York: Cambridge University Press.

Spero, J.E. (1980), *The Failure of the Franklin National Bank*, New York: Columbia University Press.

Vietor, Richard (1987), 'Regulation Defined Financial Markets: Fragmentation and Integration in Financial Services' in Hayes, Samuel (ed.), *Wall Street and Regulation*, Cambridge: Harvard Business School Press.

Walter, I. (1985), *Barriers to Trade in Banking and Financial Services*, London: Trade Policy Research Center.

Watson, M., Mathieson, D., Kincaid, R. and Kalter, E. (1988), 'Structural Changes in International Financial Markets' in Norton, Joseph Jude (ed.), *Prospects for International Lending and Reschedulings*, Matthew Bender.

Wellons, P. (1987), *Passing the Buck: Banks, Governments and Third World Debt*, Cambridge, MA: Harvard Business School Press.

White, E. (1983), *The Regulation and Reform of the American Banking System 1900-1929*, Princeton, N.J.: Princeton University Press.

Wilson, J. (1973), *Political Organizations*, New York: Basic Books.

Zysman, John (1978), 'The French State in the International Economy' in Katzenstein, Peter, ed. (1978), *Between Power and Plenty: Foreign Economic Policies of Advanced Industrial States*, Ithaca: Cornell University Press.

Zysman, J. (1983) *Governments, Markets and Growth*, Ithaca: Cornell University Press.

Organization/agency as author

American Bankers Association (1981), *The Regulation of Capital Ratios in U.S. Banking*, Washington, D.C.: ABA.

American Bankers Association (1986), *Expanded Products and Services for Banking: The Public Policy Perspective*, Washington, D.C.: ABA.

Bank for International Settlements (1986), *Recent Innovations in International Banking 1985* , Basle: BIS.

Bank for International Settlements (1986), *Fifty-Sixth Annual Report*, June.

Bank for International Settlements (1987), *Annual Report 1986/87*, Basle: BIS.

Bank for International Settlements (1991), *International Banking and Financial Market Developments*, Basle: BIS.

Bank of England, *Measurement of Capital*, September 1980.

Basle Committee on Bank Supervision (1989), *Mimeo*, Basle, Section 8.

Board of Governors of the Federal Reserve System (1990), *Annual Report*, Washington, D.C.: Federal Reserve Board.

Bureau of National Affairs, 'Final International Risk-Based Standards Adopted', *Banking Report*, 25 July 1988.

Commission of the European Communities (1990), *Report on United States Trade Barriers and Unfair Trade Practices*, Brussels: EC Commission.

Committee on Banking Regulations and Supervisory Practices (1982), *Report on International Developments in Banking Supervision 1981*, Basle.

Committee on Banking Regulations and Supervisory Practices (1983), *Report on International Developments in Banking Supervision 1982*, Basle.

Committee on Banking Regulations and Supervisory Practices (1984), *Report on International Developments in Banking Supervision 1983*, Basle.

Committee on Banking Regulations and Supervisory Practices (1986), *Report on International Developments in Banking Supervision, Report Number 5*, Basle.

Committee on Banking Regulations and Supervisory Practices (1987), *Report on International Developments in Banking Supervision, Report Number 6*, Basle.

Committee on Banking Regulations and Supervisory Practices (1987), *Proposals for International convergence of capital measurement and capital standards*, Consultative Paper, Basle: BIS.

Federal Deposit Insurance Corporation (1980), Annual Report.

Federal Deposit Insurance Corporation (1987), *Mandate for Change*, Washington, D.C.: FDIC.

Federal Financial Institution Examination Council (1980), *Capital Trends in Federally Regulated Financial Institutions*, Washington, D.C.: FFIEC.

Federal Financial Institution Examination Council (1987), *Annual Report*.

Federal Reserve Bank of Dallas (1990), 'Securities Proposal Revitalizes Glass-Steagall Debate', Financial Services Information, Spring.

Federal Reserve Bank of New York (1986), *Recent Trends in Commercial Bank Profitability: A Staff Study*.

Federal Reserve Board, *Press Release*, 6 July 1984.

Federal Reserve Board, 'Capital Maintenance: Supplemental Adjusted Capital Measure', *Press Release*, 24 January 1986.

Federal Reserve Board, *Press Release*, 21 September 1989.

Federal Reserve Board, Division of Banking Regulation and Supervision, *Memorandum*, 7 November 1983.

Independent Bankers Association of American (1990), 'SIA Reviews Glass-Steagall Position', *Washington Weekly Report*, 8 December.

International Monetary Fund (1981), *International Capital Markets: Recent Developments and Short-Term Prospects*, Washington, D.C.: IMF.

International Monetary Fund (1986), *International Capital Markets, Developments and Prospects*, Washington, D.C.: IMF.

International Monetary Fund (1988), *International Capital Markets, Developments and Prospects*, Washington, D.C.: IMF.

Morgan Guaranty Trust Co. (1986), 'Global Financial Change', *World Financial Markets*, December.

Organization for Economic Cooperation and Development (1984), *International Trade in Services: Banking*, Paris: OECD.

Organization for Economic Cooperation and Development (1985), *Trends in Banking in OECD Countries*, Paris: OECD.

Organization for Economic Cooperation and Development (1987), *Introduction to the OECD Codes of Liberalization*, Paris: OECD.

Organization for Economic Cooperation and Development (1987), *International Trade in Services: Securities*, Paris: OECD.

Organization for Economic Cooperation and Development (1989), *Economies in Transition: Structural Adjustment in OECD Countries*, Paris: OECD.

Organization for Economic Cooperation and Development (1989), *Liberalization of Capital Movements and Financial Services in the OECD Area*, Paris: OECD.

Presidential Task Force on Market Mechanisms, *Report*, January 1988, Study No. 1.

Riverside Economic Research (1993), 'The Brancalo Report', Washington, D.C., December.

Salomon Brothers Inc., 'Implications of the Federal Reserve's Proposed Capital Guidelines', Bond Market Research Publication, 12 September 1985.

Salomon Brothers Inc., Research Department, 'International Bank Capital Adequacy Proposals: Our Initial Thoughts', January 1988.

Securities Industry Association (1990), 'SIA Signals Major Policy Shift on Glass-Steagall', *Washington Report*, 12 January.

United Nations Center on Transnational Corporations (1989), *Foreign Direct Investment and Transnational Corporations in Services*, New York: United Nations.

United Nations, Department of International Economic and Social Affairs (1986), 'The changing institutional character of international financial markets in the 1980s', *Supplement, World Economic Survey 1985-1986*, New York: United Nations.

United States Department of the Treasury (1991), *Modernizing the Financial System: Recommendation for Safer, More Competitive Banks*, Washington, D.C.: U.S. Department of the Treasury.

United States General Accounting Office (1986), *International Coordination of Bank Supervision: The Record to Date*, GAO/NSIAD-86-40, Washington, D.C.: GAO.

United States General Accounting Office (1986), *U.S. Banking Supervision and International Supervisory Principles*, GAO/NSIAD-86-93, Washington, D.C.: GAO.

United States General Accounting Office (1988), *Bank Powers: Issues Related to the Repeal of the Glass-Steagall Act*, Washington, D.C.: GAO.

United States General Accounting Office (1988), *Market Access Concerns of U.S.*

Financial Institutions in Japan, GAO/NSIAD-88-108BR, Washington, D.C.: GAO.
United States General Accounting Office (1988), *Off-Balance Sheet Activities*, GAO/GGD-88-35BR, Washington, D.C.: GAO.
United States General Accounting Office (1990), *European Community, U.S. Financial Services' Competitiveness Under the Single Market Program*, GAO/NSIAD-90-99, Washington, D.C.: GAO.

Journal and newspaper articles (signed)

Aderhood, R., Cumming, C. and Harwood, A. (1988), 'International Linkages Among Equities Markets and the October 1987 Market Break', *Quarterly Review*, Federal Reserve Bank of New York, Summer.
Bardos, Jeffrey (1987-88), 'The Risk-based Capital Agreement: A Further Step Towards Policy Convergence', *Quarterly Review*, Federal Reserve Bank of New York, Winter.
Bellanger, Serge (1987), 'Regulating International Banking', *The Bankers Magazine*, November-December.
Bench, Robert and Sable, Dorothy (1986), 'International Lending Supervision', *North Carolina Journal of International Law and Commercial Regulation*, **11** (3).
Bennett, Paul and Kelleher, Jeanette (1988), 'The International Transmission of Stock Price Disruption in October 1987', *Quarterly Review*, Federal Reserve Bank of New York, Summer.
Bennett, Robert (1980), 'Is One-Stop Banking Next?', *NYT*, 28 December 1980.
Benz, Steven (1985), 'Trade Liberalization and the Global Service Economy', *Journal of World Trade Law*, **19**.
Blunden, George (1977), 'International co-operation in banking supervision', *Quarterly Bulletin*, Bank of England, September.
Boemio, Thokas and Edwards, Jr., Gerald (1989), 'Asset Securitization: A Supervisory Perspective', *Federal Reserve Bulletin*, **75**, October.
Booth, James (1989), 'The Securitization of Lending Markets', *Weekly Letter*, Federal Reserve Bank of San Francisco, September.
Boyd, John and Graham, Stanley (1988), 'The Profitability and Risk Effects of Allowing Bank Holding Companies to Merge With Other Financial Firms: A Simulation Study', *Quarterly Report*, Federal Reserve Bank of Minneapolis, Spring.
Brewer, Elijah, Fortier, Diana and Pavel, Christine (1988), 'Bank risk from nonbank activities', *Economic Perspectives*, Federal Reserve Bank of Chicago, **12** (4).
Brimmer, Andrew and Dahl, Frederick (1975), 'Growth of American International Banking: Implications for Public Policy', *Journal of Finance*, **30**.
Brittan III, Alfred, Chairman of Bankers Trust, 'Golden Goose of Investment Banks', *WP*, 15 September 1986.
Butcher, William (1981), 'Upheaval in Financial Services', *WSJ*, 15 May.
Cagan, Philip (1978), 'The Interest Saving to States and Municipalities from Bank Eligibility to Underwrite All Nonindustrial Bonds', *Governmental Finance*, **7**.
Clarke, Robert (1976), 'The Soundness of Financial Intermediaries', *Yale Law Journal*, **86** (1).
Cohen, Benjamin (1982), 'Balance of Payments Financing: The Evolution of a Regime?', *International Organization*, **36**.
Cooke, Peter (1981), 'Developments in co-operation among banking supervisory

authorities', *Quarterly Bulletin*, Bank of England, June.

Cooke, Peter (1983), 'The International Banking Scene: A Supervisory Perspective', *Bank of England Quarterly Bulletin*, March.

Cooke, Peter (1984), 'The Basle "Concordat" on the Supervision of Banks' Foreign Establishments', *Aussenwirtschaft*, **39**.

Cooke, Peter (1984), *Basle Supervisors Committee 1*, June.

Corrigan, Gerald (1982), 'Are Banks Special?', *Annual Report*, Federal Reserve Bank of Minneapolis.

Corrigan, Gerald (1986), 'On Financial System Reform', *NYT*, 29 August.

Corrigan, Gerald (1987), *Financial Market Structure: A Longer View*, Federal Reserve Bank of New York, February.

Corrigan, Gerald (1987), 'Coping With Globally Integrated Capital Markets', *Quarterly Review*, Federal Reserve Bank of New York, Winter.

Corrigan, Gerald (1990), 'Reforming the U.S. Financial System', *Quarterly Review*, Federal Reserve Bank of New York, Spring.

Crane, Dwight, and Hayes, Samuel (1983-84), 'The Evolution of International Bank Competition and Its Implications for Regulation', *Journal of Bank Research*, **14** (3).

Cumming, Christine (1987), 'The Economics of "Securitization"', *Quarterly Review*, Federal Reserve Bank of New York, **12** (3).

Dale, Richard (1982), 'Safeguarding the international banking system', *Banker*, August.

Dale, Richard (1983), 'Basle Concordat: Lessons from Ambrosiano', *Banker*, September.

de Jonquières, Guy (1989), 'The Myth of the Global Village', *Financial Times*, August.

de Larosière, Jacques (1989), 'La déréglementation a permis la "globalisation" des marchés', Agence Economique & Financière, Paris, in Deutsche Bundesbank (1989), *Auszüge Aus Presseartikeln* (62), August.

Denning, Ulrike (1986), 'Die Deregulierung des internationalen Finanzsystems seit 1975: Schein und Wirklichkeit', *Hamburger Jahrbücher für Wirtschaftsgeschichte*.

Dunn, Jeffrey (1982), 'Expansion of National Bank Powers: Regulatory and Judicial Precedent under the National Banking Act, Glass-Steagall Act, and Bank Holding Company Act', *Southwestern Law Journal*, **36**.

Dwyer, Jr., Gerald and Hafer, R.W. (1988), 'Are National Stock Markets Linked?', *Review*, Federal Reserve Bank of St. Louis, November/December.

Eglert (1970), 'The Development of Bank Holding Co. Legislation', *Bankers Magazine*, **21**.

Feileke, Norman, 'The Growth of U.S. Banking Abroad', *Federal Reserve Bank of Boston Conference Series* vol. 18 (1977).

Fischer, T., Gram, W., Kaufman, G. and Mote, L. (1984), 'The Securities Activities of Commercial Banks: A Legal and Economic Analysis', *Tennessee Law Review*, **51**.

Frieden, Jeffrey (1991), 'Invested Interests: the politics of national economic policies in a world of global finance', *International Organization*, **45** (4).

Friedman, Benjamin (1975), 'Regulation Q and the Commercial Loan Market in the 1960s', *Journal of Money Credit and Banking*, August.

Fukao, Mitsuhiro and Hanazaki, Masaharu (1987), 'Internationalisation of Financial Markets and the Allocation of Capital', *OECD Economic Studies* (8), Spring.

Gavin, Brigid (1985), 'A GATT for International Banking', *Journal of World Trade Law*, **19**.

Gehlen, Jr., James (1983), 'A Review of Bank Capital and Its Adequacy', *Economic Review*, Federal Reserve Bank of Atlanta, **68** (11) November.

Germany, J. David and Morton, John (1985), 'Financial Innovation and Deregulation in Foreign Industrial Countries', *Federal Reserve Bulletin*, **71** (10).

Giddy, Ian and Allen, D.L. (1979), 'International Competition in Bank Regulation', *Banca Nazionale del Lavoro Quarterly Review* (130).

Gilbert, Stone, and Trebing (1985), 'The New Capital Adequacy Standards', *Review*, Federal Reserve Bank of St. Louis, **12**, May.

Goldberg, Lawrence and Saunders, Anthony (1980), 'The Causes of U.S. Bank Expansion Overseas: The Case of Great Britain', *Journal of Money Credit and Banking*, **12** (4).

Gossling, Margaret (1988), 'The Capital Adequacy Framework — An Introduction', *Journal of International Banking Law*, **6** (3).

Gould, George (1987), 'Arthritic Laws Are Crippling United States Banks', *NYT*, 11 August 1987.

Gowa, Joanne (1988), 'Public Goods and Political Institutions', *International Organization*, **42** (1).

Guttmann, Robert (1987), 'Changing of the Guard at the Fed', *Challenge*, November-December.

Hackley, Howard (1966), 'Our Baffling Banking System', Part I & II, *Virginia Law Review*, **52** (4 & 5).

Hackley, Howard (1969), 'Our Discriminatory Banking Structure', *Virginia Law Review*, **55** (8).

Halpert, Stephen (1988), 'The Separation of Banking and Commerce Reconsidered', *The Journal of Corporation Law*, **13** (2).

Hammond, Thomas and Knott, Jack (1988), 'Deregulatory Snowball: Explaining Deregulation in the Financial Industry', *Journal of Politics*, **50**.

Heggestad, Arnold (1982), 'Regulation of Bank Capital: An Evaluation', *Economic Review*, Federal Reserve Bank of Atlanta, **67** (3).

Heller, H. Robert (1988), 'Banking Reform for the 1990s', *Journal of Commerce*, 26 September.

Holland, David (1986), 'Foreign Bank Capital and the United States Federal Reserve Board', *International Lawyer*, **20** (3).

Isaac, William (1982), 'Capital Adequacy and Deposit Insurance', *Annual Review of Banking*, **1**.

Isaac, William (1983), 'Instilling Discipline in the Banks', *NYT*, 7 April.

Isaac, William (1984), 'Continental Case Was Handled Well, But Shows Need to Push Deregulation', *WSJ*, 29 May.

Kane, Edward (1981), 'The Capital-Adequacy Card Game', *American Banker*, November.

Kapstein, Ethan (1989), 'Resolving the regulator's dilemma: international coordination of banking regulations', *International Organization*, **43** (2).

Kasman, Bruce and Pigott, Charles (1988), 'Interest Rate Divergence Among the Major Industrial Nations', *Quarterly Review*, Federal Reserve Bank of New York, Autumn.

Kaufman, George, Mote, Larry and Rosenblum, Harvey (1983-84), 'Implications of Deregulation for Product Lines and Geographic Markets of Financial Institutions', *Journal of Banking Research*, **14** (1).

Keeley, Michael (1988), 'Bank Capital Regulation in the 1980s: Effective or Ineffective?', *Economic Review*, Federal Reserve Bank of San Francisco, Summer.

Keeton, William (1989), 'The New Risk-Based Capital Plan for Commercial Banks', *Economic Review*, Federal Reserve Board of Kansas City, December.

Keller, Bill (1982), 'Liberation of Bank Industry This Year May be Thwarted by Fractured Finance Lobbies', *Congressional Quarterly Weekly Report*, **40**, February.

Kessel, Reuben (1971), 'A Study of the Effects of Competition in the Tax-exempt Bond Market', *Journal of Political Economy*, **79**.

Khambata, Dara (1989), 'Off-Balance-Sheet Activities of U.S. Banks: An Empirical Evaluation', *The Columbia Journal of World Business*, **24** (2).

Kool, Clemens and Tatom, John (1988), 'International Linkages in the Term Structure of Interest Rates', *Review*, Federal Reserve Bank of St. Louis, **70** (4).

Krasner, Stephen (1984), 'Approaches to the State: Alternative Conceptions and Historical Dynamics', *Comparative Politics*, **16** (1).

Lamfalussy, Alexander (1989), 'Globalization of Financial Markets: International Supervisory and Regulatory Issues', *Economic Review*, Federal Reserve Bank of Kansas City, **74** (1).

Liechtenstein (1985), 'The U.S. Response to the International Debt Crisis: The International Lending Supervisory Act of 1983', *Virginia Journal of International Law*, **25**.

Linton, Robert (1983), 'Banks, Brokers and Thrifts', *NYT*, 18 August.

Lowi, Theodore (1964), 'American Business, Public Policy, Case-Studies, and Political Theory', *World Politics*, **16**.

Macey, Jonathan (1984), 'Special Interest Groups Legislation and the Judicial Function: The Dilemma of Glass-Steagall', *Emory Law Journal*, **33**.

March, James and Olsen, Johan (1984), 'The New Institutionalism: Organizational Factors in Political Life', *American Political Science Review*, **78** (3).

Marcus, Alan (1983), 'The Bank Capital Decision: A Time Series Cross Section Analysis', *Journal of Finance*, **38**, September.

Martion, Preston, and Higgins, Bryon (1986), 'The World Financial Scene: Balancing Risks and Rewards', *Economic Review*, Federal Reserve Bank of Kansas City, **71** (6).

Mayne, Lucille (1974), 'Impact of Federal Bank Supervision on Bank Capital', *The Bulletin*, NYU Graduate School of Business Administration, Institute of Finance, No. 85-86, September.

McCall, Alan and Saulsbury, Victor (1986), 'The Changing Role of Banks and Other Private Financial Institutions', *Regulatory Review*, FDIC, April.

McCarthy, Jr., F. Ward (1984), 'The Evolution of the Bank Regulatory Structure: A Reappraisal', *Economic Review*, Federal Reserve Bank of Richmond, March/April.

Merton, R.C. (1979), 'Discussion' in *The Regulation of Financial Institutions*, Federal Reserve Bank of Boston.

Mingo, J. (1985), 'Capital Ratios: The Reg Q Fiasco of the Future', *Banking Expansion Reporter*, 21 January.

Murray-Jones, Allen and Spencer, David (1987), 'The US/UK Proposal on Capital Adequacy', *International Financial Law Review*, **6** (9).

Noonan, John and Fetner, Susan (1983), 'Capital and Capital Standards', *Economic Review*, Federal Reserve Bank of Atlanta, **68** (11).

Norton, Joseph (1989), 'Capital Adequacy Standards: A Legitimate Regulatory Concern For Prudential Supervision of Banking Activities?', *Ohio State Law Journal*, **49** (5).

Norton, Joseph (1989), 'The work of the Basle Supervisors Committee on Bank Capital Adequacy and the July 1988 Report on "International Convergence of Capital Measurement and Capital Standards"', *International Lawyer*, **23**.

Ossola, Rinaldo (1980), 'The Vulnerability of the International Financial System', *Banca*

Nazionale del Lavoro Quarterly Review (134), September.

Pardee, Scott (1987), 'Internationalization of Financial Markets', *Economic Review*, Federal Reserve Bank of Kansas City, **72** (2).

Pavel, Christine and Rosenblum, Harvey (1985), 'Banks and Non-Banks: The Horse Race Continues', *Economic Perspectives*, Federal Reserve Bank of Chicago, **9**.

Perkins, Edwin (1971), 'The Divorce of Commercial from Investment Banking: A History', *The Banking Law Journal*, **88** (6).

Pettway, Richard (1976), 'Market Tests of Capital Adequacy of Large Commercial Banks', *Journal of Finance*, June.

Plotkin (1978), 'What Meaning Does Glass-Steagall Have for Today's Financial World?', *Banking Law Journal*, **95**.

Preston, Howard (1933), 'The Banking Act of 1933', *The American Economic Review*, December.

Reinicke, Wolfgang (1983), 'Foxes Are Guarding the Henhouses...Say Critics of Regulatory System', *CQ*, September.

Reinicke, Wolfgang (1991), 'Turf Fights in Regulatory Reform', *Challenge*, November-December.

Rose, Sanford (1980), 'The Confusing Question of Capital Adequacy', *American Banker*, 11 October.

Rose, Sanford (1986), 'Random Thoughts', *American Banker*, 12 November.

Ruggie, John (1982), 'International Regimes, Transactions, and Change: Imbedded Liberalism in the Post-War Economic Order', *International Organization*, **36**.

Saunders, Anthony (1985), 'Securities Activities of Commercial Banks: The Problem of Conflicts of Interest', *Business Review*, Federal Reserve Bank of Philadelphia, July-August.

Schott, Jeffrey (1983), 'Protectionist Threat to Trade and Investment in Services', *The World Economy*, **7**.

Schumer, Charles (1983), 'A Stop Sign for Banks — For Now', *NYT*, 17 May.

Schumer, Charles (1987), 'Don't Let Banks Become Casinos', *NYT*, 26 August.

Scott, Kenneth (1977), 'The Dual Banking System: A Model of Competition in Regulation', *Stanford Law Review*, **30** (1).

Shull, Bernard (1983), 'The Separation of Banking and Commerce: Origin, Development, and Implications for Antitrust', *The Antitrust Bulletin*, Spring.

Silverberg, Stanley (1976), 'Bank Supervision and Competitive Laxity', *The Magazine of Bank Administration*, **52**.

Smith, James (1974), 'Assessing the Capital Needs of Banking', *The Journal of Commercial Bank Lending*, January.

Solomon, Frederic (1982), 'Bank Agencies' Capital Guidelines Differ', *Legal Times*, 26 April.

Symons, Edward (1957), 'The Bank Holding Company Act of 1956', *Stanford Law Review*, **9**.

Symons, Edward (1983), 'The Business of Banking in Historical Perspective', *George Washington Law Review*, **51**.

Verdier, Stephen and Scarborough, Keith (1988), 'The Banking Act of 1988?', *Independent Banker*, February.

Wall, Larry (1983), 'Will Bank Capital Adequacy Restrictions Slow the Development of Interstate Banking?', *Economic Review*, Federal Reserve Bank of Atlanta, May.

Wall, Larry (1989), 'Capital Requirements for Banks: A Look at the 1981 and 1988

Standards', *Economic Review*, Federal Reserve Bank of Atlanta, March/April.
Wallich, Henry (1983), 'Time Out for an Orderly Transition', *NYT*, 10 July.
Walmsley, Julian (1986), 'Rehearsing For Glass-Steagall's Repeal', *The Banker Magazine*, May-June.
Wellons, Philip (1985), 'International Debt: The Behavior of Banks in Politicized Environment', *International Organization*, **39**.
Winningham, Scott and Hagan, Donald (1980), 'Regulation Q: A Historical Perspective', *Economic Review*, Federal Reserve Bank of Kansas City, April.
Zimmermann, William (1973), 'Issue Area and Foreign-Policy Process: A Research Note in Search of a General Theory', *American Political Science Review*, **67**.

Journal and newspaper articles (unsigned)

'Accounting Loopholes Mask True Capital At Big Banks', *Savings Institutions*, August 1985.
'Agencies Adopt Capital Guidelines Applicable To Multinational Banks', *Washington Financial Reports*, **40**, 20 June 1933.
'Agreed Proposal of the United States Federal Banking Supervisory Authorities and the Bank of England on primary capital and capital adequacy assessment', *Quarterly Bulletin*, Bank of England, February 1987.
'As FDIC Views Glass-Steagall', *Bankers Monthly Magazine*, 15 September 1982.
'Bank Capital: Two Giants Feel the Heat', *Business Week*, 3 December 1984.
'Bank Size and the Management of Capital Ratios', *Bankers Magazine*, **165** (1), January/February 1982.
'Bank Underwriting Powers Expanded', *Banking Legislation and Policy*, Federal Reserve Bank of Philadelphia, **8** (3), July-September 1989.
'Bankers Are Seeking Relief Off the Hill', *National Journal*, 11 November 1988.
'Banking Agencies Focus on Capital Adequacy', *Banking Expansion Reporter*, 6 August 1984.
'Banking on a New Lobbying Strategy', *National Journal*, 5 March 1988.
'Banks Taking the Heat for Near-Panic of '82', *National Journal*, 19 March 1983.
'The bans are read for a bank and a broker', *The Economist*, 28 November 1981.
'Breaching Glass-Steagall: A Status Report', *United States Banker*, September 1982.
'Capital Adequacy: The View From the Regulators' Seat', *Bankers Monthly Magazine*, 15 December 1985.
'Capital Guidelines Adopted by Fed', *Banking Expansion Reporter*, 18 March 1985.
'Capital Requirements for Banks: A Look at the 1981 and 1988 Standards', *Economic Review*, Federal Reserve Bank of Atlanta, March/April 1989.
'Capital Requirements of Commercial and Investment Banks: Contrasts in Regulation', *Quarterly Review*, Federal Reserve Bank of New York, Autumn 1987.
'Capital Standards Examined Further', *Banking Expansion Reporter*, **2** (13), 4 July 1983.
'Comptroller, Fed Issue Capital Guidelines', *Mid-Continent Banker*, February 1982.
'Court reaffirms FDIC securities-affiliate policy', *ABA Bankers Weekly*, 14 April 1987.
'Dashing to the Finish', *National Journal*, 20 February 1988.
'The Demise of the Bank/Nonbank Distinction: An Argument for Deregulating the Activities of Bank Holding Companies', *Harvard Law Review*, 1985.
'The Desperate Search for Capital', *Institutional Investor*, January 1985.

'The Evolution and Growth Potential of Electronics-Based Technologies', *Science, Technology, Industry Review*, No. 5, Paris: OECD, 1989.

'FDIC and OCC Adopt New Uniform Capital Requirements', *Washington Financial Reports*, 18 March 1985.

'FDIC Approves Increase in Bank Capital Requirement', *Washington Financial Reports*, 18 February 1985.

'FDIC's Interpretation, Not Rule, Should be Supported, ABA Says', *ABA Bankers Weekly*, 5 November 1985.

'Fed to Seek Supreme Court Review Of Power to Curtail Nonbank Banks', *Washington Financial Reports*, 29 October 1984.

'Fed Staff Summary and Recommendations on Risk-Based Capital Plan', *Banking Report*, 8 August 1988.

'The Fight to Remove Glass-Steagall', *Euromoney*, October 1985.

'Financial Evolution and Financial Soundness', *Economic Report of the President*, Washington, D.C.: 1990.

'Garn, St. Germain and Proxmire Issue Warning To Nonbank Bank Applicants', *Washington Financial Reports*, 15 October 1984.

'Garn Will Not Seek An Extension Of OCC Nonbank Moratorium', *Washington Financial Reports*, **43**, 1 October 1984.

'Glass-Steagall Act — A History of Its Legislative Origins and Regulatory Construction', *Banking Law Journal*, **92**, 1975.

'Glass-Steagall Issues Move to the Front Burner', *United States Banker*, **92** (8), 1981.

'Glass-Steagall Revised: The Impact on Banks, Capital Markets, and the Small Investor', *Banking Law Journal*, 1980.

'The Glass-Steagall Wars', *United States Banker*, April 1987.

'IBAA Trying to Elevate Nonbank Bank Dispute To White House Level', *Washington Financial Reports*, 10 October 1984.

'IMF Boost No Bailout Administration Insists', *National Journal*, 19 March 1983.

'International Banking: United States-United Kingdom Capital Adequacy Agreement', *Harvard Law Review*, **28**, 1987.

'Ironing out those troublesome bumps', *Banker*, February 1988.

'Is Accounting Legerdemain Impending Resolution of Foreign Debt Problem?', *National Journal*, 17 December 1983.

'Lower Profits and Reduced Capital Strength', *Banker*, June 1983.

'Messrs Glass and Steagall turn in their graves', *The Economist*, 7 February 1987.

'More Capital For Banks: The Cure May be Worse Than the Disease', *Business Week*, 28 January 1985.

'More Capital Won't Cure What Ails Banks', *Fortune*, 7 January 1985.

'New Guidelines For Assessing Capital Adequacy', *Florida Banker*, **9**, April 1982.

'102nd Congress Still Earliest Date for Financial Restructuring', *Washington Report*, **19** (10), July 1990.

'OCC, FDIC Issue Capital Adequacy Regs', *Banking Expansion Reporter*, 1 April 1985.

'OCC Set To Begin Approving Nonbank Bank Applications', *Washington Financial Reports*, 8 October 1984.

'Off-Balance Sheet Activities and Financial Innovation in Banking', *Quarterly Review*, Banca Nazionale del Lavoro.

'One Bank Holding Companies: A Banker's View', *Harvard Business Review*, May/June 1969.

'One-bank Holding Companies Before The 1970 Amendments', *Federal Reserve Bulletin*, December 1972.

'Outlook for Bank Capital', *United States Banker*, **93** (12), 1982.

'Protecting Big Banks Against Themselves', *Business Week*, 3 February 1986.

'The Reagan-Regan-Baker Last Hurrah', *Independent Banker*, April 1988.

'Recipe for Stalemate', *National Journal*, 3 December 1988.

'Regulation of Bank Capital: An Evaluation', *Economic Review*, Federal Reserve Bank of Atlanta, **67** (3), 1982.

'Regulators Are at Odds On Glass-Steagall Act', *Deregulation*, **3** (3), 1983.

'Regulators Go Public With Capital Ratios', *United States Banker*, **93** (4), April 1982.

'Regulators Propose Increased Bank Capital Requirements', *Bank Executives Report*, 15 August 1984.

'The Regulatory Debate on Capital Continues', *United States Banker*, **95** (1), January 1984.

'Re-regulation', Euromoney Dossier, *Euromoney*, June 1986.

'Revised Basle Concordat on Bank Oversight', *Washington Financial Reports*, 18 July 1983.

'The Revolution in Financial Services', *Business Week*, 28 November 1983.

'Risk-Based Capital Requirements, Should They Apply to Bank Holding Companies?', *Issues in Bank Regulation*, Summer 1988.

'St. Germain Says No Action Planned This Year on House Banking Bill', *Washington Financial Reports*, **43**, 24 September 1984.

'Securitization', *Zeitschrift für das Gesamte Kreditwesen*, **40** (8), 1987.

'Senate Approves Omnibus Financial Reform Bill With Few Alterations', *Washington Financial Reports*, **43**, 17 September 1984.

'Sens. Proxmire, Garn Urge Fed to Allow BHCs to Underwrite Debt, Equity Securities', *Daily Report for Executives*, Bureau of National Affairs, 4 November 1988.

'Supreme Court Affirms Fed Approval of Bankamerica Takeover of Schwab', *Washington Financial Reports*, **43** (2), 1984.

'Tenth Circuit Court Invalidates Fed Action to Block Nonbank Banks', *Washington Financial Reports*, 1 October 1984.

'What the BIS Stands For', *The Banker*, 1979.

'What regulators are saying now about capital adequacy', *ABA Banking Journal*, **74** (4), 1982.

American Banker

'Capital Ratios Hurting Bank Growth', *American Banker*, 26 March 1980.

'CofC May Trim Definition of Capital, Lift Loan Limit', *American Banker*, 24 July 1980.

'Mandatory Capital Ratios?', *American Banker*, 30 July 1980.

'Proposed Comptroller Rules Would Eliminate Three Items From the Definition of Capital', *American Banker*, 18 August 1980.

'Capital Adequacy Surfaces Again', *American Banker*, 12 September 1980.

'Small Banks Hit Capital Plan', *American Banker*, 15 September 1980.

'Bankers Must Act on Debt Capital', *American Banker*, 18 September 1980.

'Volcker Prods Banks on Capital', *American Banker*, 19 September 1980.

'Comptroller's New Definition of Capital Is Viewed by Banks as Too Restrictive', *American Banker*, 26 September 1980.

'RMA Urges Comptroller to Drop Plan to Redefine Capital', *American Banker*, 3 October 1980.

'Inadequate Capital Ratios "Immoral"', *American Banker*, 15 October 1980.

'Many Complain', *American Banker*, 16 October 1980.

'RMA Opposes CofC's Proposed Redefinition of Bank Capital', *American Banker*, 17 October 1980.

'If Number of Banks Shrink, Capital Difficulties Will Be Cause', *American Banker*, 27 October 1980.

'A Look at Capitalization Problems and Some Possible Solutions', *American Banker*, 7 November 1980.

'Capital Ratio Laws Seen', *American Banker*, 17 November 1980.

'Random Thoughts', *American Banker*, 25 November 1980.

'Capital Erodes Worldwide', *American Banker*, 28 November 1980.

'The Role of Capital in the Banking Industry', *American Banker*, 2 December 1980.

'Fixed Capital Ratios Assailed By Citi as Harmful to Banks', *American Banker*, 10 December 1980.

'Parity on Small-Bank Capital Sought', *American Banker*, 9 March 1981.

'Focus on Bank Underwriting Bill', *American Banker*, 18 March 1981.

'Comptroller Eases Capital Rules For Small, Well-Managed Banks', *American Banker*, 26 March 1981.

'It's Another Round in the Long Battle Between Banks and Security Interests', *American Banker*, 27 March 1981.

'CofC to Include All of Loan Loss Reserve in Capital Definition', *American Banker*, 27 April 1981.

'Reuss Cites Banks' Disunity', *American Banker*, 27 April 1981.

'SIA Urges Glass-Steagall Review Before Actions on Money Funds', *American Banker*, 30 April 1981.

'Banks Seek Congress Aid On Competitive Disadvantages', *American Banker*, 7 May 1981.

'CofC Reveals More on New Capital Guidelines', *American Banker*, 12 June 1981.

'Exam Council Tries Hand at Defining Capital', *American Banker*, 18 June 1981.

'[FFIEC] Proposed Definition of Bank Capital', *American Banker*, 22 June 1981.

'Lawmakers Getting Behind Bills That Would Ease Glass-Steagall', *American Banker*, 16 July 1981.

'Exam Council Proposes to Define All Loan Loss Reserves as Capital', *American Banker*, 3 August 1981.

'Fed Warns BHCs to Bolster Affiliates' Capital Positions', *American Banker*, 31 August 1981.

'MHT's Torell Sees Host of New Bank Powers', *American Banker*, 2 September 1981.

'Regulation and Reality: Updating Antiquated Rules', *American Banker*, 23 September 1981.

'ICI Says Bank Mutual Fund Bills Pro-Bank, Not Pro-Competition', *American Banker*, 25 September 1981.

'BofA President Urges Prompt Deregulation', *American Banker*, 30 September 1981.

'Banks Seek to Amend Underwrite Plan', *American Banker*, 20 October 1981.

'Stop the Squabbling, Garn Warns', *American Banker*, 17 November 1981.

'Bank America Seeks Schwab Brokerage', *American Banker*, 25 November 1981.

'Can BofA Beat Glass-Steagall', *American Banker*, 27 November 1981.

'Fed Approves Definition of Capital, But FDIC Remains at Odds With Other Regulators', *American Banker*, 3 December 1981.

'Capital Ratios at Banks Declining', *American Banker*, 24 December 1981.

'Bank Capital Ratios Decline in Most Western Nations', *American Banker*, 28 December 1981.

'Glass-Steagall Action Doubted', *American Banker*, 21 January 1983.

'Volcker Warns Against Excessive Caution in International Lending', *American Banker*, 3 February 1983.

'Comptroller Allows Dreyfus Corp. to Open a New Bank in New York', *American Banker*, 8 February 1983.

'Lawmakers, Banker Clash On IMF Aid', *American Banker*, 9 February 1983.

'IMF Ends Meeting With 50% Boost in Funds Expected', *American Banker*, 11 February 1983.

'Volcker: Excessive Caution Threatens World Economy', *American Banker*, 11 February 1983.

'Teeters: Cooperation Avoided Crisis', *American Banker*, 24 February 1983.

'Schwab Case Goes to Court Today', *American Banker*, 23 May 1983.

'Federal Reserve Counsel Defends Schwab Decision', *American Banker*, 25 May 1983.

'5% Capital Requirements Set for Largest Banks', *American Banker*, 14 June 1983.

'Capital-Ratio Guidelines Within Reach', *American Banker*, 27 June 1983.

'High Court to Review Schwab Case', *American Banker*, 24 January 1984.

'Supreme Court Hears Arguments In Schwab Case', *American Banker*, 25 April 1984.

'SIA Looses Bid to Keep Thrifts from Discount Brokerage', *American Banker*, 18 May 1984.

'Decision on Discount Brokerage Soon Due', *American Banker*, 1 June 1984.

'Banks to Continue Dealing in Commercial Paper', *American Banker*, 6 July 1984.

'Regulator Plan Would Require More Capital', *American Banker*, 10 July 1984.

'Fed Approves Stiffer Capital Requirements', *American Banker*, 24 July 1984.

'Federal Reserve Decisions Based On Capital Standards', *American Banker*, 30 October 1984.

'Comptroller Steps Up Pressure on Big Bank Capital Adequacy', *American Banker*, 19 November 1984.

'Study Finds Glass-Steagall Act Merits Serious Reconsideration', *American Banker*, 28 November 1984.

'Securities Groups to Unite in Suit Against FDIC', *American Banker*, 29 November 1984.

'Court Rulings Shape Banking Industry, but Confusion and Controversy Reign', *American Banker*, 21 December 1984.

'Those Who Look Through Glass-Steagall Darkly see Bank Subsidiaries Underwriting Securities', *American Banker*, 4 January 1985.

'New York Fed Quizzes Citicorp On Securities', *American Banker*, 7 January 1985.

'St. Germain: Congress on Threshold of Major Banking Decisions', *American Banker*, 8 January 1985.

'Citicorp Vows to Keep Corporate Underwriting Activity Separate', *American Banker*, 9 January 1985.

'Most Big Banks Have Hiked Capital In Excess of Regulatory Guidelines', *American Banker*, 25 January 1985.

'Citicorp Securities Rebuff is Setback for Banks', *American Banker*, 27 February 1985.

'What the Fed Had to Say On Citicorp Application', *American Banker*, 1 March 1985.

'Capital Guidelines Revision foreseen', *American Banker*, 29 March 1985.

'Will Fed Decision End Commercial Paper Furor?', *American Banker*, 22 April 1985.

'Fed Seeks Comment On Citicorp Plan for Underwriting', *American Banker*, 15 May 1985.

'Commercial Paper Rules Set', *American Banker*, 5 June 1985.

'New No. 3 Man at Treasury Will Review Glass-Steagall Act', *American Banker*, 17 July 1985.

'Securities Industry Launches Counteroffensive to Blunt Banks' Campaign to Expand Their Securities Beachhead', *American Banker*, 25 July 1985.

'Citicorp Strikes a New Blow in Battle with Securities Firms', *American Banker*, 22 August 1985.

'Volcker to Propose Risk-Based Capital Rule', *American Banker*, 12 September 1985.

'Securities Group Likely to Sue If Fed Backs Citicorp Bid', *American Banker*, 9 December 1985.

'Fed Nominees Agree on Giving Banks Securities Powers, Differ Elsewhere', *American Banker*, 31 January 1986.

'Securities Trade Group Asks Court To Halt Bankers Trust's Paper Business', *American Banker*, 7 February 1986.

'Fed to Decide On Citicorp's Securities Bid', *American Banker*, 28 March 1986.

'Comptroller Says Regulators May Issue One Risk-Based Capital Proposal by Fall', *American Banker*, 11 July 1986.

'Goldman to Take Japanese Bank as a Partner', *American Banker*, 7 August 1986.

'Something Foreign's in the Air', *American Banker*, 6 October 1986.

'Sumitomo's Interest Is Money, Not Control, Fed Board Told', *American Banker*, 13 October 1986.

'Approval of Sumitomo's Stake in Goldman Intrigues Industry', *American Banker*, 21 November 1986.

'Glass-Steagall's Demise is Predicted', *American Banker*, 5 December 1986.

'Bankers Trust's Commercial Paper Operation Doesn't Involve Underwriting, Court Rules', *American Banker*, 24 December 1986.

'Depression Shaped Proxmire's View of Banks', *American Banker*, 30 December 1986.

'Regulators Favor Risk Exposure to Measure Capital Requirements', *American Banker*, 5 January 1987.

'Britain Sees Capital Adequacy Measures Promoting UK/US Bank Supervision', *American Banker*, 9 January 1987.

'U.S., British Join in Bank Capital Rules', *American Banker*, 9 January 1987.

'Staff Report', Federal Reserve Board, reprinted in *American Banker*, 14, 15, 20 January 1987.

'Bankers Rethink Financial Industry Framework', *American Banker*, 19 January 1987.

'Capital Rules Will Fortify Banks, Says British Official', *American Banker*, 20 January 1987.

'Should Banks Be in the Securities Business?', *American Banker*, 2 February 1987.

'Proxmire Says Fed Lacks Authority To Allow New Bank Securities Powers', *American Banker*, 3 February 1987.

'Bankers Hope Glass-Steagall Wall Will Tumble Down This Year', *American Banker*, 20 February 1987.

'Wishing on a Star for a World Without Glass-Steagall', *American Banker*, 27 February 1987.

'Foreign Banks Have a Vested Interest in the Demise of the Glass-Steagall Act', *American Banker*, 19 March 1987.

'Bankers Seek Changes in Risk-Based Capital Rule', *American Banker*, 27 May 1987.

'US-British Capital Plan Worries Mortgage Bankers', *American Banker*, 9 July 1987.

'Volcker Urges Congress to Modify Glass-Steagall', *American Banker*, 31 July 1987.

'Independent Bankers Oppose Repeal of Glass-Steagall', *American Banker*, 3 November 1987.

'Central Bankers to Seek 8% Capital Ratio', *American Banker*, 10 December 1987.

'26 Big Banks Face Need to Raise Equity', *American Banker*, 11 December 1987.

'Britain Taking A Tough View On Capital Plan', *American Banker*, 19 January 1988.

'House Panel Deals Blow to Bank-Powers Effort', *American Banker*, 23 September 1988.

'Proxmire Asks Fed to Expand Bank Powers', *American Banker*, 4 November 1988.

'Key Players At Agencies May Remain', *American Banker*, 10 November 1988.

'Some of Banking's Staunch Friends Lose Elections', *American Banker*, 14 November 1988.

'Guidelines Give Regionals Edge', *American Banker*, 29 November 1988.

'Capital Rules to Give Small Banks a Boost', *American Banker*, 30 November 1988.

'Securities Group Splits Over Expanded Bank Powers', *American Banker*, 2 December 1988.

'Gonzales Outlines Goals of Banking Committee', *American Banker*, 10 December 1988.

'Fed to Meet on Capital Rules', *American Banker*, 16 December 1988.

'Key Securities Ruling Overturned', *American Banker*, 19 December 1988.

'Court Ruling Sends Mixed Signals', *American Banker*, 21 December 1988.

'Regulatory Turf Battles to Continue in 1989', *American Banker*, 21 December 1988.

'More US Firms Using Foreign Banks: Study', *American Banker*, 27 December 1988.

'Banks Get Nod on Corporate Debt', *American Banker*, 19 January 1989.

'Panel Members Rip Fed Chief Over Ruling', *American Banker*, 25 January 1989.

'Polls Show Foreign Banks Have Eye on Fee Income', *American Banker*, 14 February 1989.

'Necessity Links US, Japanese Firms, Investment Firms Need Local Partners in Both Markets', *American Banker*, 27 March 1989.

'Number of U.S. Banks in London Hits Low', *American Banker*, 30 March 1989.

'US Bankers Heartened by Changes in European Community Entry Rules', *American Banker*, 17 April 1989.

'Flexibility Seen in Fed Position on Firewalls', *American Banker*, 3 May 1989.

'Morgan Gains Fed Approval On Securities', *American Banker*, 20 June 1989.

'Theobald Urges Bankers to Plan Strategically for Globalized Era', *American Banker*, 22 June 1989.

'Morgan Bares Its Plans to Japanese', *American Banker*, 3 July 1989.

'Securities Group Says Fed Is Tilting the Playing Field', *American Banker*, 5 July 1989.

'Fear and Longing in the U.S.', special issue of *American Banker*: '1992 Countdown', 25 July 1989.

'Bankers Gird Themselves For Assault on Firewalls', *American Banker*, 10 August 1989.

'US Banks Told By Chase Chief to Close Ranks', *American Banker*, 21 August 1989.

'Restructuring the Industry Doesn't Require New Law', *American Banker*, 11 February 1991.

'Bush Faces an Uphill Battle for His Bank Reform Plan', *American Banker*, 11 February 1991.

'Fences May Fall As Banks Push Wider Powers', *American Banker*, 6 March 1991.
'Small Banks Intensify Assault on Reform Plan', *American Banker*, 6 March 1991.
'Banking-Commerce Link Decried', *American Banker*, 12 April 1991.
'Angry Dingell Vows to Stall Reform Unless Consulted by Its Supporters', *American Banker*, 26 April 1991.
'Senate Ready to Take Aim at Banking Bill', *American Banker*, 8 July 1991.
'Opening the Door', *American Banker*, 10 July 1991.
'Dirty Doings Behind "Reform" Plan', *American Banker*, 19 July 1991.
'Dingell Slams Bank Bill, Calls Citicorp "Insolvent"', *American Banker*, 1 August 1991.
'Senator Riegle Concedes Key Points on Reform Bill', *American Banker*, 1 August 1991.
'ABA May Pull Support For a Major Overhaul', *American Banker*, 6 August 1991.
'What If Citicorp Agreed With Dingell?', *American Banker*, 11 September 1991.
'Brady Tells Top Bankers He Will Play Hardball on Bank Reform Bill', *American Banker*, 12 September 1991.
'Dingell Bill Would Be Blow For Morgan', *American Banker*, 23 September 1991.
'Enmity Toward Big Banks Hurts Nation', *American Banker*, 16 October 1991.
'Setback for Industry on Bank Bill', *American Banker*, 25 October 1991.
'Bush's Banking Reform Bill: From Nirvana to Nightmare?', *American Banker*, 28 October 1991.
'White House Threatens to Veto Bill', *American Banker*, 30 October 1991.
'Banks Fight Moratorium On New Securities Powers', *American Banker*, 8 November 1991.
'Reform Fiasco Presages a Bleak Future for Banks', *American Banker*, 3 December 1991.
'Unable to Win, Diverse Lobbies Scuttled Reform', *American Banker*, 5 December 1991.
'Congress Likely to Put Banks on Backburner', *American Banker*, 24 December 1991.
'Morgan to Break Underwriting Barrier', *American Banker*, 15 February 1992.

Congressional Quarterly

'House Votes Emergency Aid for Ailing Savings & Loans; Senate Weighs Broader Bill', *CQ*, 31 October 1981.
'Bankers Deposit Big Political Money', *CQ*, 6 February 1982.
'Liberation of Banking Industry May be Thwarted This Year by Fractured Finance Lobbies', *CQ*, 6 February 1982.
'House Banking Panel Votes Net Worth Guarantee Plan to Aid Ailing Thrift Industry', *CQ*, 15 May 1982.
'House Passes Bill to Shore Up Thrift Industry, Aid Housing', *CQ*, 22 May 1982.
'Limited Banking Reform Bill Awaits Floor Action in Senate', *CQ*, 28 August 1982.
'Congress Is Balking At Plan to Increase IMF Loans', *CQ*, 15 January 1983.
'Congress Hears Pleas for More IMF Support', *CQ*, 19 February 1983.
'IMF Measure Attracts Amendments', *CQ*, 7 May 1983.
'Bank Loan Requirements Added to IMF Bill', *CQ*, 14 May 1983.
'Senate Approves Increase in IMF Funding', *CQ*, 11 June 1983.
'Administration Seeks Banking Law Revisions', *CQ*, 23 July 1983.
'IMF Increase Runs Aground Under Barrage by Lobbyists', *CQ*, 23 July 1983.
'House Approves IMF Funds; Bank Provisions Criticized', *CQ*, 6 August 1983.
'Interstate Forays by Big Banks Revive Interest in Legislation', *CQ*, 5 May 1984.
'Senators Seek Consensus on Banking Bill', *CQ*, 5 May 1984.

'Bipartisan Bill Offered in House', *CQ*, 26 May 1984.
'Rescue of Continental Bank Fires Deregulation Debate', *CQ*, 2 June 1984.
'Banking Chairman: Secretive but Successful', *CQ*, 8 September 1984.
'"Professor" Runs the Show at House Banking', *CQ*, 8 September 1984.
'Bailing Out the Banks: How Much Is Too Much?', *CQ*, 15 September 1984.
'Senate Endorses Further Banking Deregulation', *CQ*, 15 September 1984.
'More Non-Bank Banks Approved', *CQ*, 3 November 1984.
'Bank Deregulation Issues Await Action; Hurdles Remain', *CQ*, 2 February 1985.
'Prospects Dim for Legislation To Aid Ailing Thrift Industry', *CQ*, 8 March 1986.
'Change in Banking Policy Expected', *CQ*, 8 November 1986.
'Banking Chairmen in No Hurry to Give Regulators More Power', *CQ*, 15 November 1986.
'Bailout of S&L Insurance Fund Approved by Senate Banking', *CQ*, 14 March 1987.
'Independent Fed Has Shifted With Political Winds of the Past', *CQ*, 25 July 1987.
'Senate Panel Set to Debate Bank Deregulation', *CQ*, 28 November 1987.
'Congress Set to Consider New Banking Powers', *CQ*, 27 February 1988.
'Senate Panel Approves Bank Deregulation Bill', *CQ*, 5 March 1988.
'House Panel Caucuses on Bank-Deregulation Bill', *CQ*, 19 March 1988.
'House Banking-Deregulation Bill Under Scrutiny', *CQ*, 9 April 1988.
'House Panel Nears Action on Bank Regulation Bill', *CQ*, 9 July 1988.
'Weary House Panel OKs Bank Deregulation Bill', *CQ*, 30 July 1988.
'Energy/Commerce Seeks Tight Reign on New Bank Powers', *CQ*, 24 September 1988.
'Prospects for New Bank Powers Fade in Congress' Final Days', *CQ*, 24 September 1988.
'A Flicker of Life Remains In Drive for New Bank Powers', *CQ*, 8 October 1988.
'Caught in House Turf Battle, Banking Deregulation Bill Dies', *CQ*, 15 October 1988.
'Banks Follow Glass-Steagall, Thrifts watch FSLIC Rescue', *CQ*, 26 November 1988.
'Riegle to Head Senate Banking Reform', *CQ*, 3 December 1988.
'Gonzales Sets Broad Agenda for Banking Panel', *CQ*, 10 December 1988.
'Fed's Bank-Powers Decision Defies Hill Concern Over Turf', *CQ*, 21 January 1989.
'Next on Agenda: Glass-Steagall', *CQ*, 27 May 1989.
'Regulators Urge New Powers', *CQ*, 30 September 1989.
'Bank Regulation', *CQ*, 2 December 1989.
'Administration Spells Out Plan to Reform Financial System', *CQ*, 9 February 1991.
'Why We're Here', *CQ*, 9 February 1991.
'Treasury's Hardline Strategy', *CQ*, 18 May 1991.
'Big Banks Win First Round in Pursuit of New Powers', *CQ*, 29 June 1991.
'Lobbyists Storm Capitol Hill, Clash Over Banking Bill', *CQ*, 24 August 1991.
'Banking Overhaul Losing Ground to Complexity, Controversy', *CQ*, 2 November 1991.
'Deposit Insurance Overhaul Bill', *CQ*, 14 December 1991.
'Marketplace Forces Hold Key to Future Bank Legislation', *CQ*, 4 January 1992.

Financial Times

'Rejection of supervision plan clouds convention', *Financial Times*, 18 April 1983.
'Deregulation gains that add up to zero', *Financial Times*, 29 August 1985.
'Volcker Proposes Rise in U.S. Bank Capital Ratios to 9%', *Financial Times*, 18 September 1985.
'On risk, off balance sheet', *Financial Times*, 19 September 1985.

'BIS warns of effect of capital market changes', *Financial Times*, 29 October 1985.

'Closer Control of International Banking Urged', *Financial Times*, 26 November 1985.

'The battle to keep tabs in the face of rapid change', *Financial Times*, 23 February 1986.

'Central bankers to issue warning on financial market innovation', *Financial Times*, 11 March 1986.

'Bankers agree on hidden risk guidelines', *Financial Times*, 17 March 1986.

'Financial innovation opens a Pandora's Box', *Financial Times*, 21 April 1986.

'The dangers of deregulation', *Financial Times*, 9 May 1986.

'Deregulation means one big pool', *Financial Times*, 23 May 1986.

'Shadows on the bright dawn of deregulation', *Financial Times*, 2 January 1986.

'World bankers debate regulation', *Financial Times*, 22 October 1986.

'Call for reform of banking laws in US', *Financial Times*, 28 October 1986.

'Standards for global bankers', *Financial Times*, 30 October 1986.

'Bank supervisors move in step', *Financial Times*, 9 January 1987.

'Japan banks plead to UK and US on capital ratio', *Financial Times*, 13 May 1987.

'Japanese banks to give more data to Fed', *Financial Times*, 21 May 1987.

'Japan puts life into bank capital accord', *Financial Times*, 12 June 1987.

'Japan close to deal on levels of bank capital', *Financial Times*, 25 September 1987.

'US banking act move goes ahead', *Financial Times*, 29 October 1987.

'Central banks agree standards on capital ratio requirements', *Financial Times*, 9 December 1987.

'Step towards a sounder base for banking', *Financial Times*, 11 December 1987.

'Banking on the equity capital', *Financial Times*, 14 December 1987.

'Sigh of relief from UK bankers', *Financial Times*, 15 December 1987.

'Brussels set to outline rules for reciprocity after 1992', *Financial Times*, 19 October 1988.

'Fed warns EC against reciprocity in banking', *Financial Times*, 3 November 1988.

'The Fed weighs the risks', *Financial Times*, 22 January 1989.

'Fed accused of rewriting bank law', *Financial Times*, 26 June 1989.

'EC Commissioner challenges US to open banking market', *Financial Times*, 16 July 1989.

'Brussels stands firm on banking access', *Financial Times*, 21 September 1989.

'US Securities Industry to ease banking differences', *Financial Times*, 2 December 1989.

'Moves to shatter Glass-Steagall', *Financial Times*, 3 October 1990.

New York Times

'Banking Issues for Congress', *NYT*, 9 February 1979.

'Revenue Financing Tempts Bankers', *NYT*, 27 June 1979.

'Investment Companies', *NYT*, 20 February 1980.

'Bankers Meet in Discord', *NYT*, 2 June 1980.

'Fast Growth for Foreign Banks', *NYT*, 29 July 1980.

'Fed Permits Banks to Sell Commercial Paper', *NYT*, 30 September 1980.

'Becker Investment Suit', *NYT*, 16 October 1980.

'Bank Target: Glass-Steagall Act', *NYT*, 3 March 1981.

'Banks Square Off Against the Fed', *NYT*, 14 June 1981.

'Underwriting Memories', *NYT*, 29 June 1981.

'Ruling on Paper Sale', *NYT*, 29 July 1981.

'Senate Bill Asks Bank Decontrol', *NYT*, 8 October 1981.
'Treasury Backs Change in Savings Bank Aid', *NYT*, 20 October 1981.
'Bankers Goal: More Leeway', *NYT*, 23 November 1981.
'Bank Bids $53 Million for Broker', *NYT*, 25 November 1981.
'Banks Hail 2 Plans for Broker Tie', *NYT*, 27 November 1981.
'Warning on Bank Decontrol Dispute', *NYT*, 11 February 1982.
'Bank Reform Needs a Nudge', *NYT*, 25 February 1982.
'Citibank Said to Plan Broker Tie', *NYT*, April 1982.
'Chemical's Discount Broker Plan', *NYT*, 22 July 1982.
'Stock Group to Sue U.S.', *NYT*, 14 September 1982.
'Commercial Paper Sale By Banks Ruled Legal', *NYT*, 3 November 1982.
'F.D.I.C., Fed Clash On Dreyfus', *NYT*, 14 December 1982.
'U.S. to Let Big Bank Concern Go Into Brokerage Business', *NYT*, 8 January 1983.
'Banks' Decontrol Bid in States', *NYT*, 26 March 1983.
'Bank's Role As Discounters', *NYT*, 19 April 1983.
'"Nonbank" Trend Assailed', *NYT*, 27 April 1983.
'Bankers Split Over Fed Stand', *NYT*, 4 May 1983.
'Moratorium On Bank Deals', *NYT*, 10 May 1983.
'Underwriting By Banks to be Topic of Hearing', *NYT*, 21 May 1983.
'Safety of Deregulation of Banking is Debated', *NYT*, 18 July 1983.
'Garn Supports Bank Deregulation Bill', *NYT*, 19 July 1983.
'Fed to Let Banks Serve as Discount Brokers', *NYT*, 11 August 1983.
'Growing Japanese Role In California Banking', *NYT*, 25 August 1983.
'Deregulation Peril to Thrift Units Seen', *NYT*, 14 September 1983.
'SEC Seeks Tighter Rules for Most Banks That Offer Full-Line Brokerage Services', *NYT*, 28 October 1983.
'Federal Banking Rules, or 50?', *NYT*, 24 April 1984.
'Outlook for Broad Bank Bill Dims', *NYT*, 7 June 1984.
'Banking Regulators Split Over Bill', *NYT*, 13 June 1984.
'High Court Puts Limits On Banks', *NYT*, 29 June 1984.
'Volcker Backs Bank Powers', *NYT*, 16 August 1984.
'Securities Role Given Bank Units', *NYT*, 20 November 1984.
'New Rule For Banks', *NYT*, 11 February 1985.
'New Bank Rules by Fed', *NYT*, 2 March 1985.
'Volcker Revives Bank Fears', *NYT*, 13 September 1985.
'Morgan Fed Proposal', *NYT*, 11 October 1985.
'Similar Standards For Banks Are Set By U.S. and Britain', *NYT*, 9 January 1987.
'Treasury Now Favors Creation of Huge Banks', *NYT*, 7 June 1987.
'Why Bigger Isn't Better Banking', *NYT*, 28 June 1987.
'Fed Lets 6 Banks Offer New Security', *NYT*, 16 July 1987.
'Volcker Sees Nations in Bank Pact', *NYT*, 31 July 1987.
'For Proxmire the Fleece Goes On', *NYT*, 28 September 1987.
'Keep Banks From the "Manu" Market', *NYT*, 8 November 1987.
'Glass-Steagall Shift Gaining Support', *NYT*, 11 November 1987.
'New Capital Rules Affect Some Banks, Fed Officials Says', *WSJ*, 30 December 1987.
'Prospects of Action On Bank Legislation', *NYT*, 4 January 1988.
'What Banks Want...', *NYT*, 8 January 1988.
'Senator Glass and Congressman Steagall Discuss the Crash of October 1987', *NYT*, 26

January 1988.
'Banking Plan Seen Impending Mergers', *NYT*, 1 February 1988.
'American Manufacturers Question Why Free Enterprise Doesn't Apply To American Banks', *NYT*, 29 February 1988.
'One Barrier to Banks Due to Fall This Week', *NYT*, 29 February 1988.
'Bill in House Would Limit Banks' Underwriting Power', *NYT*, 24 March 1988.
'Testing an Iron Fist', *NYT*, 12 April 1988.
'Justices Permit Banks to Widen Securities Role', *NYT*, 14 June 1988.
'Panel Chairman Offers Bank Powers Bill', *NYT*, 8 July 1988.
'Agreements On Banks' Capital Set', *NYT*, 12 July 1988.
'Capital Plan Feared as Burden on Banks', *NYT*, 15 July 1988.
'Fed Approves Rules Requiring More Capital at All Banks', *NYT*, 4 August 1988.
'Federal Reserve Acts to Let Banks into Bond Trading', *NYT*, 19 January 1989.
'Bentsen Warns Europeans Not to Set Trade Curbs in '92', *NYT*, 7 April 1989.
'U.S. Banks' Global Role', *NYT*, 10 May 1989.
'Fed Further Widens Rights Of Banks to Sell Securities', *NYT*, 14 September 1989.
'Regulatory Shift Allows U.S. Banks to Trade Stocks', *NYT*, 21 September 1990.
'J.P. Morgan's Pioneering Offspring', *NYT*, 25 December 1990.
'Excerpts from an Interview with the Fed's Chairman', *NYT*, 31 January 1991.
'Plan to Limit Deposit Insurance is Defended', *NYT*, 4 February 1991.
'Administration Presents Its Plan for Broad Overhaul of Banking', *NYT*, 6 February 1991.
'Company News: Citicorp Appeals Ruling by the Fed', *NYT*, 8 February 1991.
'For Banks, Suitors May Be Few', *NYT*, 9 February 1991.
'Fed to Fight Part of Plan on Banks', *NYT*, 5 March 1991.

Wall Street Journal

'Many Banks Now Face Their Biggest Problems Since '73-75 Recession', *WSJ*, 10 January 1980.
'Major Banks Take Steps to Raise Capital As Protection Against Unexpected Losses', *WSJ*, 31 July 1980.
'Thriving on Trouble, Settlements Bank Sees Its Influence Growing', *WSJ*, 10 October 1980.
'Curbs on Bank-Like Services of Big Firms is Major Issue for Brokers at SIA Meeting', *WSJ*, 1981.
'Money Market Funds Face Mounting Drive For Stiffer Regulation', *WSJ*, 11 March 1981.
'Commercial Banks Are Warned by SEC on Use of Rights Granted Them by Fed', *WSJ*, 19 March 1981.
'Banks Wishing to Sell Commercial Paper Receive Setback in U.S. Judge's Ruling', *WSJ*, 29 April 1981.
'Major Bill to Decontrol Banking Industry is Seen Getting Before Congress This Year', *WSJ*, 15 September 1981.
'Bill Giving Banks and S&Ls More Powers Introduced by Senate Banking Panel Head', *WSJ*, 8 October 1981.
'Regan Outlines Deregulation Plan for Banks', *WSJ*, 16 October 1981.
'White House Backs Thrust of Senate Bill to Decontrol Banking, Thrift Industries', *WSJ*,

20 October 1981.

'Bankers' Plea Draw A Withering Retort From Sen. Garn', *WSJ*, 21 October 1981.

'Regan Plan Expands Securities Services for Smaller Banks', *WSJ*, 16 November 1981.

'Industry Disputes Stall a Measure to Restructure Banking Industry', *WSJ*, 30 November 1981.

'Regan Tells Wall Street Banks' Roles Will Grow', *WSJ*, 4 December 1981.

'Banking Bummer', *WSJ*, 9 March 1982.

'Banking's Evolution Is Improvised As Disputes Stall Deregulation Plan', *WSJ*, 29 March 1982.

'FDIC Says State Banks Not in Fed System Can Have Units in the Securities Business', *WSJ*, 2 September 1982.

'Brokers Being Added at Bank of America', *WSJ*, 21 October 1982.

'Banks Set Agenda for the Entire Industry as Regulation Loosens', *WSJ*, 18 November 1982.

'Blending of Roles of Banks, Other Firms Should be Curbed, Fed Official Says', *WSJ*, 22 March 1983.

'Non-Banks Face '83 Moratorium By Comptroller', *WSJ*, 6 April 1983.

'FDIC Wants To Let State Banks Underwrite Corporate Securities, Rejecting Fed View', *WSJ*, 18 May 1983.

'Regan Weighs Curbs on S&Ls, Easing for Banks', *WSJ*, 8 July 1983.

'The Bank Law Debate', *WSJ*, 25 July 1983.

'Onward the Revolution in Financial Services', *WSJ*, 16 September 1983.

'Justices to Decide if Banks Can Compete With Securities Firms in Corporate IOUs', *WSJ*, 4 October 1983.

'SEC Considers Regulating Banks, Thrifts That Are Entering Stock-Broker Business', *WSJ*, 20 October 1983.

'Bills to Slow Down Banking Deregulation To Be Offered by Influential GOP Senator', *WSJ*, 3 November 1983.

'Bank-Insurer Dispute Over Roles Revives As Wider Policy Sales Urged in New York', *WSJ*, 16 February 1984.

'U.S. Banks Try New Businesses Abroad That Could Be Wave of Future at Home', *WSJ*, 24 April 1984.

'Bill to Outlaw Consumer Banks and Curb Other Activities Introduced by St. Germain', *WSJ*, 26 May 1984.

'Banks Await Court Rulings on Services', *WSJ*, 18 June 1984.

'Justices Uphold Banks' Offering Broker Services', *WSJ*, 29 June 1984.

'Regulators Charged With "Timid" Action On Continental Illinois in House Hearings', *WSJ*, 19 September 1984.

'Comptroller Urges Bankers to Establish Consumer Banks Fast, Ignore Congress', *WSJ*, 25 October 1984.

'Banks Find They Don't Need Congress To Help Them Expand Into Other Fields', *WSJ*, 31 December 1984.

'Minimum Capital For Banks Raised By New Fed Rule', *WSJ*, 4 March 1985.

'Judge Rules Certain Banks Can Underwrite Securities', *WSJ*, 24 April 1985.

'Chemical asks Fed to Let Unit Buy and Sell Securities', *WSJ*, 16 May 1985.

'Bankers Trust Can Distribute Paper, Fed Says', *WSJ*, 5 June 1985.

'Higher Capital to Cover Risk Urged For Banks', *WSJ*, 19 July 1985.

'Top Banking Regulator Says Increase in Capital Ratio May Encourage Risks', *WSJ*, 23

October 1985.

'Fed Proposes Requiring More Capital At Banks That Have Riskier Investments', *WSJ*, 16 January 1986.

'Comptroller Considers Linking Levels of Banks' Capital to Investment Risks', *WSJ*, 17 January 1986.

'U.S. and U.K. Propose a Rule on Bank Capital', *WSJ*, 9 January 1987.

'Wrong-Way Corrigan', *WSJ*, 26 February 1987.

'Senate Banking Panel Clears Measure Putting a Ban on New Powers for Banks', *WSJ*, 11 March 1987.

'State Banks That Aren't in Fed System May Own Securities Units, Court Rules', *WSJ*, 8 April 1987.

'Fed Grants Powers to 3 Bank Firms For Underwriting', *WSJ*, 30 April 1987.

'Greenspan Is Expected to Break Down Banking Limits that Volcker Espoused', *WSJ*, 4 June 1987.

'High Court Lets Lower Ruling Stand, Allows Banks to Sell Commercial Paper', *WSJ*, 23 June 1987.

'Carter's Comptroller Frets Over Globalization', *WSJ*, 8 September 1987.

'Proxmire Plans to Sponsor A Repeal of Glass-Steagall', *WSJ*, 24 September 1987.

'Seventeen Industrial Nations Draft Pact On Big Banks', *WSJ*, 23 October 1987.

'Officials Say Crash Shouldn't Prevent Bank Law Changes', *WSJ*, 29 October 1987.

'Treasury Drops Effort to Allow Banks to be Real Estate, Insurance Brokers', *WSJ*, 4 November 1987.

'Ruder Says Banks Should Be Allowed to Compete in the Securities Business', *WSJ*, December 1987.

'Ways to Boost Global Banking Stability Proposed by 12 Industrialized Nations', *WSJ*, 11 December 1987.

'St. Germain Orders a Bill Expanding Banks' Sphere', *WSJ*, 18 December 1987.

'Banks Win Round in Appeals Court Over Underwriting', *WSJ*, 9 February 1988.

'Big U.S. Banks May Have to Shrink to Satisfy New Capital Standards', *WSJ*, 7 April 1988.

'Greenspan Notes Pressure on Banks to Increase Rates', *WSJ*, 13 May 1988.

'Demand for Banking Reciprocity in EC May Spur Market Reform in U.S., Japan', *WSJ*, 21 June 1988.

'Securities Powers in Banking Advance in House, but Insurance Limits Imposed', *WSJ*, 28 July 1988.

'Large U.S. Banks Should Easily Meet Fed's New Capital Rules, Analysts Say', *WSJ*, 5 August 1988.

'EC Panel Seen Endorsing Reciprocal Trade Policy', *WSJ*, 19 October 1988.

'Four Banks Ask Fed for Broad Powers To Underwrite, Deal in Corporate Issues', *WSJ*, 26 October 1988.

'Likely Banking Chairman Is Fiery Populist', *WSJ*, 11 November 1988.

'Riegle, No Longer the Maverick, Faces Challenge as Senate Banking Panel Head', *WSJ*, 1 December 1988.

'Fed Plans to Keep Minimum Capital Rules for Banks', *WSJ*, 19 December 1988.

'Banks Risk Red-Ink Woes on Wall Street', *WSJ*, 20 January 1989.

'Bill Urging Big Changes In Fed Introduced in House', *WSJ*, 3 July 1989.

'Three More Banks to be Cleared to Deal in Corporate Debt', *WSJ*, 27 July 1989.

'U.S. Banks Are Losing Business to Japanese At Home and Abroad', *WSJ*, 12 October

1989.

'Fed Allows J.P. Morgan to Underwrite Stocks', *WSJ*, 21 September 1990.

'Three More Banks Win Clearance for Underwriting', *WSJ*, 16 January 1991.

'Street Fight: J.P. Morgan Expands Role in Underwriting, Irking Securities Firms', *WSJ*, 13 November 1991.

Washington Post

'A.G. Becker, SIA Appeal Fed's Decision on Brokers', *WP*, 29 October 1980.

'Foreign Banks Are Stalking The U.S. Market', *WP*, 7 June 1981.

'Where the New Money Is', *WP*, 23 October 1981.

'Reagan to Push Expansion of Bank Services', *WP*, 4 February 1982.

'Agencies Seek Control of Banking Changes', *WP*, 5 February 1982.

'Suit Filed to Stop Banks' Money Funds Ventures', *WP*, 22 May 1982.

'Sen. Garn Says He Still Plans to Push Banking Bill Vote', *WP*, 6 August 1982.

'Some Banks Get Right to Deal in Securities', *WP*, 2 September 1982.

'Senate Passes Bill Widening Bank Powers', *WP*, 25 September 1982.

'Conferees Agree On Bill to Rescue Troubled S&Ls', *WP*, 30 September 1982.

'Banks Win Commercial Paper Suit', *WP*, 3 November 1982.

'Inside: The Banking Agencies', *WP*, 4 May 1983.

'FDIC Plan Stirs Securities "War"', *WP*, 19 May 1983.

'Trying to Alter Banking Laws', *WP*, 4 July 1983.

'Regan Urges Swift Passage of Bank Bill', *WP*, 19 July 1983.

'Heinz Backs Banking Curbs, Proposes Closing Loopholes', *WP*, 3 November 1983.

'Regan Asks Bank Bill Soon', *WP*, 10 April 1984.

'Bank Bill Approved By Senate', *WP*, 14 September 1984.

'Regan Sees Need to Reform Bank Insurance System', *WP*, 30 October 1984.

'Financial Services Deregulation Still An Issue', *WP*, 13 January 1985.

'Judge Rules Against Bankers Trust', *WP*, 5 February 1986.

'Old Laws for the Banks...', *WP*, 11 August 1986.

'Paralysis on the Banking Bill', *WP*, 22 October 1986.

'Easing of Curbs on Underwriting Urged', *WP*, 28 October 1986.

'Bankers Say Wider Powers Needed to Compete', *WP*, 29 October 1986.

'Fed Approves Goldman, Sachs Deal', *WP*, 20 November 1986.

'Banking in the New Style', *WP*, 21 November 1986.

'Banking System Seen as Sound', *WP*, 23 November 1986.

'Fed Will Consider Letting Bank Firms Underwrite Securities', *WP*, 25 December 1986.

'Baker Asks "Drastic Overhaul of Banking"', *WP*, 13 January 1987.

'Court Upholds More Discount Brokerages for Banks', *WP*, 15 January 1987.

'Financial Coalition Is Formed', *WP*, 21 January 1987.

'Reforming the Bank Laws', *WP*, 11 February 1987.

'Pressure Grows As Nature of Banks Changes', *WP*, 22 February 1987.

'Impact of Proxmire Departure Weighed', *WP*, 28 August 1987.

'Proxmire Bill Would Repeal Glass-Steagall', *WP*, 23 September 1987.

'Proxmire, Garn Huddle Over Bank Bill Drafts', *WP*, 13 November 1987.

'Regulators: Collapse Shouldn't Keep Banks Out of Securities', *WP*, 29 October 1987.

'Groups Fight Deregulation of Banking', *WP*, 3 December 1987.

'A Cautious Cushion for Banks', *WP*, 8 February 1988.

'Poll on Glass-Steagall', *WP*, 18 February 1988.
'Bank Bill Unveiled', *WP*, 14 April 1988.
'Key to Bank Deregulation: Dingell's Help', *WP*, 24 April 1988.
'Banks Across Borders', *WP*, 8 May 1988.
'Central Banks Pushed Minimum Capital Rules', *WP*, 13 July 1988.
'Fed Adopts Rules', *WP*, 4 August 1988.
'Bank Bill Advances in House', *WP*, 23 September 1988.
'Mr. St. Germain Departs', *WP*, 11 November 1988.
'Fed Grants New Powers to 5 Banks', *WP*, 19 January 1989.
'New Wave in California', *WP*, 12 November 1989.
'Who's Minding the Managers', *WP*, 19 August 1990.
'Banks Take Step Into Securities', *WP*, 21 September 1990.

Unpublished sources

Robert J. Clarke, Comptroller of the Currency, Address to the American Bankers Association, San Francisco, 27 October 1986.
Gerald Corrigan, 'Coping With Globally Integrated Capital Markets', remarks before the Overseas Bankers Club Annual Banquet, 2 February 1987.
George Fitchew, Director-General for Financial Institutions and Company Law, Commission of the European Communities, *Press Briefing*, London, 9 September 1988.
Folkerts-Landau, David and Mathieson, Donald (1987), 'The Process of Innovation, Institutional Changes and Regulatory Response in International Financial Markets', paper prepared for the Financial Services Regulation Project of the American Enterprise Institute, December.
Frankel, Jeffrey (1988), 'International Capital Mobility and Exchange Rate Volatility', paper prepared for a conference on international imbalances, Bald Peak, New Hampshire, 5-7 October.
John Heimann, Comptroller of the Currency (1979), 'Supervision of International Bank Lending' in *International Conference of Bank Supervisors*, 5 and 6 July, Record of Proceedings.
H. Robert Heller, Member, Board of Governors, Federal Reserve System, 'Managing the Banking and Monetary Challenges of 1989', speech to the World Economic Forum, Davos, Switzerland, 1 February 1989.
H. Robert Heller, 'Improving America's Competitiveness', speech to the Richmond Society of Financial Analysts, 23 March 1989.
W. Lee Hoskins, President, Federal Reserve Bank of Cleveland, 'Assessing Risk, Structure, and Regulation', speech to the Community Bankers of Pennsylvania Annual Convention, 29 August 1989.
Pierre Jaans, Commissioner of Banks, Luxembourg, 'Measuring Capital and Liquidity Adequacy for International Banking Business', and panel contributions by S. Bürger, Deutsche Bundesbank and N.J. Brady, Reserve Bank of Australia, in *International Conference of Bank Supervisors*, 5 and 6 July 1979.
Markus Lusser, Vice Chairman of the Governing Board of the Swiss National Bank, in a speech delivered in Boppard am Rhein, 13 March 1987.

H.J. Müller (1986), 'Capital and Risk', paper presented to the *Fourth International Conference of Banking Supervisors*, Amsterdam, 22 and 23 October 1986.

Press Release, *Fourth International Conference of Banking Supervisors*, Amsterdam, 22 and 23 October 1986.

Wolfgang Reinicke, 'Creating the National Interest: U.S. Commercial Banks and the Globalization of Finance', paper presented at the ECPR Inaugural Pan-European Conference, Heidelberg, 16-20 September 1992.

J.L. Robertson, Vice Chairman of the Board of Governors of the Federal Reserve System, 'An Inside Look at Federal Bank Regulation', address before the State Bank Division meeting of the ABA's 94th Annual Convention, 30 September 1968.

David Ruder, Chairman of the Securities Exchange Commission, to the Annual Convention of the Securities Industry Association, 2 December 1988.

Congressional hearings

Bretton Woods Agreements Act Amendments and International Lending Supervision, Report to the Senate Committee on Banking, Housing and Urban Affairs, 16 May 1983.

Changes in Our Financial System: Globalization of Capital Markets and the Securitization of Credit, Hearings Before the Senate Committee on Banking, Housing and Urban Affairs, 13 and 14 October 1987.

Competition and Conditions in the Financial System, Part I, 28 April 1981.

Competition and Conditions in the Financial System, Hearings Before the Senate Committee on Banking, Housing and Urban Affairs, 13 May 1981.

Competitive Equity in the Financial Services Industry, Hearings Before the Senate Committee on Banking, Housing and Urban Affairs, 16 January 1984.

Competitive Equity in the Financial Services Industry, Hearing Before the Senate Committee on Banking, Housing and Urban Affairs, 21 March 1984.

Comprehensive Reform in the Financial Services Industry, Hearings Before the Senate Committee on Banking, Housing and Urban Affairs, 8 May 1985.

Deposit Insurance and Financial Services Restructuring, Hearings Before the Senate Committee on Banking, Housing and Urban Affairs, 31 July 1990.

FDIC Securities Proposal and Related Issues, Hearings Before the Subcommittee on Securities of the House Committee on Energy and Commerce, 16 June 1983.

Financial Institutions Oversight, Part I, Senate Committee on Banking, Housing and Urban Affairs, 6 April 1983.

Financial Institutions Safety and Consumer Choice Act of 1991, Hearings Before the Subcommittee on Financial Institutions Supervision, Regulation and Insurance of the House Committee on Banking, Finance and Urban Affairs, 21 March 1991.

Financial Services Restructuring, Hearings Before the House Committee on Energy and Commerce, 11 April, 20 June, 10 and 31 July, 1 August, 13 September 1991.

Financial Restructuring Proposal, Hearings Before the Senate Committee on Banking, Housing and Urban Affairs, 5 August 1987.

Global Economic Outlook, Hearings Before the Senate Committee on Foreign Relations, Subcommittee on International Economic Policy, 10 January 1983.

Globalization of Financial Markets and Related International Banking and Supervisory Issues, Hearings Before the House Subcommittee on Financial Institutions Supervision,

Regulation and Insurance, 30 July 1987.

Globalization of Securities Markets, Hearings Before the House Subcommittee on Telecommunications and Finance, 5 August 1987.

Globalization of the Securities Markets and S.646, The International Securities Enforcement Cooperation Act of 1989, Hearings Before the Subcommittee on Securities, Senate Committee on Banking, Housing and Urban Affairs, 14 June 1989.

Impact of Bank Reform Proposals on Consumers, Hearings Before the House Committee on Banking, Finance and Urban Affairs, 10 April 1991.

International Debt, Hearings Before the Subcommittee on International Finance and Monetary Policy, Senate Committee on Banking, Housing and Urban Affairs, 14, 15, 17 February 1983.

International Financial Markets and Related Matters, Hearings Before the House Committee on Banking, Finance and Urban Affairs, 21 December 1983.

International Financial Markets and Related Problems, Senate Committee on Banking, Housing and Urban Affairs, 2 February 1983.

The Internationalization of Capital Markets, Hearings Before the Senate Committee on Banking, Housing and Urban Affairs, 26 and 27 February 1986.

Legislative Proposals to Restructure Our Financial System, Hearings Before the Senate Committee on Banking, Housing and Urban Affairs, 1 December 1987.

Modernization of the Glass-Steagall Act, Hearings Before the Senate Committee on Banking, Housing and Urban Affairs, 30 July 1987.

New Securities Powers for Bank Holding Companies, Hearings Before the Senate Committee on Banking, Housing and Urban Affairs, 6 August 1987.

Oversight Hearings on the Condition of U.S. Financial and Industrial Base, Hearings Before the Senate Committee on Banking, Housing and Urban Affairs, 11, 13, 19 July and 14-15 November 1989.

Oversight Hearings on the European Community's 1992 Program, 26 September 1989.

Reform of the Nation's Banking and Financial Systems, Parts I & II, Hearings Before the House Subcommittee on Financial Institutions Supervision, Regulation and Insurance, 1987.

Restructuring of the Banking Industry, Parts I & II, Hearings Before the Subcommittee on Financial Institutions Supervision, Regulation and Insurance of the House Committee on Banking, Finance and Urban Affairs, 18 April and 30 April 1991.

Review of the International Lending Supervision Act of 1983, Hearings Before the Subcommittee on International Finance and Monetary Policy, Senate Committee on Banking, Housing and Urban Affairs, 25 June 1986.

Risk-Based Capital Requirements for Banks and Bank Holding Companies, Hearings Before the Subcommittee on General Oversight and Investigations of the House Committee on Banking, Finance and Urban Affairs, 21 April and 30 April 1987.

Role of Financial Institutions, Hearings Before the Subcommittee on Telecommunications and Finance, House Committee on Energy and Commerce, 5 October 1987.

Securities Activities of Depository Institutions, Hearings Before the Subcommittee on Securities of the Senate Committee on Banking, Housing and Urban Affairs, 4 February 1982.

Status of the U.S. Financial System, Hearings Before the Senate Committee on Banking, Housing and Urban Affairs, 18 June 1987.

Strengthening the Safety and Soundness of the Financial Services Industry, Hearings Before the Senate Committee on Banking, Housing and Urban Affairs, 21 January

1987.

Strengthening the Supervision and Regulation of the Depository Institutions, Part I & II, Hearings Before the Senate Committee on Banking, Housing and Urban Affairs, 26 February, 11 and 25-26 April, 7-9 and 15-16 and 22 May, 25 November 1991.

Structure and Regulation of Financial Firms and Holding Companies, Hearings Before the Subcommittee on Consumer and Monetary Affairs of the House Government Operations Committee, 1986.

U.S. Access to Japanese Financial Markets, Hearing before the Senate Budget Committee, 6 May 1987.

Congressional documents and reports

Bank Holding Company Act Amendments, 1966, SR1179, 89th Congress, 2nd Session, Washington, D.C.: GPO.

The European Community: 1992 and Reciprocity, CRS Report 89-227, Washington, D.C.: Congressional Research Service, 1989.

'Glass-Steagall Act: Should Bankers Be Brokers?', *CRS Issue Brief*, 21 February 1991.

House Committee on Banking and Currency, *The Growth of Unregistered Bank Holding Companies — Problems and Prospects*, 91st Congress, 1969.

House Committee on Banking, Finance and Urban Affairs, *Non-bank Loophole Legislation*, 12 June 1984.

House Committee on Foreign Affairs, Subcommittee on Europe and the Middle East, Subcommittee on International Economic Policy and Trade, *Europe 1992: The Financial Services Industry*, April 1989.

House Committee on Government Operations, report on *Modernization of the Financial Services Industry*, 30 September 1987.

House of Representatives, *International Recovery and Financial Stability Act Report*, 16 May 1983.

HR No. 175, 98th Congress, 1st Session, 1983.

International Competition in Services, Office of Technology Assessment, Washington, D.C.: OTA, 1987.

Jackson, William (1987), *The Separation of Banking and Commerce*, CRS Report No. 87-352E, Washington, D.C.: Congressional Research Service.

Joint Economic Committee, Congress of the United States, *Europe 1992*, 18 November 1988.

Murphy, M. Maureen (1988), *Glass-Steagall Act: The Legal Landscape of Financial Restructuring*, CRS-Report 88-335A, Washington, D.C.: Congressional Research Service, April 21.

SR No. 122, 98th Congress, 1st Session, 1983.

SR No. 77, 73rd Congress, 1933.

Stock Exchange Practices, Parts 5 & 6, Senate Committee on Banking and Currency, 72nd Congress, 2nd Session, January-February 1933.

Stock Exchange Practices, Parts 1-8, Senate Committee on Banking and Currency, 73rd Congress, 1st Session, February-April 1933.

Subcommittee of the House Committee on Energy and Commerce, report on *Restructuring Financial Markets: The Major Policy Issues*, July 1986.

Subcommittee of the Senate Banking and Currency Committee, *Hearings on the*

234 Banking, Politics and Global Finance

Operation of the National and Federal Reserve Banking Systems, SR71, 71st Congress, 3rd Session, 1931.

Subcommittee of the Senate Banking and Currency Committee, *Hearings on the Operation of the National and Federal Reserve Banking Systems*, SR4115, 72nd Congress, 1st Session, 1931.

Super-Banks: Prospects and Policy Choices, CRS Report No. 87-725E, Washington, D.C.: Congressional Research Service, 1987.

Miscellaneous documents

BIS Press Review, No. 121.
Federal Bar & News Journal, 35/4, 1988.
Federal Reserve Bulletin, February 1973 and 1983.
Federal Reserve Bulletin, January 1982.
International Legal Materials, **22** (4), July 1983.

Index